Here's to a good
Friend
Don M. Mustun

You Can
Control
Your Thoughts

You Can Control Your Thoughts

Don M and Arda Jean Christensen
Mary Christensen Latimer

Salt Lake City, Utah
1996

Library of Congress Catalog Card Number
96-96158

ISBN 1-57008-248-0

Printed in the United States of America

Let virtue garnish thy thoughts unceasingly.

Doctrine and Covenants 121: 45

Acknowledgments

The authors thank all those who assisted in the preparation of this book. So many hours of research, typing, editing, and proofreading, plus myriad other errands required for the many quotations and scriptural references were done by many people. We mention Tami Larson, Don's secretaries Linda Mano and Jeri Stevens; our daughter-in-law Angela Christensen; our granddaughter Lexia Dew; and particularly our daughter Ruth Hocker for meticulous editing.

We are grateful to the following people who read the manuscript and made helpful suggestions: Gerald Avery, David Clayton, Richard Coleman, George Fassler, Raby Ficklin, Eric Fredrickson, Stacey Jensen, Jeffery Jones and DeWayne Warnock.

Thanks also to our family: Rolf D. and Jean Larie Dixon, William S. and Jolene Dew, Kyle D. Latimer, Martin D. and Sherri Christensen, Evan W. and Sonja Christensen, Rachel and Jeremiah K Clark, Glenn L. and Angela Christensen, and Jeffrey C. and Ruth Angela Hocker, for reading the manuscript and making comments. The many years of paying tuition have been well rewarded.

Special thanks to Mary's children: Emily Jean, Andrew Kyle, and Eliza Ruth, for "donating" their mother for the writing of this book over the several years it was in process. They stood next to the word processor for eons, patiently waiting for mom to "finish just one more page."

All the chapters were a cooperative effort, and separate authorship is not established.

We express sincere appreciation for the beautiful cover, original artwork by our daughter Jean Dixon, M.A.

Please note that source citations within the text refer to author, book title, and page numbers. Full publishing information is available in the bibliography.

Contents

Section I

You Can Control
Your Thoughts

1

Why Are Thoughts
So Important?

Many have commented that they have troublesome thoughts. Some are bothered in their conscience, and some even feel controlled by these thoughts. Some seek help from Priesthood leaders when these thoughts don't seem responsive to their efforts to remove them. Many go for professional counseling. Why are thoughts so important? Why is it that "mere thoughts" can be such a distressing factor in people's lives? Is it necessary that we examine what is going on inside our minds and hearts, and if so, can we do anything about it? Our exploration on these questions revealed a great treasure of knowledge on significant topics.

Thoughts are gateways. They open doors to achievement. Ideas are constructive, productive, formulative. They are not only the blueprints, plans and specifications, but also the building materials for accomplishment. Indeed, creative ideas are what make it possible for us to rise above the animal condition, aspire to and achieve preservation of life, comforts, civilization, music, art, literature, storage and retrieval of information, expressions of love and caring, even worship. Such ideas should be nurtured and encouraged. On the other hand, baseness, crassness, ideas that destroy or degrade, harm or hurt, should be kept under control and dismissed. Such ideas are also productive but result in insult, injustice, and injury. Thoughts are important because they are *beginnings*.

We Are What We Think

Proverbs 23:7 tells us: "For as [a person] thinketh in his heart, so is he."

Your thoughts are a reflection of who you really are. The thoughts you have in quiet contemplation emerge from the deepest areas of your self, your spirit, your soul, or whatever word you choose to describe the essence of you. You can tell much about yourself by carefully and honestly examining your thoughts to learn what motivates you, what entertains you, what compels you, what frightens you, what enslaves you, what excites you, what is joyful to you, what happiness means to you. Becoming acquainted with this inner person can be rewarding or disquieting, depending on what you find there.

In pondering this passage of scripture, one might ask these questions: Who are you? Do you know yourself? Are you comfortable with your inward desires, at peace with your conscience? Or are you troubled with some aspects of your life? Are you in control of your actions at all times? Or do you have an uneasy feeling inside that there must be a better way? Is your mind energetic and creative? Or do you ever feel you want to escape from reality, because you cannot face your own private thoughts? Are you content with your inner self? Or do you have an anxious feeling that, no matter how much others seem to think of you, you have something to hide?

All of us are born with a director, the Light of Christ, that tells us right from wrong. This inner compass impels us to goodness, compassion, love, caring, preservation of life, and aspiration to higher situations and noble endeavors. If we listen to this director, we can know where we are in relation to ourselves, to those with whom we associate, to our eternal creator, and to the earth and universe where we live. Peace of mind is an indication that we are doing what we truly desire to do, and have no great conflict with our inner guide. A disturbing feeling indicates that one's actions or state of being do not always conform to that light.

In the beginning, we are innocent, pure—the offspring of deity. In this mortal, carnal world, we encounter influences which lead us in directions contrary to our pure beginnings. From birth, we are subjected to situations, inducements, and allurements, which tend to lead us away from our original innocence, to deaden us, even brutalize us, and make us insensitive to our higher instincts.

We become what we choose to think. The quoted passage in Proverbs 23:7 means not only that your thoughts reflect who you are, but also that your thoughts shape you. Think about it! Who you are, your inner person, depends on what you have become as you have acted and reacted throughout the circumstances you have encountered in your life. Some feel they have no control over who and what they are, but are a product of heredity or environment or both, with no ability to change their circumstances or their character. Nothing is further from the truth. We are in certain situations because of birth or conditions beyond our control, but what we do with our lives, how we react to these situations, what we think about, what actions we take, we do by choice. We even shape our character by the choices we make. Those choices, particularly in regard to our thoughts, are our own.

Unwanted thoughts sometimes come unbidden to our minds, but we need not harbor and entertain them, nor do we need to let them entertain us. If we feed ourselves upon good thoughts we become good, but if we spend life thinking evil thoughts we will become evil. We are the product of our thoughts, be they high or low. President David O. McKay explained: "A noble and godlike character is not a thing of favor or chance, but is a natural result of continued effort in right thinking, the effect of long-cherished association with godlike thoughts. An ignoble and bestial character by the same process is the result of the continued harboring of groveling thoughts." (*Pathways to Happiness*, p. 278.)

President George Albert Smith tells how a boyhood experience taught him this very important truth, which in turn helped him make important choices regarding his thoughts:

> As a child, thirteen years of age, I went to school at the Brigham Young Academy. . . . I cannot remember much of what was said during the year that I was there, but there is one thing that I will probably never forget. . . . Dr. Maeser one day stood up and said:
> "Not only will you be held accountable for the things you do, but you will be held responsible for the very thoughts you think."
> Being a boy, not in the habit of controlling my thoughts very much, it was quite a puzzle to me what I was to do, and it worried me. . . . About a week or ten days after that it suddenly came to me what he meant. . . . *Why of course you will be held accountable for your thoughts, because when your life is completed in mortality, it will be the sum of your thoughts.* That one suggestion has been a great blessing to me all my life, and it has enabled me upon many occasions to avoid thinking improperly, because I realize that I will be, when my life's labor is complete, the product of my thoughts. (*Sharing the Gospel with Others*, pp. 62-63, emphasis added.)

Thoughts Influence Actions

Thoughts are powerful. Our thoughts are directly related to our actions. What we cherish and harbor in our minds becomes a directing influence on what we do. In Arda Jean's notebook when she was a student at BYU was written "Whether you think you can or you can't, you are right." President Spencer W. Kimball used the same idea in *The Miracle of Forgiveness*, (see pp. 105-06) and referred to James Allen's masterful little book *As a Man Thinketh*: "He who cherishes a beautiful vision, a lofty ideal in his heart, will one day realize it. Columbus cherished a vision of another world, and he discovered it; Copernicus fostered the vision of a multiplicity of worlds and a wider universe, and he revealed it." (pp. 51-52.)

President David O. McKay called thoughts the "seeds of acts," (*Stepping Stones to an Abundant Life*, p. 206) and Elder Boyd K. Packer called them "the switchboard, the control panel governing our actions." (*That All May Be Edified*, p. 33.)

President David O. McKay liked to quote this verse about the relationship between our thoughts and eternal life:

> Sow a thought, reap an act;
> Sow an act, reap a habit;
> Sow a habit, reap a character;
> Sow a character, reap an eternal destiny.
> —E. D. Boardman
> (*Pathways to Happiness*, p. 332.)

This idea of sowing a thought and reaping the rewards of that thought is expressed by James Allen, who likens our minds to a garden:

> A man's mind may be likened to a garden, which may be intelligently cultivated or allowed to run wild; but whether cultivated or neglected, it must, and will, *bring forth*. If no useful seeds are *put* into it, then an abundance of useless weed seeds will *fall* therein, and will continue to produce their kind.
>
> Just as a gardener cultivates his plot, keeping it free from weeds, and growing the flowers and fruits which he requires, so may a man tend the garden of his mind, weeding out all the wrong, useless, and impure thoughts, and cultivating toward perfection the flowers and

fruits of right, useful, and pure thoughts. By pursuing this process, a man sooner or later discovers . . . how the thought forces and mind elements operate in the shaping of his character, circumstances, and destiny. (*As A Man Thinketh*, pp. 17-18, emphasis included.)

The mind, like a garden, produces good fruit or bad fruit depending on what we put into it, and what we do with that which comes involuntarily. Cultivation represents how we control it. If we let it go without supervision, the weeds will take over. As we choose pure thoughts, we plant the seeds of salvation, and if we cultivate these seeds, we can achieve our destiny of eternal life. To do so, we must cast out the destructive weeds, and cultivate, nourish and treasure up the good thoughts.

Elder Neal A. Maxwell spoke of our *desires*: "Actually, everything depends—initially and finally—on our desires. These shape our thought patterns. Our desires thus precede our deeds and lie at the very core of our souls, tilting us toward or away from God. . . . One's individual will thus remains uniquely his. God will not override it nor overwhelm it. Hence we'd better want the consequences of what we want!" (CR *Ensign*, November 1995, p. 23.)

Our whole eternal destiny begins with our thoughts. With the goal of eternal life in front of us, we can strengthen our resolve to purify our minds and hearts. God knows and recognizes our righteous thoughts and rewards them with blessings of faith, righteousness, and strength.

The consensus is, if we think right, we will do right. Good works follow good thoughts.

Thoughts Precede Emotions

Our thoughts also govern our emotions. This is an important key to understanding ourselves and our motivations.

Scripturally we find many references to our hearts as well as our minds as being the seat of thinking. In a general way, we can divide them thus: references to our *minds* concern our thinking, and references to our *hearts* concern our emotions. With this differentiation, we can receive insight into how our thoughts can produce our emotions, which can in turn convert into actions.

Jesus taught us plainly, "A good man out of the good treasure of his heart bringeth forth that which is good; and an evil man out of the evil treasure of his heart bringeth forth that which is evil: for of the abundance of the heart his mouth speaketh." (Luke 6:45.) That which we treasure up in our hearts (that is, our emotions) motivates our actions.

How does this happen? We act upon what we feel. When you ask yourself why you did something, you can find feelings that impelled you to do it. A young man "in love" acts according to the emotion swelling within him. A mother seeing her toddler reaching for a hot pan acts instantly, out of the emotion she feels. A businessman may seek revenge against a competitor, due to the emotion within. An angry man, giving in to his deep emotion, may do violence against his estranged wife. Hurt feelings may motivate any of us to carry grudges, choosing to avoid meeting certain people.

What kind of thoughts do you have about people whom you treasure as friends? Positive, uplifting thoughts, such as esteem, acceptance, sympathy, understanding, and support generate feelings (emotions) of love, caring, charity, unselfishness, compassion, and benevolence. On the other hand, negative thoughts such as impatience, annoyance, suspicion, and mistrust can produce the negative emotions of contempt, jealousy, hostility, aversion, malice, even hatred, which destroy our most important relationships.

An example of this is an attitude of criticism, which begins a chain that can damage marriage and family relationships. Thinking critical thoughts actually generates emotions of animosity toward a mate, a child, or a parent. These feelings in turn generate the deeds which destroy our love.

We knew a couple who had an unhappy marriage. Things the husband did annoyed the wife, and she would not forgive him for them. She dwelt in her mind on all the times he had offended her, and became angry and cross. These negative unforgiving thoughts produced disapproving emotions, which in turn produced unkind actions. His response to this was exasperation and disgust. This cycle was destroying their marriage relationship.

When this destructive sequence was pointed out to them, the husband agreed to be more careful and more caring. The wife in turn agreed to forgive him of all offenses, past and present, and to be more accepting of his efforts to please. Energy and effort were required on the part of each to remove the accusing, critical thoughts from their relationship, but as they did, it made room for constructive, uplifting thoughts and positive feelings. When their thinking changed, their emotions of love and regard increased; their behavior toward each other improved; their whole marriage was transformed. Sometime later they reported that they were both very happy.

We have the ability to choose our thoughts. Deliberately replacing hurtful thoughts with encouraging, ennobling thoughts will change the course of our emotions and our actions.

Evil Thoughts Lead to Sin

Likewise, before we sin, we first *think* of sinning. Moreover, unrighteous deeds grow out of unrighteous thoughts of the heart; the scriptures are full of statements reinforcing this idea:

> Hear, O earth: behold, I will bring evil upon this people, *even the fruit of their thoughts*, because they have not hearkened unto my words, nor to my law, but rejected it. (Jeremiah 6:19, emphasis added.)

> For from within, *out of the heart of men*, proceed evil thoughts, adulteries, fornications, murders,
> Thefts, covetousness, wickedness, deceit, lasciviousness, an evil eye, blasphemy, pride, foolishness:
> All these evil things come from within, and defile the man. (Mark 7:21-23, emphasis added.)

> But behold, hearken ye unto me, and know that by the help of the all-powerful Creator of heaven and earth *I can tell you concerning your thoughts, how that ye are beginning to labor in sin*, which sin appeareth very abominable unto me, yea, and abominable unto God. (Jacob 2:5, emphasis added.)

It is so important to use our God-given right of choice to select patterns of thinking that will lead us to where we want to be. President Kimball affirms, "Yes, as a man thinketh, so *does* he. If he thinks it long enough he is likely to do it, whether it be theft, moral sin, or suicide. Thus the time to protect against the calamity is when the thought begins to shape itself. Destroy the seed and the plant will never grow. Man alone, of all creatures of earth, can change his thought pattern and become the architect of his destiny." (*The Miracle of Forgiveness*, p. 114.)

An area in which our thoughts have a powerful effect on our actions is that of moral or sexual transgression. The Savior talked about the necessity of controlling our thoughts in this regard: "Ye have heard that it was said by them of old time, Thou shalt not commit adultery: But I say unto you, That whosoever looketh on a woman to lust after her hath committed adultery with her already in his heart." (Matthew 5:27-28.)

President Ezra Taft Benson also emphasized the necessity of controlling our thoughts to stay morally clean: "The first seeds of immorality are always sown in the mind. When we allow our thoughts to linger on lewd or immoral things, the first step on the road to immorality has been taken." (*Ensign*, December 1987, p. 67.)

Lust after men or women is sin, but if continued, leads to the greater sin of adultery. President Kimball gave this example of indulgence in impure thoughts leading to the heartbreak of moral transgression:

> When the thought is born which starts a chain reaction, a sin has already been committed. If the thought is sown, then develops into lust, it is almost certain to bring eventually the full harvest of the act of the heinous sin, adultery. . . .
>
> A graphic example of this came to my attention some years ago. In a community in the North, I visited a man occasionally who had above the desk in his printing establishment a huge picture of a nude woman. He laughed at the idea of its being destructive to his morals. But one day years later he came to me with a stained soul—he had committed adultery. His house had fallen in on him. Certainly the thoughts provoked by the things always before his eyes must have had a deteriorating effect on him. There may have been other factors, but surely this one played its part. (*The Miracle of Forgiveness*, pp. 113-14.)

President David O. McKay told another story illustrating how thoughts precede acts:

> Many years ago a young man came to me while I was president of the European Mission and made a confession of a wrong and sinful act. He justified himself by saying that he happened to be in a bookstore at the closing hour, and when the door was locked he yielded to temptation. He rather blamed the *circumstances* for his fall.
>
> But I said, "It wasn't the circumstances; it wasn't the locked door, nor the enticement. You had thought of that before you went to that

bookstore. If you had never thought of that act, there would have been no circumstance strong enough to entice or to tempt you, a missionary, to fall. The thought always precedes the act." (*Instructor,* March 1965, p. 86.)

This incident illustrates clearly: first we think, then we do. Our thoughts influence our actions, and even leave their imprint on our inner selves. President McKay explained that there is no such thing as an insignificant evil thought, saying, "Whether found out or not, all pay the penalty of sin and of indiscretion. The intent that precedes the act leaves its indelible impression upon the character. . . . No one can hide from his thoughts nor escape from their inevitable consequences. (*Pathways to Happiness*, p. 320.)

If we continually think evil thoughts, sooner or later we do evil acts. It is important to manage our thoughts at all times and in all places. It is clear that if we wish to keep our actions and our lives pure, the first step is to control our thoughts.

We Are Commanded to Purify Our Thoughts

Though we may think we can hide our thoughts from others, we cannot hide them from the Lord. He knows them. In Alma 18:32 we read, "Yea, and [God] looketh down upon all the children of men; and he knows all the thoughts and intents of the heart." Furthermore, He has told us we will be judged according to our thoughts. "For our words will condemn us, yea, all our works will condemn us; we shall not be found spotless; *and our thoughts will also condemn us*; and in this awful state we shall not dare to look up to our God; and we would fain be glad if we could command the rocks and the mountains to fall upon us to hide us from his presence." (Alma 12:14, emphasis added.)

We may feel it is impossible to control our thoughts, especially if we have allowed ourselves to sink to degradation and shame. But Heavenly Father holds us responsible for doing so. In every dispensation He has taught us through His living prophets the necessity of purifying our hearts. In the Old Testament Jeremiah reminds us that controlling our thoughts is possible: "O Jerusalem, wash thine heart from wickedness, that thou mayest be saved. How long shall thy vain thoughts lodge within thee?" (Jeremiah 4:14.)

In Doctrine and Covenants 88:74 our Savior teaches us how it is to be done: "Yea, purify your hearts, and cleanse your hands and your feet before me, that I may make you clean." First, with the help of God, we make a great effort ourselves to clean up our minds and our actions through repentance, then the Savior's Atonement will take effect in our lives, and we become clean.

He has commanded us, and He knows it is possible for us to accomplish it. Keep in mind God's promise that He will not give us commandments we cannot keep. "If it so be that the children of men keep the commandments of God he doth nourish them, and strengthen them, and provide means whereby they can accomplish the thing which he has commanded them." (I Nephi 17:3.)

Elder Marvin J. Ashton reminded us: "Roadblocks to eternal progress are cast aside when resolves are made that no man needs to walk alone. It is a happy day when we come to know that with God's help nothing is impossible for us." (CR, *Ensign*, May 1979, p. 69.)

We control our lives, whether we realize it or not. We make the choices as to what we think, and what we become. With God's help we can become pure in heart as we have been commanded.

In the penetrating language of the scriptures, we are admonished to make the effort to choose right thoughts, and we are promised wonderful blessings will follow: "Let thy bowels also be full of charity towards all men, and to the household of faith, and *let virtue garnish thy thoughts unceasingly*; then shall thy confidence wax strong in the presence of God; and the doctrine of the priesthood shall distil upon thy soul as the dews from heaven.

"The Holy Ghost shall be thy constant companion, and thy scepter an unchanging scepter of righteousness and truth." (D&C 121:45-46.)

We can obtain these marvelous blessings. We have the choice. The Spirit of Christ guides us to His light, and through obedience, we can call on our Father in Heaven to strengthen us and send the Holy Ghost to help us succeed in matters of eternal importance. This book will teach you to make those right choices. Your upward path will be exciting, enlightening, and strengthening. Your ability will increase as you persist in your effort.

2

The Difference Between Good and Evil Thoughts

Good Cometh From God

We learned in the last chapter the need to develop wholesome thought patterns and reject evil thoughts. Though some thoughts are obviously evil, others may be more difficult to identify as the kind of thoughts we must remove from our minds. How can we know which thoughts are healthful and proper?

The scriptures give us this guideline for how we can tell the difference between good and evil thoughts:

> Wherefore, all things which are good cometh of God; and that which is evil cometh of the devil; for the devil is an enemy unto God, and fighteth against him continually, and inviteth and enticeth to sin, and to do that which is evil continually.
>
> But behold, that which is of God inviteth and enticeth to do good continually; wherefore, *every thing which inviteth and enticeth to do good, and to love God, and to serve him, is inspired of God.* (Moroni 7:12-13, emphasis added.)

Those thoughts which invite and entice to do good, those thoughts which encourage us to love God and our fellow beings, those which influence us to serve Him, are inspired of God. This is the test. If we apply this to our thoughts we will be able to distinguish evil from good. This will enable us to avoid being deceived by the cunning traps of Satan, and will be a guide as we weed out the evil thoughts and keep the good thoughts.

Simply, all good things come from God, and all evil things come from the devil.

In the pre-mortal existence, we had our agency. We were presented with ideas which were according to God's eternal plan, as well as other ideas that sounded good, but did not correlate with God's plan and purposes. The concepts sounded good, but the underlying idea was that Lucifer would usurp the power and glory of God. Some of our brothers and sisters were led away to follow these conflicting proposals. They had their choice, exercised it, and received the consequences.

In our earthly existence, as part of Heavenly Father's plan, we still have that power of choice. We are required to walk by faith, having a veil drawn across the memory of our previous experiences. However, when we hear the gospel presented, there is a familiarity to it. It sounds wholesome and good, and the ideas seem right to us. The Spirit of Christ, given to each of us when we were born into this life, is a guide and a steering device to help us return to our heavenly home. Gospel principles and ideas are affirmed and attested to by this Spirit, so we feel comfortable with them and desire to follow after them. We must, however, attune ourselves to this guide, and by our own free will and faith, choose to follow.

Lucifer, or Satan as we now know him, is still at work trying to persuade us away from God's plan of happiness. He still tries to take away the glory of God by snatching followers away from Heavenly Father. In his rage at having been denied his selfish ambition, and being denied the privilege of coming to earth to receive a body, he and others who followed after him use their powers of persuasion to deceive us and try to make us miserable like they are. All these points are adequately taught in the scriptures. Our understanding is enlarged when we study for the purpose of learning so that we can follow the Lord's plan.

Part of our reason for coming to this earth was to gain a body. Thus we know that, being here, we heeded God's pleadings and chose to follow Him. Those who did not forfeited their birthright as spirit children of divine Parents, were cast out with Lucifer and are serving him. Another reason for coming to earth was to be tested and tried, proven to see if we will do all things our Father may require of us. We still have the gift of agency which enables us to make the choices that will lead us back to our Heavenly Father, according to the eternal plan, or away from the right to His holy presence. Much is expected of us. Much is required of us. The rewards are infinite and eternal, and the price is high.

What, then, is the difference between good and evil thoughts, and how can we tell the difference between them? The true good comes from God. Disguised good, evil in insidious, covert forms that may seem good, comes from the devil. Outright evil we recognize clearly. Other kinds of evil are deliberately masked in order to deceive us. The test is recognition and avoidance.

Elder Bruce R. McConkie explained the kinds of thoughts we must avoid, saying, "Part of man's mortal probation is to see if he can control his thoughts in accordance with righteous principles. The saints are commanded, 'Cast away your idle thoughts' (D&C 88:69), which obviously includes all *evil thoughts, all those that do not edify, and all that are unproductive.* Thoughts are idle if they do not work to further man's peace in this life and eternal reward in the next." (*Mormon Doctrine*, p. 792, emphasis added.)

If we think in terms of all our thoughts being either good or bad we can learn to recognize thoughts that come into our mind disguised as good, but are really bad.

Evil Thoughts

There is so much in this world that is evil. Satan is having great success in luring away the souls of men. Some spend their lives producing evil so they can disseminate it and persuade others to follow them down the path to hell.

Evil thoughts that lead us away from our Father in Heaven include bitterness, jealousy, hatred, revenge, unforgiveness, selfishness, envy, gossip, dishonesty, uncontrolled anger, immoral fantasies, coveting, lies, pornography, dirty jokes, vulgarity, profanity, obscenity. All these things invite us and entice us to sin.

The devil tries to put into our hearts the proposal that his thoughts are not evil. When we find ourselves rationalizing "this is not so bad," or "something else is worse," or "this once won't hurt," or "I can handle it," or worse, when we decide the bad thoughts are really good, we will know Satan has a hold on us. We had better break free immediately before he binds us to be his own.

In Moses 4:4 we read: "And he became Satan, yea, even the devil, the father of all lies, to deceive and to blind men, and to lead them captive at his will, even as many as would not hearken unto my voice."

If thoughts entice us to sin, no matter how beautifully packaged they may be, they are evil. If we listen to the inner voice of the Spirit of

Christ, or the quiet urging of the Holy Ghost, we can discern the difference.

Negative Thoughts

Negative thoughts are unproductive and will become a destructive force in our lives. They will discourage us and prevent us from accomplishing righteous goals. Such damaging thoughts include fear, depression, covetousness, feelings of inferiority or inadequacy, jealousy, suspicion, apprehension, indecision, or skepticism. All of us have times in which such thoughts or feelings assail us. What we do with them is the test.

The story is told of one woman who recognized the damaging effect of negative thoughts in her life:

> One woman found that when she allowed herself to think continually about clothing and household furnishings she couldn't afford, she felt discouraged, particularly when she compared her life with the lives of others who had accumulated more wealth and material possessions than she had.
>
> But she decided that she could learn to control her thoughts, and she made an effort to focus not on what she didn't possess, but on the kind of person she wanted to become. She studied the scriptures, concentrating on the Savior's life and on patterning her life after his. She prayed more earnestly, and she developed a strong desire to become more Christlike.
>
> As she did this, she became more sensitive to the needs of those around her. With her new perspective, she found that her problems seemed to shrink and her testimony and her family became more precious to her. She felt more grateful for her blessings and felt a greater spirit of charity. She began to admire Christlike character in others more than she had admired worldly wealth. ("Charity Thinketh No Evil," *Ensign*, August 1988, p. 61.)

If we are alert to the negative thoughts that come into our minds, we will be able to take off their disguise and see them for what they are— destructive thoughts sent from the devil. We must learn to detect them and evict them before they can do any damage to our souls.

Most negativism is a form of selfishness—of dwelling too much on our own desires and yearning. There is always someone who has more of what we want than we have, and there is always someone who seems better in some way than we do. On the other hand, there are many who have less. The best cure for a negative attitude is to seek outward and upward, looking for someone we can serve, someone who needs the help we can offer, and giving gratitude to God for the very real blessings each of us enjoys.

Thoughts That Lead Us Closer to God

Some thoughts are good, and will lead us closer to our Father in Heaven. Such thoughts invite and entice to do good, to love God, and to serve Him. They are based on honesty . . . justice . . . hope . . . love . . . faithfulness . . . unselfishness . . . truthfulness . . . humility . . . a broken heart and contrite spirit . . . a thirst after righteousness . . . optimism . . . mercy . . . cleanliness of heart . . . enlightenment . . . charity . . . repentance . . . enthusiasm . . . nobility . . . obedience to God . . . service . . . excellence . . . cheerfulness . . . virtue . . . desire to do God's work . . . forgiveness . . . and concern for the welfare of others.

These uplifting thoughts may be the sweet whisperings of our "conscience", the Light of Christ, and to faithful members of the Church, the edifying inducements of the Holy Ghost. The Prophet Joseph Smith spoke of the spirit of revelation giving us "sudden strokes of ideas," and the feeling of "pure intelligence flowing" into us. (*Teachings of the Prophet Joseph Smith*, p. 151.) He also taught of the impact of the Holy Ghost: "This first Comforter or Holy Ghost has no other effect than pure intelligence. It is more powerful in expanding the mind, enlightening the understanding, and storing the intellect with present knowledge . . ." (p. 149.) These are precious experiences. When our minds have felt the joy of illumination by the Spirit of revelation, we long to remain in that influence.

The Holy Ghost will never encroach on our agency, nor force us, but will entice us toward the light, toward sweetness and goodness, which will lead us gently in the path of happiness. We have the choice. It is our opportunity and blessing to choose the right.

The Happy Results of Right Choices

Think how happy we would be if we had the Holy Ghost to be a constant companion, to teach, guide, direct, and comfort us, and bring us peace of mind. The only way we can hope to receive these most welcome blessings is by taking control of our own thoughts and lives, choosing good so Satan can no longer entice our minds. Elder Carlos E. Asay said, "Can one hope to enjoy the companionship of the Holy Spirit when one is double-minded—when his mind shares time with the evil one? I think not." ("The Companionship of the Holy Ghost," *Ensign,* April 1988, p. 15.) By controlling our minds we shut him out. By not listening to the "father of lies", we bind him, and destroy his power over us.

Happily, when we control our thoughts in righteousness, we make a suitable place for the influence of the Holy Spirit. He will strengthen us, encourage us to good works, enlighten our minds with creative and attractive ideas, enhance the spirit of love in our hearts, and replace our sorrows with peace and faith. This enlightenment will reach into all areas of our lives. We will find ourselves making fewer errors of judgment. We will be warned of dangers. We will be assisted in solving our problems. Our relationships with our spouses and children, with our business associates, and with our social contacts will improve. Many have testified of experiences of this nature taking place in their lives as they move along the upward spiral toward joy.

What do the scriptures teach us will be the result of taking righteous control of our thoughts? When we have succeeded in making the right choices, the promises of the Lord are very straightforward and clear. From the New Testament we select two such beautiful, specific promises. In Romans 8:6 we are told: "For to be carnally minded is death; but to be spiritually minded is life and peace." A spiritual mind is a lively mind, enjoying freedom from the bondage of sin, freedom from the turmoil and darkness that torment the carnal mind: in two words, *life* and *peace.*

James admonishes us, "Cleanse your hands, ye sinners; and purify your hearts, ye double minded"; then promises, "Draw nigh to God, and he will draw nigh to you." (James 4:8.) This is a beautifully comforting thought to those who have struggled with the servitude of a sin-racked soul. To have the Lord draw near to one who has felt so unworthy and unclean is a blessing of the highest magnitude.

Remember the fervor with which Alma recounted his purification of soul?

> Now, as my mind caught hold upon this thought [the Atonement],
> I cried within my heart: O Jesus, thou Son of God, have mercy on

me, who am in the gall of bitterness, and am encircled about by the everlasting chains of death.

And now, behold, when I thought this, I could remember my pains no more; yea, I was harrowed up by the memory of my sins no more.

And oh, what joy, and what marvelous light I did behold; yea, my soul was filled with joy as exceeding as was my pain!

Yea, I say unto you, my son, that there could be nothing so exquisite and so bitter as were my pains. Yea, and again I say unto you, my son, that on the other hand, there can be nothing so exquisite and sweet as was my joy. (Alma 36:18-21.)

Elder M. Russell Ballard relates a modern day story of a man who had sunk to the depths of sin and then worked his way back. He came to know this man when he performed the temple sealing ordinances for him and his family.

Elder Ballard says, first quoting from a letter the man wrote to him:

"I was born into the Church and was taught the gospel at my mother's knee. Through her diligence and perseverance, she kindled a small ember of testimony that never left me even through some of the roughest times of my life. In my teen years Satan hit me hard. It was during the late 1960s and early 1970s, a time of great turmoil, and Satan was hard at work on me. I was taken with the practice of free drugs, free love, free fun, and the rest of the world be damned. Beginning with my first drink of alcohol, I began to slowly deteriorate. After alcohol, other drugs were that much easier to use. In order to take drugs, you must become a good liar. You learn to do whatever it takes to conceal your behavior from others.

"After many years of living this way, all my moral fiber seemed to be completely eroded away. I had a minimal amount of conscience and had sunk to the depths of despair and depression. I watched friends die from drugs and suicide. As time passed, my friends and I were exposed to the criminal justice system. In fact, many of my former friends are still in prison. Had it not been for the small flicker of testimony instilled in me by my mother when I was a child, to know that Heavenly Father could still love me, I have reservations as to whether I would even be writing this letter today."

Some parents might have given up hope on this prodigal son, but not this man's mother. She continued to believe that he would find

his way back to the teachings of his childhood and once again place
his trust in the Lord Jesus Christ. With the loving support of his
family and friends, that is exactly what he did. Let me read again
from his letter:

"If there is one thing I have learned, it is that no matter how lost
you feel, no matter how low you may have sunk, there can be forgiveness and peace. I learned that the further one drifts from the
Lord, the harder it is to return to Him and His teachings. But once
I opened my heart and called out in prayer to Heavenly Father to help
me in the name of His Son Jesus Christ, I came to know the power
of repentance and the blessings of obedience to God's
commandments."

Brothers and sisters, I wish all of you could have been with us in
the temple that day to feel the joy of hope fulfilled. (CR, *Ensign*,
November 1992, pp. 32-33.)

This man and his family experienced, as Alma did, the eternal joy
that comes through repentance and making right choices.

The latter-day scriptures also give beautiful promises to us: "And
now, verily, verily, I say unto thee, put your trust in that Spirit which
leadeth to do good—yea, to do justly, to walk humbly, to judge righteously; and this is my Spirit. Verily, verily, I say unto you, I will
impart unto you of my Spirit, which shall enlighten your mind, which
shall fill your soul with joy." (D&C 11:12-13.) The companionship of
the Spirit brings light to the mind and joy to the soul. The joy of the
Lord is indescribable to one who has never felt it, but is of utmost worth
and desirability. Would we not be willing to sacrifice the puny pleasure
of sin for such a blessing?

Moving upward in worthiness and commitment, we find even more
blessings available: "Behold, the Lord requireth the heart and a willing
mind; and the willing and obedient shall eat the good of the land of Zion
in these last days." (D&C 64:34.) Zion is both a place for the gathering
of the Lord's people, and a state of being for those worthy to gather
there. "And the Lord called his people ZION, because they were of one
heart and one mind." (Moses 7:18.) People worthy of these blessings
will have put the temptations of Satan away from them, will feel the
Savior's joy, and will be willing to give their minds and hearts to the
Lord and to building up His Kingdom.

And even more specific blessings will be reserved for those who lose
themselves sufficiently in the mind and will of the Lord. "And again,

verily I say unto you that it is your privilege, and a promise I give unto you that have been ordained unto this ministry, that inasmuch as you strip yourselves from jealousies and fears, and humble yourselves before me, for ye are not sufficiently humble, the veil shall be rent and you shall see me and know that I am—not with the carnal neither natural mind, but with the spiritual." (D&C 67:10.) Truly, "eye hath not seen, nor ear heard, neither hath entered into the heart of man, the things which God hath prepared for them that love him." (1 Corinthians 2:9.)

With this vision before our eyes as to the beauties and glories of the clean, chaste, pure mind, our motivation should be strong enough to carry us into what Alma called "an experiment upon my words." (Alma 32:27.) The quest to find the way to cleanse our minds and open our hearts to the sweetness of light and spirit will be one of excitement and challenge. We will find the way engrossing and the goals fulfilling as we move forward step by step into a new realm of mental and spiritual light. Relish the search!

How Can We Control Our Thoughts?

The Law of the Harvest

The Doctrine and Covenants teaches us that "when we obtain any blessing from God, it is by obedience to that law upon which it is predicated." (D&C 130:21.) In other words, keeping the Word of Wisdom brings us certain blessings, which are predicated upon obedience to the Word of Wisdom. Attendance at the temple brings us certain blessings which are predicated upon temple attendance. Choosing to think pure thoughts will bring us blessings predicated upon thinking pure thoughts. And so on. This is sometimes referred to as the Law of the Harvest: "For whatsoever a man soweth, that shall he also reap." (Galatians 6:7.)

When we keep the full Gospel law, we are entitled to receive the Lord's blessings, and if we are not getting the desired results, we need to learn the law better and to follow it more strictly. By His own word, the Lord is bound when we do what He tells us to. Also by His word, if we do not follow the law upon which a blessing is predicated, we have no promise. (See D&C 130:20-21 and 82:10.)

Where Are You Headed?

"You will arrive at where you are going unless you change direction." This statement seems simplistic enough, but it is amazing how many times we ignore it. We have in mind what we want to happen, and we are astounded and disappointed when it does not happen, even though the things we have been doing are leading directly away from the desired result.

We see examples of this: parents who want their children to behave in a way contrary to what the parents themselves are doing; teachers who wonder why children in a Primary class are rowdy and disinterested in a lesson poorly prepared and poorly presented; a slovenly husband who wonders why his wife is cranky and upset at his table manners. Be sure, as you approach the process of controlling your thoughts, that your methods are in harmony with the "law of the harvest", leading you toward the beautiful goal you desire. It has been said that the chief cause of failure and unhappiness in this life is trading what you want most for what you want at the moment. Why do we do that?

When you are contemplating a situation with which you are not satisfied in your life, ask yourself, "Where is this behavior or practice taking me?" Then, "What is my real goal—what do I really want to happen?" And finally, "What behavior or practice will take me there?" More simply put, "What do I want?" and "Why don't I have it?" Relate this exercise to your eternal, long-term goals.

For example, perhaps you are uneasy about watching too much television. You want to accomplish some important goals such as scripture study, meaningful family time, and a better evening routine, but so often you find yourself, and possibly the whole family, plunked down in front of the television, soaking up the dubious values there presented.

You ask yourself, "What happens because we watch so much television?" Your answer may be, "We don't talk to one another very much. Everyone seems so short-tempered. Important evening tasks such as chores or homework are overlooked."

Then you ask yourself, "What do I really want to happen?" Your answer is, "I want my home to be a place of nurturing, where we draw together as family members in love and mutual support. I want our hours to be filled with useful activity, fun, and learning." Of course your greatest long-term goal is eternal life for yourself and your family. A home such as you long for is a vital part of achieving this goal.

Finally you ask yourself what practices will take you there, and what do you need to do to initiate them. This may sound like a tall order, but when you look at the situation in this light, you realize that the first thing you must do is tame the electronic beast. You decide you will make some family rules limiting how much television will be watched in your home, and *what* will be watched. And *you* commit to follow the rules along with your children.

Limiting TV watching will create a vacuum in your home, so to fill it, you need to make plans for some of these goals: regular family home evening, interviewing your children, a chore system to teach your children to work, adding fun family activities to your schedule, daily family scripture study, reading aloud for pleasure, and so on. Of course these things cannot be integrated into your family life instantly, but if you plan to introduce them one at a time, they will become part of the fabric of your family life.

Applying this approach to the issue of controlling thoughts, if you are having a problem in this regard, you know where your current behavior has taken you. The first two chapters have focused on the fact that pure thoughts are essential to your peace of mind and progress toward eternal life. With this information you may now want to purify your mind, to focus on the solutions, the practices that will take you where you want to go.

This is a step-by-step program. An overview of the five points will help you the reader to evaluate your own circumstances. You will find that the points overlap and interlock, but your best success will result from concentrating on one point at a time, and trying to accomplish it, meanwhile keeping the others in mind and working on them as led by the Spirit. Approach each step with a repentant heart and a willingness to change.

A Five-Point Plan for Controlling Thoughts

1. Pray for the Lord's help.
2. Take responsibility for all of your thoughts.
3. Cut off the flow of trash.
4. Replace evil thoughts with something good.
5. Be engaged in a good cause.

Remember that the second principle of the gospel is repentance. All of us have need of this principle, and it is of utmost importance that we come forward with a humble heart and a contrite spirit, in the spirit of repentance, willing to change established patterns of behavior in preference for those that will more directly lead us to where we want to go. We pray earnestly that your heart will be touched to feel this way as you begin to use this five point plan for purifying your thoughts.

Step One: Pray for the Lord's Help

Purification Begins with Prayer

When we are really in earnest about making changes in our lives that will result in controlling our thoughts and cleansing our lives, we need help. We may have fallen to levels from which we are unable to lift ourselves. The bombardment of evil thoughts, accompanied as they always are by actions which we now regret, seems too heavy and too difficult to recover from by our own power. Rather than giving in to such feelings it is essential to appeal to that Source which has power to lift us up. This is a vital step in learning to control our thoughts and cleanse our lives.

Bishop H. Burke Peterson advised us to begin this purification of our minds with prayer: "The secret of cleansing the spirit of impurities is not very complicated. It begins with prayer every morning and ends with prayer every night. This is the most important step I know in the process. It may simply be a prayer for strength to turn from bad habits or a prayer that sin will be distasteful to you, remembering not all prayers are answered the same day or even the next day. Sometimes it takes a long time. But with this step in place, I've seen hundreds of miracles take place." ("Clean Thoughts, Pure Lives," *Ensign*, September 1984, p. 73.)

Prayer is more than just a supplication, even more than a communication with your Father in Heaven. There is power in prayer, a tapping into the forces that create and generate, govern and regulate throughout the universe. Did He not create all things? Are we not His sons and daughters? He has assured us these powers are available to us, if we make ourselves available to Him. The scriptures are full of promises of power through prayer:

> Humble yourselves in the sight of the Lord, and he shall lift you up. (James 4:10.)

> Be thou humble; and the Lord thy God shall lead thee by the hand, and give thee answer to thy prayers. (D&C 112:10.)

> All victory and glory is brought to pass unto you through your diligence, faithfulness, and prayers of faith. (D&C 103:36.)

We will be strengthened against Satan's temptations if we pray. Jesus said, "Behold, verily, verily, I say unto you, ye must watch and pray always lest ye enter into temptation; for Satan desireth to have you, that he may sift you as wheat.

"Therefore ye must always pray unto the Father in my name." (3 Nephi 18:19.)

Remember to always pray to the Father in the name of Jesus Christ, our Savior, our Mediator, our Advocate with our Father.

Nephi asked the Lord for a very special gift: "O Lord, wilt thou redeem my soul? Wilt thou deliver me out of the hands of mine enemies? *Wilt thou make me that I may shake at the appearance of sin?*" (2 Nephi 4:31, emphasis added.)

Nephi asked the Lord to make him detest sin so much that he would shake at its very appearance. We can also ask for this gift. The Lord can cause us to abhor sin. We need to ask Him. He already knows what we need; essential to the process is to open the door by asking. Part of the strengthening process is confessing to Him that we want to keep His commandments, asking for help to cleanse the mind of all unrighteousness, and pleading for the strength to live a righteous life.

Pray to your Father in Heaven for help. Ask Him to lift you up and make you equal to the task of controlling your thoughts. Be specific about what you want. Pray that evil thoughts will become distasteful to you. Pray that you will abhor evil no matter where it comes from. Pray for the influence of the Holy Spirit. Your Father in Heaven loves you; He will help you. "Verily, verily, I say unto you, even as you desire of me so it shall be done unto you." (D&C 11:8.)

The Lord wants to help us overcome evil thoughts, and He only waits for us to ask Him. Elder Eldred G. Smith assures us: "If you ask the

Lord for help, he will give you strength, power, and ability to overcome Lucifer and withstand his efforts, and thus you will be strengthened and made more perfect. . . . The Lord has made no promise to those who try to go it alone." ("Decisions," *Ensign*, December 1971, p. 46.)

Adversity and Prayer

Often we find it takes adversity to cause us to turn to the Lord for help. Adversity is an integral part of this mortal life. With the help of the Lord, adversity can be one of our greatest teachers. President Spencer W. Kimball said we can be stronger for the struggle: "Is there not wisdom in [God's] giving us trials that we might rise above them, responsibilities that we might achieve, work to harden our muscles, sorrows to try our souls? Are we not exposed to temptations to test our strength, sickness that we might learn patience, death that we might be immortalized and glorified?" (*Faith Precedes the Miracle*, p. 97.)

The scriptures also promise us our afflictions will ultimately be for our good. "Therefore, he giveth this promise unto you, with an immutable covenant that they shall be fulfilled; and all things wherewith you have been afflicted shall work together for your good, and to my name's glory, saith the Lord." (D&C 98:3.)

Lehi said to his son Jacob, who had suffered much tribulation in his life, "Thou knowest the greatness of God; and he shall consecrate thine afflictions for thy gain." (2 Nephi 2:2.) Adversity has a sanctifying effect, if we remain faithful.

The Lord is in charge of this world. He knows our circumstances. He will bless, guide, and help us as we live our lives. He will "order all things for your good, as fast as ye are able to receive them." (D&C 111:11.) There is a lovely idea embodied here, that of making ourselves ready for a higher good, which the Lord holds ready to give us, when we are able to receive.

The trials we undergo are evidence of the Lord's love for us. "My son, despise not thou the chastening of the Lord, nor faint when thou art rebuked of him: For whom the Lord loveth he chasteneth, and scourgeth every son whom he receiveth." (Hebrews 12:5-6.)

If you are chastised by the Lord, remember He chastens those He loves. Take the chastisement in good spirit. Repent as necessary, put your life in order, do what pleases your Heavenly Father.

Although adversity is part of our earthly experience and cannot be completely avoided, there is a great amount of suffering that can and should be avoided, because it is a result of sin. President Kimball said, "There are many causes for human suffering—including war, disease, and poverty—and the suffering that proceeds from each of these is very real, but I would not be true to my trust if I did not say that the most persistent cause of human suffering, that suffering which causes the deepest pain, is sin—the violation of the commandments given to us by God." (*Teachings of Spencer W. Kimball*, p. 155.)

We avoid unnecessary suffering in this life by keeping the commandments. This includes controlling our minds. If we let our thoughts go uncontrolled, sin and suffering lie at the door. Overcoming evil thoughts is one of the trials we face in this life, and if we are successful, the struggle prepares us for the eternities to come. We must strive to become pure in heart. Elder O. Leslie Stone said, "If we strive to be like God, then we will do all we possibly can to cast from our minds and actions all unholy and ungodly things, that our motives will be honorable and our hearts pure." (CR, *Ensign*, November 1974, p. 32.)

Remember, the Lord is the great healer. He can heal our minds. Elder Bruce R. McConkie said, "The growth of faith in the heart of an earthbound pilgrim, and the healing, as it were, of the soul of man, is as great a miracle as—nay, a far greater miracle than—the healing of the physical body." (*The Mortal Messiah*, Vol. 2, p. 12.)

Our faith is required if our minds are to be healed. Elder James E. Talmage said, "Read the record of the youthful demoniac whose agonized father brought his son to the Master, pleading pitiably "If thou canst do any thing, have compassion on us and help us." To this qualified intercession Jesus replied "If thou canst believe" and added "All things are possible to him that believeth." (Read Mark 9:14-29). The faith requisite to the healing was not that of the Healer alone, but primarily faith on the part of the suppliant." (*The Vitality of Mormonism*, p. 80.)

In the pre-mortal existence we eagerly accepted the opportunity to come to earth knowing that we would have joy and sorrow. We also knew that we could have eternal life if we were faithful. President Kimball emphasized our eagerness in the preexistence to accept the conditions of mortality:

> We knew before we were born that we were coming to the earth for bodies and experience and that we would have joys and sorrows, ease and pain, comforts and hardships, health and sickness, successes

and disappointments, and we knew also that after a period of life we would die. We accepted all these eventualities with a glad heart, eager to accept both the favorable and the unfavorable. We eagerly accepted the chance to come earthward even though it might be for only a day or a year. Perhaps we were not so much concerned whether we should die of disease, of accident, or of senility. We were willing to take life as it came and as we might organize and control it, and this without murmur, complaint, or unreasonable demands. (*Faith Precedes the Miracle*, p. 106.)

We prevent all the suffering we can through good choices, obedience to the commandments, and avoidance of sin. However, mortality will always include adversity, and we knew before we came into mortality that we would be tested. President Marion G. Romney said, "Our mission, as a church, is to bring people to a knowledge of Christ and thus avoid all unnecessary suffering. We are aware, however, that should all men accept and live his teachings, adversity and affliction would still abound because, in the words of the Prophet Joseph Smith, 'Men have to suffer that they may come upon Mount Zion and be exalted above the heavens.' (*Documentary History of the Church* 5:556)

"This does not mean that we crave suffering. We avoid all we can. However, we now know, and we all knew when we elected to come into mortality, that we would here be proved in the crucible of adversity and affliction." (CR, October 1969, p. 57.)

As we struggle to control our thoughts, we will become stronger, and we will learn things we would never have learned if we had not been tried and tested. President Brigham Young said all our experiences can be for our good if we treat them as learning opportunities: "There is not a single condition of life that is entirely unnecessary; there is not one hour's experience but what is beneficial to all those who make it their study, and aim to improve upon the experience they gain." (*Journal of Discourses*, 9:292.)

President Spencer W. Kimball added, "Suffering can make saints of people as they learn patience, long-suffering, and self-mastery. The sufferings of our Savior were part of his education." (*Faith Precedes the Miracle*, p. 98.)

Even though we know the Lord tests us through adversity, keep in mind that God does not tempt us. In the New Testament we read, "Let no man say when he is tempted, I am tempted of God: for God cannot be tempted with evil, neither tempteth he any man." (James 1:13.)

We must trust the Lord when He tells us that all our trials will be for our good. Someday we will understand the reasons for everything that happens in this life. Elder Delbert L. Stapley said, "Sometime in the eternities to come, we will see that our trials were calculated to cause us to turn to our Heavenly Father for strength and support. Any affliction or suffering we are called upon to bear may be directed to give us experience, refinement, and perfection." (CR, *Ensign*, November 1977, p. 20.)

If we put our trust in God He will support us in our trials. Alma told his son, "Whosoever shall put their trust in God shall be supported in their trials, and their troubles, and their afflictions, and shall be lifted up at the last day." (Alma 36:3.)

Prayer: An Armor of Protection Against Temptation

Many of our problems are the result of our bad choices, or our sins. Prayer helps to protect us from that situation. President Kimball reminded us of the protective power of prayer: "Let us all revive our individual and family prayers. Prayer is an armor of protection against temptation and I promise you that if you will teach your children to pray, fervently and full of faith, many of your problems are solved before they begin." (*Teachings of Spencer W. Kimball*, p. 117.)

If we pray with all our hearts for help in resisting our temptations and then use all the control we can muster, the Lord will strengthen us and we will win out over temptation. The Savior said, "Watch and pray, that ye enter not into temptation: the spirit indeed is willing, but the flesh is weak." (Matthew 26:41.)

When we are striving to overcome temptation, prayer can be our shield. President George Q. Cannon, formerly of the First Presidency, called prayer "the bulwark of the Saints. It shields and protects those who offer it in sincerity and faith. Without prayer, man is exposed to wicked temptations and to every evil. When he goes unto the Lord in humility, He shows him his weaknesses and the dangers by which he is surrounded. This prompts him who prays to seek unto God for strength to overcome his weaknesses and to resist every temptation. His faith is strengthened by having his prayers answered. He has communion with his Heavenly Father through the Holy Ghost, and that Spirit becomes his constant companion and guide." (*Gospel Truth*, pp. 411-412.)

Jesus Christ promised His people "I will be [your] shield." (D&C 35:14.) The psalmist wrote, "The LORD is my strength and my shield." (Psalms 28:7.) "But thou, O LORD, art a shield for me." (Psalms 3:3.) We need this shield against Satan's temptations. The Lord provides it if we will put our faith in Him and keep His commandments, and pray for the blessing. "And inasmuch as ye are humble and faithful and call upon my name, behold, I will give you the victory." (D&C 104:82.)

Prayer can strengthen us to overcome temptation! In a recent missionary homecoming sacrament meeting, the enthusiastic young elder told this story about a woman he taught while on his mission. She wanted to join the Church, but she found it very difficult giving up coffee. She was in her sixties and had drunk coffee her whole life. Finally one day she triumphantly announced to the missionary that she had overcome her desire to drink coffee. "How did you do it?" he asked. She replied, "Well, I took my coffee pot and put it under the bed. That way, in order to get it, I had to get down on my knees. While I was on my knees I figured I might as well go ahead and pray, and when I prayed, I no longer wanted the coffee!"

This good woman took literally Alma's admonition to "call on his holy name, and watch and pray continually, that ye may not be tempted above that which ye can bear." (Alma 13:28.) Through prayer she found the strength she needed to overcome a lifelong habit.

Always remember that all of God's children were born with a certain amount of self-control. If we use the self-control we have to the fullest degree, then pray wholeheartedly for more control, He will strengthen us. President Kimball said, "We pray for righteousness but do not expect the Lord to *make us good*. He will help us to perfect ourselves, and as we pray for controls and exercise those controls, we grow toward perfection." (*Faith Precedes the Miracle*, p. 203.)

We use our own strength to withstand Satan's temptations, and the Lord adds to that strength, making us equal to any trial. We can use this procedure to avoid any kind of temptation—we can become strengthened to the point that it has no effect on us.

We should ask for the specific strength or help we need. For example, perhaps we have ugly thoughts that come into our minds over and over again. In this case, we can cry unto the Lord that He will stop these ugly thoughts from coming into our minds, and that He will strengthen us so we can control our minds.

When we are tempted to dwell on or enlarge on a bad thought we can remind ourselves to use our own self-control to get rid of the bad thought, and then pray. At this point God will strengthen us and we will avoid enlarging on the bad thought.

Our Savior was tempted as we are. How did He respond to temptation? In D&C 20:22 we read, "He suffered temptations but gave no heed unto them." When you are tempted, pray until the temptation leaves, and it will leave. With our own self-control and strength from God, we, like the Savior, will not give heed to temptation.

When Satan puts a bad thought into your mind, cast it out immediately. Do it sharply, positively, and promptly; close the discussion. If you allow Satan into your mind, you tread on dangerous territory. Walk away from it. When you are tempted, President Kimball suggests, say to Satan, as the Savior did: "'Get thee hence, Satan,' meaning, likely, 'Get out of my sight—get out of my presence—I will not listen—I will have nothing to do with you.' Then, we read, 'The devil leaveth him.'" (*The Miracle of Forgiveness*, p. 216.) If you follow this procedure, the devil will leave you also.

Temptation is most severe in our areas of personal weakness. Elder Delbert L. Stapley tells us that: "Satan and his followers are constantly looking for weakness in our armor of spiritual protection, and when it is found, every pressure and stratagem is placed upon it to infiltrate our souls and destroy us." ("Our Responsibility: To Save the World," *Ensign*, December 1971, pp. 94-95.)

We cannot compromise with this destroyer. We make sure we cut him off without response. We do not listen to his enticements or entertain his thoughts. We do not cross into his territory. We do not risk one R-rated movie, watch one immoral TV show, or choose one corrupt video. We elect to be clean in every area of our lives.

The Lord said, "Ye shall bind yourselves to act in all holiness before me." (D&C 43:9.) In our morning prayer we can bind ourselves—commit ourselves—for that day to do what we know the Lord would have us do. We should discuss with Him the weakness we are trying to overcome and ask for strength; then promise to strive all that day to use all the self-control we have to withstand temptation.

Evil Thoughts and Unrepented Sin

It may be that recurring evil thoughts are a result of unrepented sin. Bishop H. Burke Petersen advised, "When necessary, receive the blessing that comes with the confession process. Too many are harboring the inner feeling of guilt resulting from unrepented mistakes. Part of the repentance process is confession. If you happen to be one of those who has this need, I plead with you to go see your bishop before the sun sets today." (*Ensign*, September 1984, p. 73.)

As you know, all major sins must be confessed to the bishop. If you have unresolved sins, see your bishop at once. Do willingly what he asks you to do. Be humble and fully repent; you can get rid of the burden of guilt that follows unrepented sins. You will be so glad you did. Great happiness will fill your soul as you put your life in order.

True repentance will effect changes in behavior. After one recognizes wrong behavior, remorse brings a desire to change lives for good. At this point, commit yourself to keep all of God's commandments. Go the extra mile in serving the Lord. Search for ways to reach out and render service to others. "Godly sorrow worketh repentance to salvation not to be repented of: but the sorrow of the world worketh death." (2 Cor. 7:10.)

Elder F. Burton Howard described it thus: "In order to be forgiven, a transgressor must experience godly sorrow. (See 2 Cor. 7:10.) He must have anguish of soul and genuine regret. This sorrow must be strong enough and long enough to motivate the additional processes of repentance, or it is not deep enough. Regret must be great enough so as to bring forth a changed person. That person must demonstrate that he is different than before by doing different and better things." (CR, *Ensign*, May 1983, p. 59.)

Humble yourself before the Lord. Be willing to forego your previous habits and indulgences in favor of a higher course. Let your godly sorrow work repentance unto forgiveness in your own life. Then when you have fully complied, when your repentance is complete and the works of righteousness have been fulfilled, allow your faith in Christ's Atonement to bring peace to your heart.

Elder Richard G. Scott explains that we should not continue to relive sins after true repentance: "Suffering does not bring forgiveness. It comes through faith in Christ and obedience to His teachings, so that His gift of redemption can apply. . . . Can't you see that to continue to suffer for sins, when there has been proper repentance and forgiveness of the Lord, is not prompted by the Savior. . . . Satan would encourage you to continue to relive the details of past mistakes, knowing that such thoughts make progress, growth, and service difficult to attain." (CR, *Ensign*, May 1986, pp. 10-11.)

Hope is a glorious gospel principle. The Lord provided a way for us. The good news of the gospel is "Peace on earth", and Jesus Christ came to provide that hope. Nephi exulted: "Awake, my soul! No longer droop in sin. Rejoice, O my heart . . . Do not slacken my strength because of mine afflictions . . . yea, my soul will rejoice in thee, my God, and the rock of my salvation." (2 Nephi 4:28-30.)

The Lord's Grace

When we exercise faith in Christ by relying completely on Him, He helps us understand where our weaknesses lie, so we can work to overcome them with His help. This formula is given to us in the Book of Mormon: "And if men come unto me I will show unto them their weakness. I give unto men weakness that they may be humble; and my grace is sufficient for all men that humble themselves before me; for if they humble themselves before me, and have faith in me, then will I make weak things become strong unto them." (Ether 12:27.)

Christ is speaking of the grace which He affords to the humble to make weak things become strong. Grace has a great depth of meaning. One meaning is the gift of resurrection which is given to us freely by the grace of Christ. "There is no flesh that can dwell in the presence of God, save it be through the merits, and mercy, and grace of the Holy Messiah, who layeth down his life according to the flesh, and taketh it again by the power of the Spirit, that he may bring to pass the resurrection of the dead, being the first that should rise." (2 Nephi 2:8.) Another is His bridging the gap between justice and mercy, and taking upon Himself our sins. "For all have sinned, and come short of the glory of God; Being justified freely by his grace through the redemption that is in Christ Jesus." (Romans 3:23-24.) The Bible Dictionary refers to *grace* as "an enabling power that allows men and women to lay hold on eternal life and exaltation after they have expended their own best efforts." (p. 697.)

In all these instances, grace has reference to power from God beyond that of our mortal ability, an "enabling power" which bridges the gap between what mortals are able to do for themselves, and the desired result. "Nevertheless, the Lord God showeth us our weakness that we may know that it is by his grace, and his great condescensions unto the children of men, that we have power to do these things." (Jacob 4:7.)

Being brought face to face with our weaknesses and shortcomings is a very humbling experience. As we become aware of our personal deficiencies, we must in meekness believe that Jesus Christ can help us, and then we must *ask* for His help.

There is great power available to the faithful humble seeker. This power, the grace of Christ, can enable us to overcome any weakness. Elder Boyd K. Packer described it: "But you yourself can call upon a power that can renew your body. You yourself can draw upon a power that will reinforce your will. . . . Oh, if I could only convince you that you are a son or a daughter of Almighty God! You have a righteous, spiritual power—an inheritance that you have hardly touched. You have an Elder Brother who is your Advocate, your Strength, your Protector, your Mediator, your Physician." (*Devotional Speeches of the Year,* Provo, Utah: Brigham Young University Press, 1978, p. 40.)

Christ, our Savior, has the power to transform our lives. Through Him our natures can literally be changed. We can change from what we are to the person we hope to become. President Benson reaffirmed this truth when he said, "The Lord works from the inside out. The world works from the outside in. . . . Christ changes men, who then change their environment. The world would shape human behavior, but *Christ can change human nature.* . . . Yes, Christ changes men, and changed men can change the world." (*The Teachings of Ezra Taft Benson,* p. 79, emphasis added.)

Jesus Christ, speaking to the Nephites, taught them not to cast out an unworthy person from their places of worship, saying there was hope such a person might choose to be healed by the power of Christ: "Nevertheless, ye shall not cast him out of your synagogues, or your places of worship, for unto such shall ye continue to minister; for ye know not but what they will return and repent, and come unto me with full purpose of heart, and I shall heal them; and ye shall be the means of bringing salvation unto them." (3 Nephi 18:32.)

This hope is available to all of us through the grace of Christ. "For we labor diligently to write, to persuade our children, and also our brethren, to believe in Christ, and to be reconciled to God; for we know that it is by grace that we are saved, after all we can do." (2 Nephi 25:23.) Prayer is the way we tap into the power available through the grace of Christ.

Surrender Your Life to God

The culmination of this step is to reconcile yourself to God. Surrender your will to His. Agree to keep all His commandments. Acknowledge your great need for His help in all facets of your life, and allow Him to lead, direct and help you with all your problems. Declare your love for Him and for His Son. Thank Him for His great love. Thank Him for the answers your prayers. Thank Him for the Atonement His Son wrought in your behalf. Ask for the blessings you need. Ask Him to apply the blood of Christ to your sins. Ask Him to change your nature.

President Spencer W. Kimball explained how, with the help of the Lord, we can accomplish any righteous goal: "The man who leans heavily upon his Lord becomes the master of self and can accomplish anything he sets out to do, whether it be to secure the brass plates, build a ship, overcome a habit, or conquer a deep-seated transgression." (*The Miracle of Forgiveness*, p. 176.)

"Lean heavily upon the Lord"—what a beautiful expression of the help that is available. He will bear you up. He will support your efforts. He will hear and answer your prayers. He will help you become the master of yourself, help you break your bad thought habits, and make you clean.

Alma promised deliverance to those who trust in God, saying, "I would that ye should remember, that as much as ye shall put your trust in God even so much ye shall be delivered out of your trials, and your troubles, and your afflictions, and ye shall be lifted up at the last day." (Alma 38:5.)

To receive these blessings, we must more than simply believe in Christ. President Ezra Taft Benson advised us to rely totally on the Lord: "Faith in Him is more than mere acknowledgment that He lives. It is more than professing belief. Faith in Jesus Christ consists of complete reliance on Him." (CR, *Ensign*, November 1983, p. 8.)

In our prayers we should acknowledge our complete dependence on Him who created us. When we have faith in Him, love Him, depend on Him, and lean heavily upon Him, we prepare ourselves to receive His strength. We exercise our own power of choice to subject ourselves to His will and make ourselves ready for His blessings, trusting that He knows what is best for us, and wants what is best for us.

"Therefore, cheer up your hearts, and remember that ye are free to act for yourselves—to choose the way of everlasting death or the way of eternal life. . . . Reconcile yourselves to the will of God, and not to the will of the devil and the flesh; and remember, after ye are reconciled unto God, that it is only in and through the grace of God that ye are saved." (2 Nephi 10:23-24.)

Praying from the Extremity of Need

There is a deeper level of prayer that is reached in our deepest need, when we fully realize our need for our Father in Heaven, and the impossibility of accomplishing what we need without His help.

This level of prayer is described in the play *Shadowlands*. The Christian author C.S. Lewis is faced with the imminent death of his beloved wife from cancer. He says, "I pray all the time these days. If I stopped praying, I think I'd stop living. . . . I pray because I can't help myself. I pray because I'm helpless. I pray because the need flows out of me all the time, waking and sleeping. It doesn't change God. It changes me." (*Shadowlands*, p. 103.)

The anguish of his great need brought supplication more profound than he had ever supposed possible. He was praying from the depths of his soul. He was changed by his need, and he was changed by his prayer. He sought grace to bridge the chasm between where he was and where he needed to be. His fervent pleading truly approached the throne of God.

Alma's missionary companion Amulek encouraged us to pray with this kind of deep humility and earnestness. He said,

> Yea, humble yourselves, and continue in prayer unto him. . . .
>
> But this is not all; ye must pour out your souls in your closets, and your secret places, and in your wilderness.
>
> Yea, and when you do not cry unto the Lord, let your hearts be full, drawn out in prayer unto him continually for your welfare, and also for the welfare of those who are around you. (Alma 34:19,26-27.)

Notice the power of this scripture! Alma says we should not merely ask, we should *cry* unto the Lord—*pour out our souls* to the Lord when seeking His help. This type of prayer is far more than just words. It is imploring from the heart for divine assistance. "I need . . . I lack . . . I desire . . . I hope . . . I ask . . . I pray . . . I plead . . . I beseech . . . I implore . . . I beg . . . I supplicate . . ." This type of prayer comes from the realization of our greatest need and the Lord's ability and willingness to help.

In the scriptures are many examples of this type of deep and fervent prayer and the answers received in return. Alma reached the point that he cried to the Lord from the depths of his tortured soul, and the Lord answered him.

Remember that Alma had been very wicked. The son of righteous parents, he nevertheless went about trying to destroy the Church of God. He and his friends sinned greatly and caused others to sin. In response to his father's continuing fervent prayer, Alma was one day stopped by an angel and fell into a state wherein he "could not open [his] mouth, neither had [he] the use of [his] limbs."

During this time he was tortured by the memory of his sins. He was "racked with eternal torment" because of the evil he had done. As he remembered his sins, his agony was so great he wished to "become extinct both soul and body, that [he] might not be brought to stand in the presence of . . . God to be judged of [his] deeds." For three days he suffered thus, the pain of the damned. Surely he reached his lowest point possible.

At this moment, however, he remembered hearing his father speak of Jesus Christ who would atone for the sins of the world. He uttered a humble, agonized prayer from the depths of his pain and need. His simple cry contained all the agony of his suffering and the intense hope that God would help him: "O Jesus, thou Son of God, have mercy on me, who am in the gall of bitterness, and am encircled about by the everlasting chains of death."

When Alma finally prayed from the extremity of his need, the Lord answered his prayer in a miraculous way. Alma says,

> And now, behold, when I thought this, I could remember my pains no more; yea, I was harrowed up by the memory of my sins no more.
>
> And oh, what joy, and what marvelous light I did behold; yea, my soul was filled with joy as exceeding as was my pain!
>
> Yea, I say unto you, my son, that there could be nothing so exquisite and so bitter as were my pains. Yea, and again I say unto you, my son, that on the other hand, there can be nothing so exquisite and sweet as was my joy. (Alma 36:10-21.)

God heard the plea that came from the depths of Alma's tortured soul, and sent relief. Alma was restored to physical and spiritual health, and he spent the rest of his life preaching the gospel.

Joseph Smith the Prophet also had an experience with this type of prayer. While a prisoner in the jail at Liberty, Missouri he reached one of the lowest points of his life. The Church was under heavy persecution and was in disarray. He had been forced from his home and was unable to protect and support his family. He was locked in a dark, filthy jail, powerless to care for the church or his family. It must have seemed like things could get no worse. At this point Joseph offered this fervent, anguished prayer:

O God, where art thou? And where is the pavilion that covereth thy hiding place?

How long shall thy hand be stayed, and thine eye, yea thy pure eye, behold from the eternal heavens the wrongs of thy people and of thy servants, and thine ear be penetrated with their cries?

Yea, O Lord, how long shall they suffer these wrongs and unlawful oppressions, before thine heart shall be softened toward them, and thy bowels be moved with compassion toward them?

O Lord God Almighty, maker of heaven, earth, and seas, and of all things that in them are, and who controllest and subjectest the devil, and the dark and benighted dominion of Sheol—stretch forth thy hand; let thine eye pierce; let thy pavilion be taken up; let thy hiding place no longer be covered; let thine ear be inclined; let thine heart be softened, and thy bowels moved with compassion toward us.

Remember thy suffering saints, O our God; and thy servants will rejoice in thy name forever. (D&C 121:1-6.)

The prophet pled with God to help him in his hour of trial. He explained the problem and asked for specific help. His prayer was answered with sweet consolation:

My son, peace be unto thy soul; thine adversity and thine afflictions shall be but a small moment;

And then, if thou endure it well, God shall exalt thee on high; thou shalt triumph over all thy foes.

Thy friends do stand by thee, and they shall hail thee again with warm hearts and friendly hands. (v. 7-9.)

Enos was another prophet who prayed in this way. President Kimball described his prayer in these words: "The supplication of Enos is written with a pen of anguish and on the paper of faith and with a willingness to totally prostrate himself that he might receive forgiveness. His words are mighty and definitive. He could have said merely, 'I want information,

Lord.' But he said, 'My soul hungered.' He could have merely prayed unto the Lord like too many pray, but in his eagerness for forgiveness, he said, 'I kneeled down before my Maker, and I cried unto him in mighty prayer and supplication for mine own soul.' (Enos 1:4.)" (*The Teachings of Spencer W. Kimball*, p. 126.)

These prayers can be examples to us. From the depth of our need, we are to be serious and earnest in our prayers, pleading for the blessings we require and expressing gratitude for the help we receive. The Lord will hear and answer our humble, sincere, thankful prayers.

When we feel the need for forgiveness as Enos or Alma did we can kneel down with anguish of soul before our maker and plead with Him for forgiveness. When Enos prayed this way, he reports, "There came a voice unto me, saying: Enos, thy sins are forgiven thee, and thou shalt be blessed." (Enos 1:5.) Imagine hearing the Lord say that to you!

As we can see from these three powerful examples, there is more to prayer than words. It is a true communication, soul to soul, with our Father, who watches us from Heaven. President Kimball writes, "If one rises from his knees having merely said words, he should fall back on his knees and remain there until he has established communication with the Lord who is very anxious to bless, but having given man his free agency, will not force himself upon that man." (*The Teachings of Spencer W. Kimball*, p. 124.)

What we are talking about here is the difference between *words* and *communication*. Sometimes the cry of an anguished soul has no words, but it communes directly with God.

Our prayer should be open and full, holding back nothing. President Kimball said "Some things are best prayed over only in private, where time and confidentiality are not considerations. If in these special moments of prayer we hold back from the Lord, it may mean that some blessings may be withheld from us. After all, we pray as petitioners before an all-wise Heavenly Father, so why should we ever think to hold back feelings or thoughts which bear upon our needs and our blessings? We hope that our people will have very bounteous prayers." (*The Teachings of Spencer W. Kimball*, p. 125.)

A sister in the Missionary Training Center had an experience that taught the importance of telling the Lord all of the thoughts and feelings of the heart. It was her second night in the MTC, and as she knelt to pray she found that her heart, instead of bursting with joy, was bursting with anger and loneliness. She says,

I didn't like my companion, I didn't like Spanish, and I didn't like myself much for being such a baby.

I started my prayer, but then realized that I didn't have anything to say. Although I desperately needed someone to talk to, it just didn't seem right to express my empty, lonely, and bitter feelings to Heavenly Father. I finally said a standard, "thank you for my health and the chance to be here," sort of prayer and crawled into bed.

Why doesn't Heavenly Father help me? If he really knows how I feel before I ask, what is he waiting for? I thought angrily.

Then I remembered the book of Enos, which I had read that afternoon. . . . His words echoed in my mind: "I did pour out my whole soul unto God" (Enos 1:9).

Had I done the same? Had I really humbly asked for Heavenly Father's help? I knew I hadn't.

I knelt again. This time I had plenty to say. I told my Father how frustrated I felt, how I couldn't learn the language, how I needed to love my companion, and how I wanted to do a good job. I cried as I explained that I felt abandoned, and I needed his help. . . .

This time I didn't say a prayer—I prayed. Again, I felt that my heart would burst, but this time with hope, peace, and love. As I climbed into bed, I still didn't know how things would work out, but I knew they would. ("A Change of Heart," Christie Ann Giles, *New Era*, November 1991, p. 11.)

When we honestly tell our Father in Heaven all of our needs, our feelings, our hopes and fears, He will be there to comfort and sustain us. Sister Jayne B. Malan, then First Counselor in the Young Women General Presidency, said,

Your Heavenly Father knows you and cares about what you are doing. He wants you to fulfill your divine mission, then come home and bring your family and friends with you. He wants you to be happy. Be on your knees daily and talk to your Heavenly Father. Share the happy times. Talk about what's hard for you. . . . Your Heavenly Father will understand. He'll be there to walk with you, and to comfort and protect you, for he has promised to those who seek him, "I will be on your right hand and on your left, and my Spirit shall be in your hearts, and mine angels round about you, to bear you up." (D&C 84:88.) (CR, *Ensign*, November 1989, p. 79.)

We gain much needed strength to solve our difficult problems when we discuss them with Him fully, explaining our desires and our purposes. When we are finished, President Kimball reminds us, "It would not hurt us, either, if we paused at the end of our prayers to do some intense listening—even for a moment or two—always praying, as the Savior did, 'not my will, but thine, be done.' (Luke 22:42.)" (*The Teachings of Spencer W. Kimball*, p. 125.)

There is a price to pay to get answers to our prayers. The Lord has promised, "Draw near unto me and I will draw near unto you; seek me diligently and ye shall find me; ask, and ye shall receive; knock, and it shall be opened unto you." (D&C 88:63.)

When we pray, let us draw near to Him with a broken heart and a contrite spirit, making ourselves worthy, and by exercising faith in our own behalf. Let's seek Him diligently by being willing to talk intimately with Him for as long as necessary, and listen for His answer. Let's ask specifically for what we need, telling him our purposes and intents. Let us listen to the Holy Spirit, who will guide our thoughts as we pray, and, when the door is opened, convey answers from our Father to us.

A spirit of humble thankfulness will open the heavenly conduit. Let's thank Him for the past answers to our prayers, and acknowledge His guiding and helping hand in our lives. Praying for the things we really need, with determination and faithfulness, will help us be worthy of the blessings we seek.

When we face something serious such as getting rid of evil thoughts, we can use this process. We can plead with the Lord to give us strength to control our thoughts. We can petition Him to send the Holy Ghost to be our guide for the entire day. We can strive to live a worthy life, and ask the Lord to put it into our hearts to abhor sin. We can pray that He will help us be faithful Latter-day Saints. Then make sure we live according to our prayers, and remember the "law of the harvest".

As you learn to pray this way, do your part by keeping your environment clean. Fortify yourself against temptation by praying morning and evening, and keeping a silent prayer in your heart. Attend only wholesome entertainment. Avoid vulgar language. Don't watch TV soaps or talk shows that use filthy language and discuss prurient topics. Read only good books. Think only Christ-like thoughts. Beseech your Father in Heaven to give you a pure heart.

If we have not received an answer to our righteous prayer, the reason may be we have not been persistent enough. We may have given up before we have paid the price for an answer. The Savior said, "Whatsoever ye shall ask the Father in my name, which is right, believing that ye shall receive, behold it shall be given unto you." (3 Nephi 18:20.)

Cleaning up our minds is a righteous desire and will be received if we persistently strive to accomplish it. The Savior commanded us to become pure in heart, and stated the promised blessing: "Purify your hearts, and cleanse your hands and your feet before me, that I may make you clean." (D&C 88:74.)

Our Savior gave, as in all things, the perfect example of the type of prayer we have been discussing—prayer that emanates from the soul in deep need and reaches God. When He was in the Garden of Gethsemane, drinking the dregs of the bitter cup of agony, He was constantly engaged in prayer to His Father. The scriptures tell us He "kneeled down, and prayed, Saying, Father, if thou be willing, remove this cup from me: nevertheless not my will, but thine, be done." In response to this prayer His Father sent "an angel unto him from heaven, strengthening him." (Luke 22:41-43.)

Our Savior reached out to His Father throughout His life. In his time of greatest trial, He did not stand alone. Remember that none of us ever need stand alone. God is always willing to help those who put their faith and trust in Him. President Kimball writes, "Man never stands alone unless his own desires are independence and egotism and selfishness. The realness and closeness and degree of communication depends upon us, his children. If we find our own paths, calculate our own best movements, continue independent of him, then of course we are estranged to that extent. Or on the other hand, our Lord is as close as we draw him to us by our righteousness and belief and faith." (*The Teachings of Spencer W. Kimball*, p. 126.)

Your Father is your greatest friend in times of personal trial, in your own "Gethsemanes," whatever they may be. Reach out to Him in this type of deep, fervent prayer, in trust that He will answer the cries of your soul as you seek for comfort and help. We testify that He will hear and answer your earnest prayers, as He has done for others, including Alma, Enos, Joseph Smith, and our Savior.

5

Step Two: Accept Responsibility for All of Your Thoughts

Blaming others for our problems seems to be a symptom of the time we live in. The courts are choked with lawsuits blaming others for accidents, emotional problems, financial woes, physical disabilities. When we encounter adversity we want "someone else" to fix it. More than that, we feel it is somehow their duty to do so. Recently we saw on the news the mother of a teenager blaming the juvenile court system that her son was in trouble with the law. Neither the son nor the mother had a feeling of responsibility for what had occurred.

If people have a hard time feeling responsible for actions, small wonder there is little accountability for controlling their thoughts. We are sure we can't control what goes on in our minds, "because we were raised wrong," "because we are exposed to too much evil in the media," "because Satan tempts us too much." Perhaps we say, "It is the fault of this permissive society," or "It is just too hard and we can't help it." A popular phrase a few years back was, "The devil made me do it."

Excuses such as these are lies, possibly whispered to our minds by Satan. He knows that we will never be able to overcome destructive thoughts until we take responsibility for our own lives and stop blaming others. These are all attempts to avoid the obligation to control our own behavior. As long as we blame our parents, school teachers, church leaders, the devil, or others for our thoughts or the resulting actions, we are not acting as responsible people.

The Gift of Agency

One of the central points of the plan of salvation is the God-given right of choice, or agency. "All truth is independent in that sphere in which God has placed it, to act for itself, as all intelligence also; otherwise there is no existence. Behold, here is the agency of man." (D&C 93:30,31.)

Satan, the father of lies, having the right to choose in the pre-mortal sphere, sought to usurp the power and glory of God. His idea was to bring us to this earth without the right of choice, and thence force us back into the presence of God, every one receiving salvation, and the glory would be given to him, Satan, rather than to God. Heavenly Father, however, knew the eternal plan from the beginning and knew that we must have the right to choose in order to learn and develop, and to test our obedience and willingness. He will never abridge our agency, or right to choose. The Lord said to Adam, "They taste the bitter, that they may know to prize the good. And it is given unto them to know good from evil; wherefore they are agents unto themselves." (Moses 6:56.) Nephi gave a concise explanation of this doctrine, including this explanation of the role of evil: "Wherefore, the Lord God gave unto man that he should act for himself. Wherefore, man could not act for himself save it should be that he was enticed by the one or the other." (2 Nephi 2:16.) "Wherefore, men are free according to the flesh; and all things are given them which are expedient unto man. And they are free to choose liberty and eternal life, through the great Mediator of all men, or to choose captivity and death, according to the captivity and power of the devil; for he seeketh that all men might be miserable like unto himself." (v. 27.)

Further, "And it must needs be that the devil should tempt the children of men, or they could not be agents unto themselves; for if they never should have bitter they could not know the sweet." (D&C 29:39.)

We have our agency, and the Lord has promised us help. Accepting responsibility for all our thoughts, good or bad, is the first step to improving them.

We Receive the Consequences of our Choices

Admittedly, society and the world in which we live have many problems, temptations, and adversity. This is essential to the plan of progression. As agents unto ourselves, we are free to choose. God will not force us to do good, and He will not allow the devil to force us to sin. The devil has power only as we permit him.

However, we are not free to choose the consequences of our acts. The results of our choices are inbuilt, and follow automatically. President

Ezra Taft Benson said, "You are the one who must decide whose thoughts you will entertain. You are free to choose—but you are not free to alter the consequences of those choices. You will be what you think about—what you consistently allow to occupy the stage of your mind." ("Think on Christ," *Ensign*, April 1984, p. 11.)

According to the scriptures, we have the right to choose. We also have the power to choose. Furthermore, we can and do choose what we think as well as what we do. This is our God-given agency. Thoughts precede action, therefore, we are accountable for our thoughts as well as our actions. They can and must be controlled. Choosing right thoughts averts most wrong actions. Understanding this will help us to break out of a spiritually defeating pattern of wrong thoughts, actions, and behavior, and into the freedom that making right choices affords us.

As previously cited, Nephi states that we are free to choose, and that we can in turn choose liberty or captivity. Our good choices result in liberty. Our poor choices bind us to the results of those choices—when we choose evil thoughts, evil actions follow. When we choose evil actions, captivity follows. We are tied to those results—we bind ourselves to that master we are following. Satan's way is destructive, "for he seeketh that all men might be miserable like unto himself." By yielding ourselves to him, we become agents of destruction to ourselves, our loved ones, and others whose lives we affect. Consequences follow in predictable sequences.

Satan entices us to be jealous. These thoughts impel us to act in a compulsive manner toward our loved one, abridging his or her independence, and bringing with it resentment and distress. Our eternal relationships suffer.

Satan entices us to take offense at words heard in General Conference, perhaps because of our transgressions. This offense leads us to harbor feelings of resentment and to speak ill of the man in authority, which undermines our faith, which leads us to try to justify our sins. It is a downward road.

All of us have unworthy thoughts at times. They are stimulated by circumstances or situations around us. We make conscious or unconscious choices when these thoughts come into our minds. We might harbor them, entertain them, and justify them, or we can cast them out in favor of thoughts which will lead us upward.

A beautiful doctrine is described by the Lord: "For the power is in them, wherein they are agents unto themselves. And inasmuch as men do good they shall in nowise lose their reward." (D&C 58:28.) We have not only the right to choose, but the power and ability to choose right. The consequences of right choices follow to our happiness just as surely as captivity follows poor choices. We are responsible for the consequences we receive. Elder Bruce R. McConkie reminds us: "The children of God were endowed with agency, the *power* and *ability* to either obey or disobey the divine will." (*Mormon Doctrine*, p 539, emphasis added.)

We Are Accountable for our Choices

In regard to freedom of choice, the Lord stated "That every man may act . . . according to the moral agency which I have given unto him, that every man may be accountable for his own sins in the day of judgment." (D&C 101:78.) A prime purpose for our agency is that we may receive according to our works, strength and development or harm in earth life, and reward for right or penalty for sins in the day of judgment. If the Lord does not hold us accountable for our misdeeds, neither will He bless us for our righteousness. The principle of accountability holds for both our good choices and our sorrowful choices.

Elder Richard L. Evans emphasized our freedom of choice and our responsibility when he said, "We *can* choose. . . . We *can* break *bad* habits; we *can* acquire *good* habits; we *can* choose what we *think* by the sheer determination to do so. God has given us our agency, the right and obligation to choose between right and wrong. . . . We can turn from a wrong road. But we are responsible, we are accountable for our thoughts, our words, our actions, and we must have the character and the conviction to keep self-control." (CR, *Improvement Era*, December 1963, p. 1113, emphasis included.)

We might remind ourselves that even our secret thoughts and secret acts are already known to God. In the Doctrine and Covenants we read that "there is none else save God that knowest thy thoughts and the intents of thy heart." (D&C 6:16.)

President George Q. Cannon also tells us that God knows every thought of our hearts: "There is not a single thought of our hearts which [God] does not comprehend; there is nothing connected with us He does not know. We may hide ourselves in the bowels of the earth, but we cannot conceal ourselves from His all-piercing sight. We may climb the highest mountains or descend into the deepest valleys, or we may go to the uttermost parts of the earth; but wherever we may go, He is there;

His power is there; His vision is there to hear and to comprehend the desires and the wishes of our hearts." (*Gospel Truth*, p. 101.)

In the final judgment all our thoughts and secret acts will be exposed: "And then shall the second angel sound his trump, and reveal the secret acts of men, and the thoughts and intents of their hearts, and the mighty works of God." (D&C 88:109.)

President John Taylor further explained what happens during that final judgment, saying, "Man sleeps for a time in the grave, and by-and-by he rises again from the dead and goes to judgment; and then the secret thoughts of all men are revealed before Him . . . we cannot hide them." (*Journal of Discourses*, Vol. 11, pp. 78-79.)

We will be judged by our secret thoughts, acts, and intents of our hearts. This should help all of us to be very careful as to the things we think about, especially secret, dishonorable thoughts. Surely the knowledge that God is aware of our secret thoughts will motivate us to discard those that are dishonorable.

Proper Motivation Develops Determination

How can we develop the determination to choose the right in what we think?

If we are properly motivated, we can do anything. For example, nothing motivates us to immediate action better than danger. Most of us would beat our own speed records if pursued by a grizzly bear! How can we motivate ourselves to choose proper thoughts?

The gospel teaches us who we are. Before we came to this earth, we lived with our Heavenly Father as spirit children. When we were born on this earth, the spirit was united with a physical body.

Elder Russell M. Nelson explains how knowing who we are helps us to gain self-mastery: "Before you can master yourself, my precious one, you need to know who you are. You consist of two parts—your physical body, and your spirit which lives within your body. You may have heard the expression 'mind over matter.' . . . I would like to . . . phrase it a little differently: 'Spirit over body.' That is self-mastery." (CR, *Ensign*, November 1985, p. 30.)

Our spirits are not only eternal, they also have the power to control our physical bodies. Elder Theodore M. Burton spoke of the power our spirits have over our bodies, and our bodily appetites:

The spirit within man is eternal, whereas his present body is mortal or temporal. Therefore, the spirit is more powerful than the body and is able to control the body. Sometimes we think ourselves sick. There are also times when we can think ourselves well. But there is no need to let the body and bodily appetites control our actions. The spirit within us is more powerful than the body, and we can use that spirit to commit ourselves to righteous actions. We *can* control the body and its bodily appetites. It is fallacious to say that we were created with propensities and appetites we cannot control. It is simply not true that people are born with such powerful appetites and passions that they are powerless to control them. God would not be a righteous God if man were created with drives he could not control.

I admit that some people have greater drives and appetites than others, but I say that a righteous God has given us minds and wills by means of which, if we desire, we can control and limit those passions and appetites. Satan has no control over us unless we give him that control. (CR, *Ensign*, May 1981, pp. 29-30.)

Our spirits were thousands of years old when we were born into this world. They were pure and holy when they entered our bodies. They are more powerful than our physical bodies. If we will let the spiritual side of us take the lead, we will do right. Satan can't control us unless we let him! With the help of God we can win this battle.

A good way to accomplish something is to make goals. Our loftiest goal should be achieving eternal life, and this thought is powerful motivation. We now know that in order to purify ourselves we must control our thoughts. If we desire it with all our hearts, we can have eternal life.

Replace Despair with Faith

We can use the agency with which our Father in Heaven has endowed us to make choices which strengthen us. If we think we can control our thoughts, we can. We will work at it until we find a way.

It may not be easy. If we have allowed our minds to fill with degrading thoughts, we may feel we are worthless. We may have been in the downward spiral so long that we feel it is impossible to change. We may have tried again and again, without success, so we feel God has forsaken us, or that we are beyond His love. Despair takes hold.

However, as we replace these negative, evil thoughts with positive thoughts, our feelings change. We begin to feel good about ourselves.

Righteous feelings help us to listen to the whisperings of the Holy Spirit, and give place for righteous desires. In this receptive mood, we can feel God's love. Despair gives way for hope. Faith—the assurance that God and Christ live, that they love us, and that they can and will assist us— enables us. Righteous desires lift us, bring peace to our hearts, encourage us, and translate into actions. As we emphasize righteous actions, they become good habits, a new approach to life's problems that transforms our lives.

One of our young families was having family home evening together, discussing King Benjamin's exhortation to the saints to love one another and to serve one another. They gave some examples of service that was on the level of their young children. After the lesson and the treats, six-year-old Peter was helping his dad tidy the kitchen and wash the dishes. "Dad," he said thoughtfully, "is this service, like King Benjamin was talking about?" "Yes, Peter," his dad assured him. A few minutes of reflective silence as they continued their work, then Peter said: "Dad, I really like doing spiritual things with you."

Can you see how important it is to think righteous thoughts? Everything of worth starts with good thoughts. It puts us ahead of Satan's enticements. Choosing to read the Book of Mormon, for example, fills our minds with righteous thoughts. Heeding the Spirit, we turn those righteous thoughts into desire and commitment so that we want to keep all of the commandments of our Father in Heaven. Keeping the commandments increases the desire to build His kingdom. The process of working in His kingdom develops a sterling character. We become faithful Latter-day Saints.

Faith enables us to stubbornly withstand the temptation to think bad thoughts. As our resistance grows stronger, we think fewer and fewer bad thoughts.

Faith enables us to ask the Lord for strength to overcome. As we pray for strength, we become stronger. By keeping the commandments and working to build the Lord's kingdom, we stay strong.

President Spencer W. Kimball's counsel: "We would all be well advised to avoid the motivation to the evil thought. If persistently resisted it will 'get the message' and stay away." (*The Miracle of Forgiveness*, p. 114.)

Let's take the prophet at his word. If we resist all evil thoughts, eventually they stay away. With faith in the Savior, and confidence in our own ability, we can replace evil thoughts with noble, uplifting thoughts that will lead us toward our goal of eternal life. The Lord did not send us here to fail. He will help us to succeed if we will make the commitment to keep His commandments in faith.

Fear is the opposite of faith. As we build our faith, fear diminishes. As we put our trust in God, our faith increases. As we serve the Lord faithfully, our faith becomes stronger and our joy and happiness increase.

President Ezra Taft Benson assures us that if we live in faith and righteousness, we need not fear. "[There are] two principle essentials for security and peace: first, trust in God; and second a determination to keep the commandments, to serve the Lord, to do that which is right. Latter-day Saints who live according to these two admonitions—trust in God and keep the commandments—have nothing to fear." (*Conference Report*, October 1950, p. 146.)

We can do this. We can choose to think positively and purely if we have sufficient faith and determination to do so. We can control our thoughts. With God's help we can become pure in heart.

Make a Conscious Choice to Desire Righteousness

As we take responsibility for our thoughts and actions, we come to realize that not only do we make the choices, we also receive the results. If we understand this fully, we also recognize that we choose our wants and desires, along with our responses and behaviors. We can choose the desire to do right. We can make a conscious decision to use our agency to make that choice.

Alma teaches us to begin to exercise faith with a desire to believe, which will work in us until we have come to the full fruition of that faith (see Alma 32). In controlling our thoughts, we must also begin with a desire to overcome.

If we are determined to gain control of our minds and thus our own lives and destiny, we can do so with the help of God. We make the choice, take full responsibility for our actions, and begin the search for ways to make it happen. As we work to develop self-mastery, we can tune our eternal spirit to the guides our Father gave us. We can discipline ourselves to change. Repentance, the second principle of the gospel, is the ability to change.

Elder Jack H. Goaslind said, "When you are pure in your heart, when you desire that which is good, true, and beautiful, then you can avoid the pitfalls of life. If you build your foundation upon the 'rock of our

Redeemer, who is Christ,' then the devil 'shall have no power over you.' (Hel. 5:12.)" (CR, *Ensign*, May 1991, p. 47.)

The work of the Lord is truly the way to happiness. We are our Father in Heaven's children. As a king's son can become a king, so as sons and daughters of our heavenly parents we can become like them. When we begin to choose right because we desire it, we are learning to accept responsibility for what we think, what we say, and what we do. Let's keep our minds riveted on the big picture, eternal life. Let's not get distracted in the worldly ways that are so prevalent. Although we are in the world, let us not be of the world. Let's take joy in being found in holy places doing the work of the Lord. The temple, the chapel, and our homes are holy places.

Even though we must live in the world we don't have to become like the world. We can remain absolutely honest in our daily work. We can use clean language. We can be caring and concerned about others. We can set an example of what a saint should be. We can lead those around us to come unto Christ. As we choose to live out our lives in service to our Father in Heaven, our lives will be sweet and purposeful.

"Pure Dogged Determination"

Consider this statement by Elder S. Dilworth Young: "We . . . will find the key which opens the door to the solution of [our] problems by the practice of this simple but potent word—determination. Without it the gospel will not affect us very much." (CR, *Improvement Era*, December 1963, p. 1088.)

Determination! What a plain yet profound word. It is one we often hear associated with success in the material world, and yet it is even more important and rewarding in our spiritual lives.

If we truly want to change our lives we must be determined. Our covenanted "re-birth" must be given great emphasis. We must stand resolved at all cost to *live* the gospel principles that make the change possible. We must be, in the words of the Prophet Joseph Smith, "determined to serve [the Lord] at all hazards." (Teachings, p. 150.) Continuing, Elder Young echoed the prophet's words: "That is the word, and that is what we need today—*determination*—voluntary determination to serve [the Lord] at all hazards." (CR, *Improvement Era*, December 1963, p. 1088, emphasis included.)

By being determined to serve Jesus Christ at all hazards we put the proper emphasis on gospel principles that will help us change our lives.

When we serve Jesus Christ, we keep His commandments. Referring to the pioneers, Elder Young adds, "The past generations to which we point with solemn pride were determined to stand pure before the Lord. Each generation must in its turn show equal determination if it is to be accepted." (CR, *Improvement Era*, December 1963, p. 1088.)

The pioneers were determined to keep the faith even to the point of leaving their homes and colonizing a new land. Are we that determined? Will we give up, not our homes, but our sins to become pure in heart?

Many of our ancestors stood firm throughout their lives. Even if we are converts to the Church, the pioneers are our "spiritual ancestors," and we can look to them for strength and example. Of these spiritual ancestors President George Albert Smith said, "If we want to honor our Heavenly Father today and please him, there is no better way than for us to live up to the ideals and standards of those who came here one hundred years ago. Their determination to serve God and keep His commandments brought them success and happiness. Though they were more than one thousand miles away from civilization they believed in the promises of the Lord, that if they would be blessed and prospered they must seek first, not last, the Kingdom of God and His righteousness." (*Sharing the Gospel With Others*, pp. 41-42.)

Determination to "seek first . . . the Kingdom of God" has been a characteristic of the faithful sons and daughters of God through the ages. After Adam and Eve were driven out of the Garden of Eden they were determined to keep God's commandments. They stood firm in the gospel. We read in the Pearl of Great Price, "And after many days an angel of the Lord appeared unto Adam, saying: Why dost thou offer sacrifices unto the Lord? And Adam said unto him: I know not, save the Lord commanded me." (Moses 5:6.) Moses was determined to free the children of Israel, and with God's help he did. Jesus Christ was determined to finish the atonement in the Garden of Gethsemane and on the cross, and He succeeded. He became the Savior of the world when He paid the price for our sins. Joseph Smith was determined to translate the Book of Mormon into English and restore the true church, and with God's help he did. The pioneers were determined to find a place where they could worship their Father in Heaven in peace and with God's help they did.

How determined are we? Can we withstand the pressures in our lives today? Are we determined not to see R-rated movies, evil videos, prurient talk shows and soap operas? Are we determined not to allow our minds to build upon Satan's evil thoughts? Will we cast them out immediately when they come?

Are we determined to build our own lives and strengthen others by being resourceful and creative in our thoughts? Are we determined to pray to our Father in Heaven and ask for strength to combat Satan and stay on the straight and narrow path leading to eternal life? Let us stand determined to keep God's commandments and follow His prophets at any price.

Elder Bruce R. McConkie said, "To endure to the end requires *diligence*—that is, pure dogged determination, perseverance, application to duty, zeal, industry, heed to counsel. Continuing diligence in church service is a mark of testimony, conversion, and spiritual stability. 'Be ye doers of the word, and not hearers only.' (Jas. 1:22.)" (*Mormon Doctrine*, p. 197.)

Let's endure to the end with pure dogged determination! Let's make our commitment to become pure in heart, and then with determination live the gospel principles which will make our lives happy and successful, and enable us to endure to the end.

President N. Eldon Tanner said, "May we as individuals have the determination, the courage, the ability to stand up and do those things which we know are right, realizing that we are the spirit children of God, with the potential to make it possible to be like him if we will follow his teachings to keep his commandments. And while we are doing it we will be happier, more successful, more respected and loved than if we were doing anything else, because this is the work of the Lord." (CR, *Improvement Era*, December 1968, p. 93.)

There are other blessings that come with our determination to live the Gospel. Elder ElRay L. Christiansen promised: "Contentment and peace will come only when we trust in God and admit our sins and forsake them and then with determination '. . . live by every word that proceedeth forth from the mouth of God.' (D&C 84:44.)" (CR, *Improvement Era*, December 1964, p. 1098.)

Let's be more determined to live the principles that will help us control our thoughts. Let's take delight in living up to all the commitments we have made to God. Let's recommit ourselves to living the principles that will help us become pure of heart.

Elder Neal A. Maxwell describes a friend's struggle to purify his mind: "I was a nearby witness to the manner in which [my] friend did make strong determination to be chaste of mind and heart, persisting in that promise and anguishing his soul no more . . . Thus the energy of his soul could be expended in good causes, being no more wearied down by endless enticements." (*Of One Heart*, p. 33.)

We can also get to the point where we give no heed to the temptation to think impure thoughts. Then we too can channel our energy into good causes. Thus we go on the offensive—a much easier way to fight Satan. Moving ahead in service and good works, reaching out to others in need, and building up the Kingdom of God put us in a position of strength in our struggle against evil. No longer need we fight discouragement, anxiety, and allurements. We can become masters of ourselves by letting our pure spirits rule our bodies and our lives instead of letting the lusts of the flesh rule us. President Brigham Young said, "Let each person be determined, in the name of the Lord Jesus Christ, to overcome every besetment—to be the master of himself, that the Spirit God has put in your tabernacles shall rule." (*Discourses of Brigham Young*, pp. 265-66.)

This is a righteous cause. If we pray to God for help He will strengthen us. As we become stronger we will be able to move along on the road to becoming pure in heart. If we seek first the Kingdom of God, putting our Father in Heaven first in our lives, everything will fall into its proper place and our lives will be right. Many before us have succeeded. We can too.

So, as we begin the process of cleansing our minds, let's do it with determined hearts. President Joseph Fielding Smith said, "Let us be faithful and humble. Let us live the religion of Jesus Christ, put away the weaknesses of the flesh, and cleave to the Lord and his truth with undivided hearts, with full determination to fight the good fight of faith, and continue steadfast to the end." (CR, *Improvement Era*, December 1968, p. 42.)

Then after we have repented of all our sins let us stand determined to endure to the end. Let us be faithful to our Savior every day of our lives. Let us correct our inconsistencies, put away our follies, and stand firm as saints in His church.

Commit to the Plan: Learn It and Follow It

This chapter has encouraged us to take responsibility for our thoughts and not blame others for what we think or do. We have learned that there are consequences to all our choices, and that happiness comes from making prudent choices, misery comes from disobedience to gospel law. We have learned that we have the ability and power to choose right, and that we will be held accountable for our choices. We have learned that we can make a goal of achieving eternal life by being determined to obey the commandments of the Lord, beginning with controlling our thoughts and purifying our minds.

Our missionaries, as a group, live very close to the Lord. One reason for this is that they have made a commitment to do so. Another is that they have a definite plan for keeping themselves close to Him, and as they follow it, they receive the blessings afforded by it. Basically, they are taught to PRAY, STUDY, and WORK. If we adopt this format, we will find our quest for self-mastery to be much easier.

When we begin our commitment by letting the desire for a better life work in us, we should prayerfully dedicate our efforts to the Lord. Then we continue with fervent *prayer* on a daily basis, even hourly as we find ourselves tempted, or faced with decisions. *Study* consists of reading and pondering the scriptures daily, with full intent of heart to learn the principles of the gospel and apply them as tools to implement change in our lives. Thus we fill our minds with good things to the exclusion of the troublesome thoughts we are trying to erase. The *work* to be done will be learned as you proceed, step by step, for changing any habit or behavior is hard work. It requires determination and diligence. As we move forward into the next step of the plan and begin to change, we should strive to be steadfast in praying for help and accepting responsibility for our thoughts and actions. The chapters following will help with further steps—guidelines and principles perhaps not previously understood.

God bless you in your determined effort!

6

Step Three: "Cut Off the Flow of Trash"

Our Minds Partake of All We Hear and See

The environment in which we lives our lives, in which we move about day by day, is one of the greatest predictors of what passes into our minds.

Elder J. Thomas Fyans explained:

> One interesting feature about [the rivers of South America] is their different colors. The Madiera, for example, is called a white river because its waters carry fine clay particles along its course. The black color of the Rio Negro comes from decaying organic materials picked up in the forests through which it passes. Still other rivers flow over white sands and often appear emerald green or turquoise blue.
>
> Just as these rivers are colored by the substances picked up as they flow along, so the streams of our thoughts are colored by the material through which they are channeled. (In Conference Report, Buenos Aires Area Conference 1975, pp. 28-29, as quoted in "Duties and Blessings of the Priesthood," Basic Manual for Priesthood Holders, part B, 1987, pp. 272-73.)

Our minds partake of all the things we hear and see. Like the river that takes on fine particles along its course, discoloring its water, so our thoughts are colored by what we pass through them. A clean, wholesome atmosphere will produce a clean mind. On the other hand, there is no such thing as partaking of evil entertainments and not becoming tainted.

Bishop H. Burke Petersen says if we want to cleanse our minds we must first, in his words, "cut off the flow of trash": "Sometimes our minds may be so cluttered with filth and pollution that they are unable to be a spiritual strength to us and to our families. . . . To avoid this impure condition . . . we must [first] stop the flow into our minds of these unhealthy and unwholesome streams of experiences and thoughts. Evil acts are preceded by unrighteous thoughts, and unrighteous thoughts are born of vulgar stories, jokes, pictures, conversations, and a myriad of other evils or foolish products." ("Clean Thoughts, Pure Lives," *Ensign*, September 1984, p. 72.)

"No Dumping Allowed"

So, as we begin the process of cleaning up our minds, we first stop any more pollution from entering our minds through the channels of our senses.

Elder Boyd K. Packer spoke of the methods he uses to keep his mind free from unwanted waste:

> Years ago I put up some signs in my mind. They are very clearly printed and simply read: No Trespassing, No Dumping Allowed. On occasions it has been necessary to show them very plainly to others.
>
> I do not want anything coming into my mind that does not have some useful purpose or some value that makes it worth keeping. I have enough trouble keeping the weeds down that sprout there on their own without permitting someone else to clutter my mind with things that do not edify.
>
> I've hauled a few of these away in my lifetime. Occasionally I've tossed these thoughts back over the fence where they came from, when it could be done in a friendly manner. (*That All May Be Edified*, p. 65.)

What are some of the sources of mental pollution we are to shun?

The First Presidency stated in 1972, "We . . . are deeply concerned about this growing obscenity in print, on record and tape, on television, and in motion pictures. We therefore urge Latter-day Saint parents to teach their children to avoid smut in any of its many insidious forms." (First Presidency Statement, *Church News*, 7 October 1972, p. 5.)

The obscenity that alarmed the First Presidency at that time has increased a great deal since then, to now include print, records, tape, and CDs, television, motion pictures, computer games, videos, telephone, even cartoons and children's toys. So also the results of this obscenity have increased frightfully in the lives of people and in society itself. If we are to avoid its disastrous effects in our lives, we need to redouble our efforts to avoid not only obscenity, but violence, brutality, and cruelty as well.

President Ezra Taft Benson reaffirmed this stance when he said:

> Consider carefully the words of the prophet Alma to his errant son, Corianton, "Forsake your sins, and go no more after the lusts of your eyes" (Alma 39:9).
>
> "The lusts of your eyes." In our day, what does that expression mean?
>
> Movies, television programs, and video recordings that are both suggestive and lewd.
>
> Magazines and books that are obscene and pornographic.
>
> We counsel you, young women, not to pollute your minds with such degrading matter, for the mind through which this filth passes is never the same afterwards. Don't see R-rated movies or vulgar videos or participate in any entertainment that is immoral, suggestive, or pornographic. And don't accept dates from young men who would take you to such entertainment. (CR, *Ensign*, November 1986, p. 84.)

President Benson specifically said we should not see R-rated movies or vulgar videos. We sometimes hear of the rating "R-but." This rating is spoken of by people who go to a movie that is "rated R, but it really wasn't that bad," "R, but it only had a few bad scenes," or "R, but it was worth seeing anyway." Can anything be worth doing if it contradicts the teachings of the prophet? Many PG or PG-13 movies are not fit to look at. If we go to a movie and find that it is not right we should have the courage to get up and leave.

Bishop H. Burke Petersen gave an excellent talk in which he unflinchingly detailed the evils available in modern media and society, and counseled us to avoid partaking of and engaging in them. He said,

> Some contribute to . . . personal weakness when they read filthy magazines, watch unwholesome movies, television shows and videos, or remain in a group where unclean discussions occur. Some married couples will even joke about sexual matters. Each of these kinds of experiences will weaken any spirit and make it less able to withstand the fiery darts of the adversary.

Now, my brothers and sisters, beware of loose thinkers. The subtlety of their influence can be disarming and destructive. Regardless of what others may do, we should not view or talk about suggestive movies. Shun them as you would the plague. A good movie with only a little pornography or vulgarity is not a good movie. Avoid pornographic magazines or pictures or music—and I plead with you, be careful of the music—or retelling filthy jokes or crude stories.

We're in the Lord's army. It is up to us to fight His battles. How do we do this? Bishop Peterson continued:

Once in a while we should stop and ask ourselves, "In whose army are we fighting? Whose battle lines are we defending, Satan's or the Savior's?" We are in one or the other, and, like it or not, our actions signal our true allegiance. Do you have the courage to walk away from an off-color movie or video? Or do you watch, listen, absorb, and suggest to yourself, "This soon will pass" or "Everyone is doing it; it must be acceptable entertainment"? Have you the courage to keep out of your home television shows and videotapes that are filled with suggestive sexual conversation and even visual experiences? (*Ensign*, September 1984, p. 72.)

In order to cut off the flow of trash, we must make difficult decisions for ourselves and our families. What does Elder Peterson advise? Do not listen to or repeat dirty jokes, or engage in unclean discussions. Don't read sexually oriented magazines. Be careful of the music you listen to. Do not attend movies with "only a little" pornography or vulgarity. Do not purchase or rent videotapes, or watch television programs that have suggestive or outright sexual portrayals or conversation. Do not watch graphic depictions of violence, murder, and other hideous forms of brutality.

Although movies, videos, and TV are frequently mentioned as things we need to be cautious of, there are other sources of mental pollution. President Ezra Taft Benson said,

Today, with the abundance of books available, it is the mark of a truly educated man to know what not to read. "Of making many books there is no end" (Ecclesiastes 12:12). Feed only on the best. As John Wesley's mother counseled him: "Avoid whatever weakens your reason, impairs the tenderness of your conscience, obscures your sense of God, takes off your relish for spiritual things, . . . increases the authority of the body over the mind."

The fact that a book is old does not necessarily make it of value. The fact that an author wrote one good work does not necessarily mean that all his books are worthy of your time. Do not make your mind a dumping ground for other people's garbage. It is harder to purge the mind of rotten reading than to purge the body of rotten food, and it is more damaging to the soul. ("In His Steps," *1979 Devotional Speeches of the Year*, p. 61.)

Disastrous Effects of Pornography

We should be embarrassed to recommend a movie to others which compromises moral or Church standards in any way. By compromising our standards we weaken ourselves, and become that lower thing. As we witness more filth of any kind we are gradually addicted to it. Satan binds us to himself. First we fantasize the immoral acts we have been witnessing. Soon we are trying them. If we don't repent and repent quickly, we may find it is too late.

Is it possible that a little thing like an improper movie can eventually have such devastating effects in our lives? President Gordon B. Hinckley said, "Speaking to the Prophet Joseph Smith in 1831, the Lord said: 'Out of small things proceedeth that which is great.' (D&C 64:33.) It is so with good or evil, my brothers and sisters. Small, kind acts can grow into mammoth good institutions. . . . It is so likewise with evil things. Small acts of dishonesty, small acts of an immoral nature, small outbursts of anger can grow into great and terrible things." (CR, *Ensign*, May 1984, p. 81.)

Draw the line when it comes to reading filthy magazines, watching unwholesome movies, videos, and TV. This includes talk shows and "soaps" when the language and content are foul and sordid. Just as one cigarette, one alcoholic beverage and one use of cocaine leads to more, reading one filthy magazine, watching even one unwholesome movie, video, or TV program fills our mind with images and ideas that recur and color our actions. Not only our own destiny is at risk, but the entire fabric of the society we live in is gradually being destroyed. We must cut off the flow of filth totally and completely.

Elder Joseph B. Wirthlin advised us that "pornography in all its forms —found at the movie theater, on television, and in printed form—constitutes a spiritual poison that is addictive and destructive. Every ounce of pornography and immoral entertainment will cause you to lose a pound of spirituality. And it will only take a few ounces of immorality to cause you to lose all of your spiritual strength, for the Lord's Spirit will not dwell in an unclean temple." ("Little Things Count," *New Era*, May 1988, p. 7.)

The result of continued ingestion of slime is spiritually devastating. As we watch increased amounts of filth and pollution, our testimonies weaken. We drive away the Holy Spirit. Our ability to make good decisions will be hampered. With our minds cluttered, we think less clearly. Satan has more control over us. If we don't exercise our faith, repent, and come back to the teachings of Christ we may find that Satan has us bound, that we are addicted to pornography, brutality, and the ideas of the world. This loss of spiritual strength is probably the most ruinous effect of pornography on the soul. Bishop H. Burke Peterson said,

> Every time you go through one of these experiences, the spirit steps down little by little. As I have reviewed Church court cases over the years, I have found that the tragedies that occur in the lives of men and women do not occur overnight in a hurry. They are a step-by-step process. Now, I am not suggesting that if you see immorality displayed in a movie you are going to be involved in immorality. Some will, in the process. But I do know this: there will be a dilution of the spiritual strength within you that will have its long-term effect, even if you never get involved in an immoral act. Every time you put some of this material into your mind, your righteousness and your power to do good, to think clearly, and to make decisions that are proper will be diluted. (*Ensign*, September 1984, p. 72-73.)

President Spencer W. Kimball points out the path to immorality, saying, "Certainly the tragedy of abortion often begins with a visit to an X-rated motion picture theater or fingering through an obscene magazine. The path to the grievous sins of fornication, adultery, and homosexuality can begin, too, with the viewing of some of the sex- and violence-oriented programs now being shown on television, including network television." (CR, *Ensign*, November 1976, p. 6.)

Great tragedy can begin with one bad experience. Making a clear conscious decision to avoid pollution can keep us from starting down this ugly path, and we won't wind up degraded as some do. We must choose proper entertainment, and occupy our minds with things wholesome. There is too much danger in this area.

Keeping Our Homes Pure

It takes courage, determination and action to keep these things out of our homes. When the first bit of filth shows its ugly head, turn off the TV, turn off the video, discard the magazine, turn off the radio, close the book. Do it immediately. Be an example of good in your home. Your children will follow you in keeping these things out of your home and out of their future homes. Our children develop wholesome appetites when we lead the way.

Elder David B. Haight admonishes us as parents to warn our children, saying, "Parents, discuss with your children of appropriate age, and in sensitive ways, the harmful effects and addictive nature of such material. Rigidly monitor the selection of television programs, movies, video-cassettes, music, and other forms of entertainment for your family. Let us never, by purchasing these damaging materials, contribute to the financial success of those who deal in this material." (CR, *Ensign*, November 1984, p. 72.)

Parents must take an active role in training the children to acquire a taste for good, wholesome media. When family home evening is held every week and meritorious lessons are given, when we go as a family to proper entertainment, we and our children learn to choose and enjoy that which will lead us upward. Not only that, but as the demand for good entertainment increases, the supply will also increase.

In this world where obscenity is so readily available, we have to instruct our children by word and example about its dangers. The opposite is unthinkable. It is addictive. Even small exposure to evil materials produces an appetite and an addiction grows. Their minds take on the ideas they are seeing and hearing. It is exciting and stimulating. We must teach our children to recognize the danger, and teach them how to make a courageous decision to not continue watching. They need the strength of character to leave if they find a movie they are seeing is inappropriate.

Do you take your family and societal values from the TV? Think how "soaps" affect our morals. Of them, Elder H. Burke Peterson said, "I think one of the subtle dangers that we face are the so-called 'soaps.'

They tell, teach, and display the deterioration in morals and in marriage. Have you thought lately how effective these shows are in piercing even the strongest spirit? We must not feed ourselves a diet of trash. We become what we think; we think about things we hear and read and see." (*Ensign*, September 1984, p. 72.)

Allowing corrupt television programs or movies to be shown in your home is like having raw sewage dumped on your family room floor. In fact, the evil programs are worse because you could clean up the mess and sanitize your floor, but it is very difficult to get these vile pictures out of your mind once you place them there.

You will find that the TV will be the hardest media to control. Keep the TV where you can see what is playing. If a worldly show comes on, turn it off. Talk with your children about the reasons for doing this. Train your children to be selective of what they watch. Note that this means *you* will also have to be very selective about what *you* watch.

Many people have gotten rid of their TVs. One man came home from work, saw the filth that was on TV, and was so enraged that he put his foot through the picture tube. We don't recommend you do this. However, if you can't control your TV, it would be better to get rid of it.

Do not just change the channel. When you do this, you will find that while you are going from channel to channel you may see and hear some suggestive or vulgar scenes. These indecent scenes will keep coming back to you as you continue your day, and will be a constant obstacle for you in trying to control your thoughts. Instead, get the TV schedule, pick out the program you want to see, then turn to that channel as you turn the TV on. If your TV is like mine, before you can see the picture you will be on your station. If this show starts to get off the strait and narrow, turn the TV off. Look through the TV schedule and find another program you want to watch. If you can't find a good program by this method, keep the TV turned off.

Sometimes while watching the news a report will come on that you know you won't want to hear. Just press your mute button or turn off the TV until it is over. Do the same with commercials that are not fit to watch.

Strengthen Our Youth

Help your children avoid exploitation, first by controlling what is available to be seen on TV or on their computers, and second by teaching them to make choices, even hard choices, as to what they allow into their minds. Perhaps before we are aware, children are making their own choices, and with so much filth and violence available, their minds may be brimming with scenes, sensations, images and ideas we would prefer they did not have. We have learned how damaging such things are to adult minds, and children are still forming their values and morals.

Make the effort to know what your children are watching and playing. Avoid toys and games that teach violence, destruction, and disregard for life. Make the effort to search out entertainment that is wholesome and worthwhile. It is possible to block out certain channels so they cannot come into your home, but you cannot control what they will watch in someone else's home unless the desire to choose right is built into them.

Today's youth need strong testimonies of the gospel in order to stand against Satan and all of his pollution that surrounds them in the media and increasingly in the society at large. Without this strength they may be lost. There is too much risk to allow ourselves to take the situation for granted.

Prayer is a great help. We should teach them to love their Father in Heaven, and turn to Him in their personal prayers night and morning, and to ask for help whenever they feel the need. Our children have learned to pray this way. They say it helps them to remain calm before a test in school and remember what they have studied. This faith and strength also helps them when they are confronted with daily choices, or when someone teases them to see an objectionable movie or video. As they pray and get answers to prayer they grow stronger in the Gospel. Heavenly Father, who knows all of their thoughts, will hear each prayer. Teach them to thank Him right at the time they are being blessed, hour by hour.

Priesthood blessings should be given on a regular basis. A blessing for each of the children before they go back to school each year is a great strengthening factor. They should also be given special blessings to help them solve the problems that come up in their lives. To feel the Spirit as the blessings are given is an assurance that the priesthood power is real and effective. Children who are thus blessed on a regular basis recognize the strength it gives them, and come to ask for their blessings. These priesthood blessings help shield them from the powers of Satan, and their testimonies grow in the gospel of Jesus Christ.

Our children have had many experiences when they have been faced with the decision whether to "sit through" inappropriate entertainment or to leave. We have tried to set the proper example for them.

Several years ago we took our three oldest daughters on a trip to Mexico. It was a wonderful time for us to focus in on them, as they were all in their teens and beginning to explore the world outside our home. We enjoyed swimming at the beach, attending the Ballet Folklorico, visiting the ruins of ancient civilizations.

One evening we went to a stage show, unaware of the burlesque nature of the program. As we sat there we all became more and more uncomfortable with the presentation. It was a small theater, and we were seated in the center of the audience. There was no way to slip quietly out. We could see our daughters looking at us to see what we would do. It was time for action! We all got up and walked out of the theater, the eyes of the performers and the audience upon us.

Several years later we had a rather humorous experience which showed us that our example had been noticed and followed.

One of our younger daughters, at the time a teenager, and some of her friends went to a movie (rated PG) that was touted as being quite good. As the movie got worse and worse, they began to think they should leave. She said the dead giveaway was when they sneaked looks at each other and found that they were all sitting there with their hands over their eyes! They all agreed that they should leave.

Behind them was a row of teenage boys, and as they got up to leave one of the boys said to them, "What's the matter, can't you take it?" Our daughter turned to them and said, "I don't *have* to take it!"

She and her friends went to the store and bought some treats, then returned to our home. When they arrived they were greeted by two of our married daughters and their husbands. They too had gone to a movie which had also turned out to be inappropriate, and they too had walked out. Finding themselves near our home and the evening still early, they had also bought treats and come for a visit. Everyone had a good laugh over the coincidence and quite enjoyed the evening together!

Find or make entertainment that is clean and more fun than that which destroys the soul. Use your imagination and other resources to make happy options available for yourself and your children.

Now is the time to begin to teach our children that *they* must control what enters their minds. In a society permeated with sin, as ours is, tomorrow may find our precious children already in deep trouble.

The Gospel: Our Shield

Even though it is difficult to avoid the harmful effects of inappropriate entertainment, we have a great gift to help us to keep these things out of our lives—the gospel. Elder Marion G. Romney explained how the gospel protects us: "We know that to qualify us to prevail against Satan and his wicked hosts, we have been given the gospel of Jesus Christ. We know that the Spirit of Christ and the power of his priesthood are ample shields to the power of Satan. We know that there is available to each of us the gift of the Holy Ghost—the power of revelation which embraces the gift of discernment by which we may unerringly detect the devil and the counterfeits he is so successfully foisting upon this gullible generation." (CR, *Ensign*, June 1971, pp. 36-37.)

We can win the battle against pollution with our whole family if we are willing to band together against all kinds of smut. The gospel teaches us to read the scriptures daily, have our personal and family prayers, and make ourselves worthy of the Holy Ghost. He will help us detect evil around us and give us strength to withstand it.

People have said, "I wish I could get rid of the evil thoughts I have in my mind." If you have such a problem, I plead with you to cut off the flow of trash today. Put the gospel to work in your life. Pray to your Father in Heaven for help. Do your part by resolutely keeping all the commandments and living a worthy life. Ask your bishop for an assignment in the Church. Volunteer to serve others and help build the Kingdom of God. Get the influence of the Holy Ghost back again, then stay on the strait and narrow path.

Make an agreement with yourself that you will pray for strength to resist looking at improper shows, TV, and magazines every time you become tempted. If we humble ourselves before God He will give us the strength to withstand this trash. We must pray every time we are tempted.

It is up to us to make these decisions. No one else can safeguard our minds for us. President Spencer W. Kimball, speaking in the women's conference, said that we are individually responsible to sort truth from trash: "You read the papers, you watch television, you hear the radio, you read books and magazines, and much that comes to your consciousness is designed to lead you astray.

"Much of what you read is scurrilous. It is to tempt you. You are intelligent women. You have learned from your infancy what is right. You must make your own decisions in determining if it is right or wrong." ("The Blessings and Responsibilities of Womanhood," *Ensign*, March 1976, p. 71.)

We must discipline ourselves to reject evil and choose good. It may be a lonely battle, because most of the world lives by a much lower standard. But if we put our faith in Jesus Christ and pray sincerely, He will give us the strength we need. This *will* work. We *can* prevail over the evils that threaten to overwhelm us.

This is the third point of the five-point program. We have learned the necessity for prayer, we have accepted responsibility for our actions and have committed to cut off the flow of trash into our lives. Next we learn some exciting principles about what to put in its place. Life is meant to be invigorating and energizing. You will find it so on the Lord's side of the line.

7

Step Four: Replace Evil Thoughts with Something Good

In our search for purity of mind, by means of earnest prayer and effort, we have now accepted responsibility for what we entertain in our minds. We have determined to cut off the flow of trash. We have made efforts to clean up the environment of our minds and are ready to remove the rubbish. This process will leave a void in our minds. Our minds will be filled with something. If our goal is to overcome evil thoughts, we must make further effort to fill the void with something good.

Elder Boyd K. Packer described the process of overcoming evil thoughts by replacing them with something good:

Do not try merely to *discard* a bad habit or a bad thought. *Replace* it. When you try to eliminate a bad habit, if the spot where it used to be is left open it will sneak back and crawl again into that empty space. It grew there; it will struggle to stay there. When you discard it, fill up the spot where it was. Replace it with something good. Replace it with unselfish thoughts, with unselfish acts. Then, if an evil habit or addiction tries to return, it will have to fight for attention. Sometimes it may win. Bad thoughts often have to be evicted a hundred times, or a thousand. But if they have to be evicted ten thousand times, never surrender to them. You are in charge of you. I repeat, it is very, very difficult to eliminate a bad habit just by trying to discard it. Replace it. Read in Matthew, chapter 12, verses 43 to 45, the parable of the empty house. There is a message in it for you. (*That All May Be Edified*, p. 196.)

The empty, bored mind is easy prey to thoughts that can reappear, even bringing in more evil. If we evict the destructive, non-paying tenant and supplant it with a good one, there will be no room for the evil thought to re-enter.

The Stage of Your Mind

President Ezra Taft Benson compares the mind to a stage:

> The mind has been likened to a stage on which only one act at a time can be performed. From one side of the wings the Lord, who loves you, is trying to put on the stage of your mind that which will bless you. From the other side of the wings the devil, who hates you, is trying to put on the stage of your mind that which will curse you.
>
> You are the stage manager—you are the one who decides which thought will occupy the stage. . . . You are the one who must decide whose thoughts you will entertain. . . .
>
> Sometimes you may have difficulty driving off the stage of your mind a certain evil thought. To drive it off, Elder Boyd K. Packer suggests that you sing an inspirational song of Zion, or just think on its words. Elder Bruce R. McConkie recommends that after the opening song, you might preach a sermon to yourself. In fact, he says the finest sermons he has ever preached have been preached to himself.
>
> . . . *Our accountability begins with how we handle the evil thought immediately after it is presented.* Like Jesus, we should positively and promptly terminate the temptation. ("Think on Christ," *Ensign*, April 1984, pp. 10-11, emphasis added.)

Thoughts may pop into your mind unbidden, but what you do with them makes all the difference. Good thoughts and bad thoughts are not compatible; bad thoughts leave the mind when good thoughts enter. You have the power of choice to replace them, which can be done in a number of ways.

Concentrate on What You Are Doing

How can we control our minds and force the bad thought out? One way is to fix the mind firmly on what is going on around us. We term this reality. When an unworthy idea appears, try this system. Instantly concentrate on reality—what you are doing, saying, seeing, and involved in—thus driving the evil thought off center stage.

Look away from the thing that triggered the evil thought. Force your mind to be involved in what is happening at the time. Really concentrate. Listen pointedly to the conversation that is going on, and become involved. Think of a new and better way to do the thing you are doing. Get totally absorbed in the color, texture, and arrangement of what you are looking at. Since the mind can only think on one thing at a time, make it think on something other than the evil thought that is striving for entry onto your stage.

You need the Lord's help. Sometimes you may throw out a thought, and it jumps back in at the earliest chance, like a TV screen flipping channels. But persistence wins out. Offer a quick, silent prayer. If you resist the thought, it will finally flee from you. You will have more control over your mind.

Consistently following this plan can train your mind to make the exchange so automatically that you will hardly notice the bad thought. It begins to work like a wheel going around, starting up instinctively when a bad thought tries to enter your mind, throwing it out and bringing your mind back to reality. Keep this up day after day, month after month, and you will see rapid improvement in your ability to control your thoughts. The more times you win, the easier it is to win. The incidents will become fewer and fewer. You will find you really can replace bad thoughts when you are determined to do so.

In quick summary, when you recognize an unwanted thought, instantly concentrate on reality, forcing the thought off center stage. Offer a quick, silent prayer, and choose what you think. It really works.

Productive Activity

A second plan is to avoid idle time by filling empty moments with productive activity. President Hugh B. Brown recommended this when he said, "It takes self-discipline to select a good book rather than a western on the TV, to enjoy a home evening with the family rather than go to a second-rate movie, to keep the mind in gear rather than let it idle, to think worthwhile thoughts in moments of relaxation, to read and memorize a verse while waiting for an appointment or a meal." (*You and Your Marriage*, p. 129.)

Organize small projects you can do when you have a few minutes to wait. Memorize scriptures, favorite hymns, or inspirational poetry. Think about the gospel. Study the scriptures. Be of service to your fellow beings.

An account was given years ago about a bus driver in a large city who had about five minutes to wait at the end of his route several times a day. There was a vacant piece of ground between the buildings which had become littered with trash. At first, he thought of putting a bag on his bus, and when he had to wait he would pick up trash and carry it away with him. Later it occurred to him that he could pull a few weeds each time he stopped. His fertile mind found other ways to use his five minute intervals, and he planted flowers and even brought a bench to put in his little "park". It was a great comfort to him when he saw people smiling at the beauty he had created, and stopping for a few minutes rest in what had previously been an eyesore.

It is important that we train our minds to be fertile and creative. Especially if we have turned off the TV, more time will be available for our own mental activities. Unless we fill it with something good, this time is particularly vulnerable to being attacked by evil thoughts. We must retrain our minds to think for themselves, rather than remaining empty and bored.

We should teach our young people to start cultivating good mental habits when they are young, and then continue to cultivate the mind throughout life. Be energetic and alert. Always have a wholesome project to be working on.

Photography is a splendid project for old or young. Art work of various forms, painting, sketching, weaving, quilting, or paper crafts, can be challenging and rewarding. Creative processes such as poetry, writing, and music are fulfilling. Computers offer so much challenge to master, to use, to program, to create with. Be careful with these new electronic devices, which can be used either for good or ill. Those activities in which you use your own mind rather than being entertained or occupied by the inventions of others are superior, and lead one on an upward path. There is literally no end to the possibilities by which one can occupy time, space, and energy in today's exploding technological society.

In all your processes, keep in touch with your personal Father and Creator. When you face a critical time where you know you may be tempted to think evil thoughts, pray to your Father in Heaven for deliverance. Ask Him to help you think only clean thoughts. Ask Him to help you concentrate on the good things you are doing. He will hear and answer your sincere, faithful prayers. He will help you win the battle.

Pray when confronted with the evil thought. Pray in your mind as you force yourself to concentrate on reality, or to fill your empty mind with something constructive. Let the prayer pass through your mind as you close your eyes and ears against tempting scenes or sounds. Fill the void with a word of praise to your Heavenly Father, who is helping you overcome a trial. Really express your gratitude.

Study the Gospel

A fourth procedure for filling the void left by the eviction of our evil thoughts, habits, or addictions is gospel study. Elder Boyd K. Packer stated, "The study of the doctrines of the gospel will improve behavior quicker than a study of behavior will improve behavior. Preoccupation with unworthy behavior can lead to unworthy behavior. That is why we stress so forcefully the study of the doctrines of the gospel." (CR, *Ensign,* November 1986, p. 17.)

Getting in your mind The Big Picture, the eternal perspective, is the most enlivening, invigorating experience an individual can have. It is hard to describe to one who has not experienced it—it is easier felt than recounted.

One of the best ways to experience this gospel excitement is to read the scriptures daily. Not only can you insulate yourself against temptation to evil by the daily devotional before you begin your work, but it puts you into enlightenment from the Holy Spirit. Have you felt the Holy Ghost giving you "sudden strokes" of ideas, information, urges, and affirmations? This is available not only for your Sunday School class lesson, but for your daily occupation as well. Jot down the ideas you receive from scripture study. They are most useful!

Listen to the scriptures on tape as you go to work and back or as you go to the grocery store and back. Listen to the Book of Mormon in your headset as you do your evening walk. Repetitious tasks like folding the laundry or mowing and weeding can be livened up by listening. It is more exciting than the current top 50, and infinitely more uplifting! Before you know it, you will have been through the whole standard works. You will find that the whole of Creation, times, seasons, principalities and powers, things both in Heaven and in earth take on new dimension and purpose. When you explore a subject, led by the Spirit from one topic to another, you will see that it all fits together into one complete whole. Your concept of daily events, activities, and issues is improved; your understanding is enlarged. Your entire outlook is energized. Technology to the rescue: books like *Jesus the Christ,* conference talks and other stimulating speakers are available on tape or on CD. Keep a gospel book in your car or briefcase, and turn to it when you have spare moments. You will have forgotten whatever was in the "hole" that is now overflowing with the vibrant and hopeful message of the gospel.

In Matthew 5:6 we read, "Blessed are they which do hunger and thirst after righteousness: for they shall be filled." What shall we be filled with? "And if your eye be single to my glory, your whole bodies shall be filled with light, and there shall be no darkness in you; and that body which is filled with light comprehendeth all things." (D&C 88:67.) The Book of Mormon rendition adds: "Blessed are they which do hunger and thirst after righteousness, for they shall be filled with the Holy Ghost." (3 Ne 12:6.) Through the Holy Ghost, we are filled with that Light of which Jesus Christ speaks.

An understanding of the Gospel in its fullness and our relationship to our Father in Heaven and our Savior will do more to fortify us against the evil one than any other activity. Truth has no end and its beauties will fill our minds with excitement and challenge to remove any place for boredom, emptiness, or dark thoughts.

Nephi expressed this great joy: "For my soul delighteth in the scriptures, and my heart pondereth them . . . my soul delighteth in the things of the Lord." (2 Nephi 4:15-16.)

Overcoming a Negative Disposition

A closely allied principle, also often misunderstood, is that negative thinking is also matter of choice. Many people say that a certain disposition to bad temper or critical thinking is "just the way they are." Quite the contrary is true, as we have learned in our consideration of the effect of evil in our minds. The Spirit of God is one of peace, love, efficacy, kindness, and charity. Negative feelings are inspired by the evil one in order to tear down our effectiveness, destroy our relationships with those we love, and make us less able to function in the Lord's kingdom on earth. In truth, the freedom of choice is active in this area of our lives. We can choose the thoughts which will build us up rather than choosing the negative thoughts which tear down our happiness and effectiveness.

Good thoughts can inspire us to greatness. If we allow our minds to dwell on the negative, we can spiral down until all we can do is sit and ponder our misfortune. On the other hand, we can be moved to lift ourselves up and put forth extra effort if we fill ourselves with inspiring thoughts from the scriptures and other good sources.

As we strive to be like Christ, some of our faults will disappear for lack of attention.

Elder Dean L. Larsen tells us how our thoughts determine our attitudes and behavior: "Thoughts have a great deal to do with how we live each day, whether we are enthusiastic or depressed, whether we experience success or failure, whether we are obedient or disobedient to the laws of God. Learning to control our thoughts is an essential part of our development here in mortal life. If we do not control our thoughts, they will eventually control us. There is that much power in thoughts." (*Free To Act*, pp. 95-96.)

Some people choose to approach life with a negative attitude. These people always seem to look for the bad in every situation. They make life miserable for themselves and those who live around them. Elder Rulon G. Craven described such people this way:

> Those who think negatively usually portray some of the following dispositions: bad temper, criticism, faultfinding, self-pity, persistent resentment, and the chronic feeling of being badly treated and disliked by others. Negative-thinking people are likely to spend their time thinking about their problems and therefore do not take time to think concerning solutions to their problems. They may also add to their own negative disposition by building on their negative thoughts. Since negative thoughts usually contain gross distortions that are bound to negatively affect their feelings, their problems continue. It becomes a vicious circle. But if they can become aware of their negative thinking, it is easier to stop thinking negatively. It is important to remember that we tend to feel the way we think. (*The Pursuit of Perfection*, p. 46.)

Do you see a little of yourself in this description? If so, perhaps you have allowed yourself to dwell on the negatives in life and thus you have become a bad-tempered person. When we allow a negative attitude to take over, we often hurt those around us. Elder LeGrande Richards spoke of this hurtful disposition thus: "An irritable man or woman is about the most objectionable creature there is. They should get down on their knees and ask the Lord to give them strength to overcome it as much as they would the habit of liquor or tobacco. Harsh words cut deeply. It takes a long while for such wounds to heal, if they ever do." (*LeGrande Richards: Beloved Apostle*, p. 25.)

Can we overcome the problem of irritability and bad temper? Can we change from being a negative to a positive person? Habitual anger is a process of continually choosing a bad or negative thought over a peaceful one. We look at a situation and allow our mind to slip into its old pattern. This or that has always "made us angry," and we presume it is the fault of the person or situation. Not so. What makes us angry is *our choice to become angry*. Another person or a thing cannot make that choice for us, therefore cannot "make us angry." Learning this one principle made an eternal difference in our home. It can make that difference in yours as well.

Understanding the anatomy of anger is helpful. Anger is a secondary emotion, following the primary emotion influenced by what we view as an unpleasant situation. When we experience the first emotion, such as jealousy, hurt pride, fear, and so on, we react by choosing anger, often as a defense against the pain of the first emotion. The first cause is generally unresolved expectations— someone or something did not perform according to our expectations—but you see, it is our own expectation that is disappointed. We cannot expect someone else to "make us happy", we make that choice according to the response we give to what happens to us or around us. We have the power to choose, and like it or not, we do choose our responses. We are responsible for our responses.

President George Q. Cannon said,

> *Everyone has the power* to close his heart against doubt, against darkness, against unbelief, against depression, against anger, against hatred, against jealousy, against malice, against envy. . . . We can help yielding to wrong influences and being quarrelsome and selfish.
>
> Whenever darkness fills our minds, we may know that we are not possessed of the Spirit of God, and we must get rid of it. When we are filled with the Spirit of God, we are filled with joy, with peace and with happiness no matter what our circumstances may be; for it is a spirit of cheerfulness and of happiness. (*Gospel Truth*, pp. 16-17, emphasis added.)

You have the power to close your heart against anger and other negative thinking! This knowledge is freeing and empowering. Instead of being the prisoner of your thoughts and feelings, you can exercise your free agency and forge the character you desire—one of patience, love, faith, humility, and hope.

The gospel principle of *hope* is one that can help us most in avoiding negative thinking and overcoming its effect in our lives. Hope is the opposite of despair. The good news brought by the Christmas angels was the gospel of hope: We can have peace on earth and good will among men! It comes through the way of life offered by Jesus Christ. There is no problem our Savior cannot help us solve. We have the hope that we will be forgiven, that we will participate in His rest and joy. Satan attacks us most severely when we are lowest in hope, or when we are in despair. Hope is the lifting principle of the gospel, enabling us to move forward with faith to cleaner, more productive lives. It moves us up to faithfulness.

Elder John H. Groberg talked about it:

> Let's not spend our time . . . worrying about justice being done to others. It will be done. Let's spend our time being *just* ourselves.
>
> One of Satan's ultimate weapons (if not the ultimate) is to remove hope from your life. He tries to convince you that you can't do it, that there is no hope. Thus, by removing hope, he removes Christ from your life, for Christ is hope. . . .
>
> *On the other hand, the thing Satan cannot fight is one who is full of hope—for he is then full of the Spirit of Christ—and when that hope is perfected or full, Satan has lost completely.* ("There is Always Hope," *BYU 1983-84 Fireside and Devotional Speeches*, p. 138, emphasis added.)

When we are discouraged, when we feel despair, we should pray that our Father in Heaven will increase our hope. Hope will return.

Another idea that can illuminate the darkness of our minds is to recognize the effect of pride in our decision-making: *pride* has a great deal to do with anger, jealousy, hatred, and doubt. We pridefully fill our minds with self-importance, and think that no one else can do it as well as we can, or that if someone else does not do as we think best, it will undermine our prominence in some way.

President Ezra Taft Benson often pointed out the scriptures that condemn the attitude of pride. It is the opposite of the humble, teachable heart that Jesus asked us to offer.

> Another face of pride is contention. Arguments, fights, unrighteous dominion, generation gaps, divorces, spouse abuse, riots, and disturbances all fall into this category of pride.
>
> Contention in our families drives the Spirit of the Lord away. It also drives many of our family members away. Contention ranges

from a hostile spoken word to worldwide conflicts. The scriptures tell us that "only by pride cometh contention." (Prov. 13:10; see also Prov. 28:25.)

The scriptures testify that the proud are easily offended and hold grudges. (See 1 Nephi 16:1-3.) They withhold forgiveness to keep another in their debt and to justify their injured feelings. (CR, *Ensign*, May 1989, p. 6.)

How do we overcome a negative disposition and develop a spirit of cheerfulness and happiness? Elder Rulon G. Craven taught us how to choose:

> A basic rule for overcoming a negative disposition is to admit to yourself that you are acting negatively and that your thinking may be the cause. Try to recognize negative conduct for what it is—self-defeating and destructive behavior. Try not to identify with, dwell on, or build on negative thoughts. Do not allow your day to begin with your mind entertaining negative, unpleasant, critical thoughts. Before you go to bed at night, reflect upon the day's activity and repent of any negative thoughts and acts. Rise in the morning with the firm objective of maintaining your mind free of negative thoughts. In so doing, you will be working toward self-perfection as well as more effective people relationships. Last, but not least, seek divine help by praying to the Lord for help in controlling negative thoughts and feelings. (*The Pursuit of Perfection*, p. 47.)

The way to change our attitude is to change our thinking. Good, healthy, positive thoughts produce a good attitude. There is a wonderful example of this in the Book of Mormon. Captain Moroni was leading the Nephites in battle when he saw that his men were being overcome with a negative thought: fear of "the fierceness and anger of the Lamanites." He realized that this negative thought was about to cause the men to *defeat themselves* by turning and fleeing from their enemies. What was Moroni's response? "Moroni, perceiving their intent, sent forth and *inspired their hearts with these thoughts*—yea, the thoughts of their lands, their liberty, yea, their freedom from bondage."

When the men's thoughts were inspired by what they were fighting for, they "turned upon the Lamanites, and they cried with one voice unto the Lord their God, for their liberty and their freedom from bondage." Now, instead of fleeing in fear, they "began to stand against the

Lamanites with power; and in that selfsame hour that they cried unto the Lord for their freedom, the Lamanites began to flee before them." (Alma 43:48-50, emphasis added.)

Notice that they not only replaced negative thoughts with positive ones, at the same time they prayed for help. The Lord blessed them, and they were able to overcome their enemies.

The idea that negative thoughts are just part of our nature is destructive in itself. Remember that through the grace of Christ, by His enabling power, our very nature can change. Anticipation of the beautiful results of this change should motivate us do everything in our power to become a positive, righteous person. Let's pray for the help we need in this area of our life.

The Golden Door

President Robert Rice, a former mission president in Columbia, tells us to visualize a golden door and a dark door. Through the golden door the Holy Ghost sends messages to us, blesses us, and helps us solve all of our problems. Through this door we receive answers to our prayers. As long as we keep this door open we are strengthened by the Lord. We can withstand temptation. We can do the Lord's work the way He wants it done. Blessings follow us throughout our days.

Satan tries to get our dark door open. If he succeeds he can tempt us to think evil thoughts. The longer the door of darkness remains open the more power he has over us. He will try to lead us down to hell and then laugh at us. Our misery is his reward.

To remove bad thoughts from our minds, we can close the dark door, then turn our minds toward to the golden door, or toward the light. Pray for the Holy Spirit. Rejoice in the Atonement of our Lord. Choose to be happy. Sing the songs of Zion. Serve others. Build the kingdom. Go to the temple. Ponder problems, pray about solutions, feel the Spirit. Become renewed. Solve problems. Move toward righteous goals.

Elder Robert E. Wells counsels us that we are the keepers of our minds:

> Before any sin is committed, the thoughts of the transgressor are out of control. As a man thinketh, so he becomes. This is one reason the Lord tells us that we are supposed to control our thoughts and that if we don't control them, we will be judged and condemned.

Alma makes it very clear when he says, "For our words will condemn us, yea, all our works will condemn us; . . . and our thoughts will also condemn us" (Alma 12:14). King Benjamin warns us in rather frightening terms, "I cannot tell you all the things whereby ye may commit sin; for there are divers ways and means, even so many that I cannot number them. But this much I can tell you, that if you do not watch yourselves, and your *thoughts*, . . . even unto the end of your lives, ye must perish" (Mosiah 4:29-30; emphasis added).

We are the keepers of our minds. We can control our thoughts. Our minds are like computers—garbage in, garbage out. We will be judged for letting garbage in instead of beautiful, uplifting, inspiring thoughts that edify our minds. ("In Control," *New Era*, September 1987, pp. 4-6.)

We choose what will occupy the stage of our minds. We are responsible for those choices. We must be keepers in righteousness. Elder Boyd K. Packer warned of the awful consequences of our poor choices: "We *must* learn to control our thoughts, or someone or something else *will* control them. Untrained, unemployed thoughts are soon enslaved." (*That All May Be Edified*, p. 32.)

We control our thoughts by filling our minds with so much good that the evil has no room to flourish.

So when you undertake the removal of the trash from your mind, remember these strategies. Immediately replace bad thoughts with something good. Concentrate on the reality around you. Pray for help. Involve yourself in productive activity. Choose to dismiss negative attitudes and thoughts. Take heart from the scriptures you are reading. Let the words of a hymn run through your mind. Think about where you came from, why you are here and where you are going after death.

Think about the Savior in a personal manner. Visualize Him blessing the little children. Think of how tenderly he healed the sick. Think of the great love he showed for His mother. Visualize Him saying, "Greater love hath no man than this, that He lay down his life for his friends." Think of Him saying "By this shall all men know that ye are my disciples, if ye have love one for another." Reach out for faith in Jesus Christ. Be humble. Pray for forgiveness and for strength to overcome.

As we practice these suggestions, we learn to think positively the way the Lord would have us do. We become more righteous. The desire grows within us for things of righteousness, and we become more like our Savior. This is the goal of all our efforts. May they be crowned with success.

Step Five: Be Engaged in a Good Cause

The Power Is in You

We have learned four steps: we acknowledge our need for the help of Jesus Christ in our repentance, and we pray earnestly for it; we have accepted the full responsibility for our own thoughts and resulting actions; we have cut off the flow of trash; we know how to replace evil thoughts with good. We are ready for the next step, which is to *act*—to strive to do as Christ would have us do. We will first fill our minds, and then fill our lives with good thoughts and deeds. We have learned that evil thoughts turn our actions toward evil. Just so, good thoughts will translate into good actions.

Keeping in mind that we become what we think about, we choose to fill our minds with enough good thoughts that we will do good. Elder Bruce R. McConkie has said, "If we are pondering in our hearts the things of righteousness, we shall become righteous." (CR, *Ensign,* January 1974, p. 48.)

Where shall we begin? Remember this scripture from the Doctrine and Covenants that tells us how to be wise servants of the Lord: "Verily I say, men should be anxiously engaged in a good cause, and do many things of their own free will, and bring to pass much righteousness;

"For *the power is in them,* wherein they are agents unto themselves. And inasmuch as men do good they shall in nowise lose their reward." (D&C 58:27-28, emphasis added.)

Think of the glory in these principles! The power is in you! You are not dependent upon what someone else does or thinks. You are not dependent upon circumstances over which you have no control. You are free. By God's own word, His children are "agents to themselves, and the power is in them." If we do good, we shall not lose our reward.

This energizing thought should help us to get started. Now that we have filled our minds with good, let us go forward with a determination to fill our lives with good as well. The power is in us! Let's look in the scriptures and recent general conference reports found in the *Ensign*. Following are some suggestions taken from these sources:

Read the Scriptures

Why is scripture study so important? Because when we feast upon the words of Christ, He can inspire our minds with ideas to guide us. Have you ever had the experience of reading the scriptures and having one specific thought or group of words stand out, literally burn themselves into your mind? This is a special kind of guidance. If we choose not to read the scriptures daily, we choose not to receive these impressions.

Our daughter Jolene told us of an experience where she found an answer to prayer while reading the scriptures. She had to have some foot surgery, and it took a couple of weeks in bed to recuperate. Their family scripture study became erratic because of her condition.

During this time she began having a problem with one of her teenagers. She tried several things, but nothing seemed to be helping. She began praying about the problem. Then as she was reading the scriptures one day Alma 31:5 seemed to leap from the page: "And now, as the preaching of the word had a great tendency to lead the people to do that which was just—yea, it had had more powerful effect upon the minds of the people than the sword, or anything else, which had happened unto them—therefore Alma thought it was expedient that they should try the virtue of the word of God."

Jolene thought about this scripture. She had tried several things— although not the sword as yet—and this scripture told her that when Alma had trouble with his people he found the word of God had the most powerful effect in helping the people to do right. She decided that her first solution should be returning to regular family scripture study. She and her family did so, and a couple of weeks later she saw a drastic difference in that teenager's attitude.

We acquaint ourselves with the Master through study of the scriptures, so we can truly serve Him. "For how knoweth a man the master whom he has not served, and who is a stranger unto him, and is far from the thoughts and intents of his heart?" (Mosiah 5:13.)

Elder Sterling W. Sill, always a champion of filling our minds with the thoughts of great men, pointed out to us the blessings that come when we fill our minds with the thoughts of the greatest one who ever lived:

Jesus rethought the same ideas many times and then said, "Follow me." What a thrilling challenge that each of us can follow him in his thinking and can develop the courage and good works that make future good thoughts possible! The more we rethink the thoughts of Deity, the deeper our mental grooves become, the broader are the marks left on our character, and the more readily we are able to mold ourselves into the image of his righteousness. How tragic when we comprehend some great Christian ideal and then say, "I never gave it another thought"! If we rethink the Master's thoughts enough times and with enough intensity, our lives will tend to respond as his did. (*The Best of Sterling W. Sill,* p. 98.)

This is why reading the scriptures every day is so beneficial. As we read and study the scriptures, we build for ourselves a new life. Our spiritual mental grooves become deeper while our character becomes more firmly rooted in righteousness.

Reading the Book of Mormon will give us strength, and specific help for the problems of today. It was written for this day, and its spirit will carry over into our lives. President Ezra Taft Benson said, "Young men, the Book of Mormon will change your life. It will fortify you against the evils of our day. It will bring a spirituality into your life that no other book will. . . . A young man who knows and loves the Book of Mormon, who has read it several times, who has an abiding testimony of its truthfulness, and who applies its teachings will be able to stand against the wiles of the devil and will be a mighty tool in the hands of the Lord." (CR, *Ensign,* May 1986, p. 43.)

Through reading the Book of Mormon we receive the word of God, and through it we can find the power to resist temptation. President Benson further said, "Not only will the word of God lead us to the fruit which is desirable above all others, but in the word of God and through it we can find the power to resist temptation, the power to thwart the work of Satan and his emissaries." (CR, *Ensign,* May 1986, p. 80.)

Serve Others

Reaching out to others begins our upward spiral to joy. If we are finding any kind of desolation, any spiritual drought or drabness in our lives, it is almost a guarantee that we are lacking in our service to others; in our ability to reach outside of ourselves. We are concentrating inwardly, thinking of our selves, denying those God-given tendencies to help and lift others.

Elder Vaughn J. Featherstone said, "I believe if you really want to be spiritual, you must first make a commitment and a decision to serve the Lord's children. If you cannot make that commitment, I don't believe you will be able to gain the level of spirituality that is necessary in this life to achieve all that we want to achieve." ("No Other Talent Exceeds Spirituality," *1976 Devotional Speeches of the Year*, p. 363.)

But whom can we serve? Most people don't step forward and say, "I need your help. My heart is breaking. I have lost my way, please come and console me, come and care for me, reach out your hand and be my friend." But the need is there. If we are attentive to the Holy Spirit, or to the Spirit of Christ which lights both the needy and those who can help, we can find opportunities to bless the lives of our brothers and sisters.

Are we always to wait to be "assigned" to do service for others? Bishop Glenn L. Pace of the Presiding Bishopric encouraged us to *find* needs and fill them. He said,

> The greatest compassionate service each of us can give may be in our own neighborhoods and communities. Wherever we live in the world there is pain and sorrow all around us. We need to take more initiative as individuals in deciding how we can best be of service. The fact that a particular activity is not sponsored by the Church does not mean it is not worthy of a Church member's support. . . . In humanitarian work, as in other areas of the gospel, we cannot become the salt of the earth if we stay in one lump in the cultural halls of our beautiful meetinghouses. We need not wait for a call or an assignment from a Church leader before we become involved in activities that are best carried out on a community or individual basis. (CR, *Ensign*, November 1990, pp. 9-10.)

The Lord spoke of slothful servants who sit and wait to be commanded in all things. In every life, in every home, in every neighborhood, there is much to be done, and singly or together, we can accomplish much good.

President Thomas S. Monson admonished us to follow the example of the Savior as we serve one another: "What power, what tenderness, what compassion did our Master and Exemplar demonstrate. We, too, can bless if we will but follow his noble example. Opportunities are everywhere. Needed are eyes to see the pitiable plight, ears to hear the silent pleadings of a broken heart; yes, and a soul filled with compassion, that we might communicate not only eye to eye or voice to ear, but in the majestic style of the Savior, even heart to heart." (CR, *Ensign*, November 1994, pp. 69-70.)

Our daughter Mary tells this story of when someone was of service to her and her family: "We had a personal tragedy that left us stricken and mourning. Our dear bishop, hearing of our trouble, came for a visit. Was there anything he could do?

"We could think of nothing. We were in good health, and our needs were not physical. It was our hearts that were bruised and aching. He comforted us during his visit and then left.

"Later that day I heard the sound of machinery outside our home. Looking out the window I saw the bishop, who was a farmer, on his tractor. He must have left our home looking for some way to be of service, and noticing that we were in a new home that we had not yet landscaped, he saw that we had a fine crop of tall weeds. He had returned to mow them down for us.

"This fine and tender man saw that we needed love more than anything else, and he showed it in the best way he could think of. Our hearts were soothed by his act of compassion every time we looked out the window."

President Gordon B. Hinckley suggests three ways we can serve others: "How great a thing is charity, whether it be expressed through the giving of one's substance, the lending of one's strength to lift the burdens of others, or as an expression of kindness and appreciation." (CR, *Ensign*, November 1990, p. 54.)

If we are sensitive to the Spirit, we may be moved upon to assist others and bring the answer to their prayers. Live so the Spirit of the Lord may dwell within you and guide you. Thus you may serve and bless the lives of others, and bring comfort and satisfaction to your own life.

Devote Yourself to Your Family

Certainly there is always something to do to strengthen our families and help our brothers and sisters, our parents, or our spouse and our children to fulfill their greatest potential. These are the ties that will remain forever, and they are our first responsibility. They also bring our greatest joy.

If we have children, the challenge is there to teach them and bring them to a knowledge of the gospel principles. This requires devotion and commitment. Elder Durrel A. Woolsey encouraged fathers to become heroes to their families. He said that to do this, "a generous amount of your time is required. Not a superficial moment here and there, not a tired and worn-out phrase, 'We'll talk about that later,' but an honest, generous piece of your day on a continuing basis, even at the sacrifice of things social, things personally entertaining, or even things financially rewarding." (CR, *Ensign*, November 1990, p. 43.)

We can make the time we spend with our children effective and enjoyable by taking advantage of teaching moments as they occur. Our daughter Mary had this special experience with her daughter Emily: "I did a project for my husband's family wherein I wrote brief biographies of all his direct ancestors who had joined the Church. I did this because I felt that I needed a resource to teach my children from—one short enough for them to share in without losing interest. One day my daughter and I went to a nearby graveyard to locate the grave of one of these ancestors. While there I pulled out this book of biographies to read to her about the ancestor whose grave we were visiting.

"I began to read this woman's testimony, spoken directly to her descendants, and my eyes filled with tears. I was unable to continue. My nine-year-old daughter took the book from me and began to read: 'I am thankful that I am worthy of being counted a good Latter-day Saint, and I bear my testimony to all who read these lines, that I know the Gospel of Jesus Christ is true . . . I hope my posterity will follow the good example of their fathers.'

"Emily paused and I said, 'Do you know who she is talking to?' Emily's eyes got wide. 'To me?' she asked. 'Yes, to you,' I replied. She continued reading: 'This is written for my future generation, God bless them all.' Through my tears I hugged my sweet daughter and said, 'She hoped that you would read her words and know that she loved you and wanted you to have a testimony like she did.' As we stood and looked at that weathered gravestone, I knew that my daughter felt the blessing that was sent, and my heart was full of joy at the connection made between this grand woman and her great-great-great granddaughter."

Nothing we can do in this life is as important as raising our children in righteousness before the Lord. President Joseph F. Smith emphasized this, saying, "What would it profit me, though I should go out into the world and win strangers to the fold of God and lose my own children? Oh! God, let me not lose my own. I can not afford to lose mine, whom God has given to me and whom I am responsible for before the Lord, and who are dependent upon me for guidance, for instruction, for proper influence." (*Gospel Doctrine*, p. 462.)

What do we do to ensure that our homes are holy places? We begin by having personal and family prayer at least twice a day, and blessing the food before we eat it. Regular family scripture study helps to teach the gospel. Then we follow through by treating all family members with love and kindness, and helping them to be able to meet their daily challenges.

President Harold B. Lee said, "There are those who have seemed to forget that the most powerful weapons the Lord has given us against all that is evil are His own declarations, the plain simple doctrines of salvation as found in the scriptures." (CR, *Ensign*, May 1986, p. 81.)

Family home evening should be held at least each week. Elder Boyd K. Packer gives this promise: "With this program [family home evening] comes the promise from the prophets, the living prophets, that if parents will gather their children about them once a week and teach the gospel, *those children in such families will not go astray*." (CR, *Improvement Era*, December 1970, p. 108, emphasis added.)

What an exciting promise! In a world where we seek anxiously for answers and assurances, here are words from a prophet. We took this promise to heart when we were rearing our children, and found family home evening to be that promised safeguard.

Even so, raising righteous children is difficult at times, but there is no greater joy than seeing children growing in the light of the gospel. Elder James E. Faust encouraged parents by reminding them of the rewards of parenting: "While few human challenges are greater than that of being good parents, few opportunities offer greater potential for joy. Surely no more important work is to be done in this world than preparing our children to be God-fearing, happy, honorable, and productive. Parents will find no more fulfilling happiness than to have their children honor them and their teachings. It is the glory of parenthood." (CR, *Ensign*, November 1990, pp. 32-33.)

We often remind those who are in the process of rearing their families to take hold of the joys of the moment, to grasp and hold to their hearts the happy times, and magnify them. This encourages them through the harder times, and helps avoid doing things that may be regretted later. Quick hugs and joyful laughter do more toward keeping the children in the right than harshness does.

Missionary Work

Many of us are worried about world peace. We see people on television protesting for peace, and we see nations building up huge armies to preserve peace. And yet our living prophets have told us there is another way. President Howard W. Hunter said, "The restored gospel of Jesus Christ can be a dynamic, moving influence, and true acceptance gives us a meaningful, religious experience. . . . This replaces turmoil and confusion with peace and tranquility." (CR, *Improvement Era*, December 1970, p. 117.)

President Ezra Taft Benson said, "We are commanded by God to take this gospel to all the world. That is the cause that must unite us today. Only the gospel will save the world from the calamity of its own self-destruction. Only the gospel will unite men of all races and nationalities in peace. Only the gospel will bring joy, happiness, and salvation to the human family." (*Teachings of Ezra Taft Benson*, p. 167.)

We need to overcome our timidity and apprehension, and share the gospel with others. When my wife and I travel, we take copies of the Book of Mormon and try to place them with people we meet. Once we took a family trip with our grown children and challenged each of them to place a Book of Mormon during the trip. They were all successful, and had some stimulating gospel discussions.

Our daughter Mary tells this experience with sharing the gospel: "My husband and I had some young entertainers from five different countries stay with us for a few days. We were delighted to find that the young people were very curious about the "Mormons," and one evening after dinner they began asking questions about our church. We spent several hours explaining the gospel to them. Before they left I made a packet for each of them containing a personal letter, several pamphlets, and a Book of Mormon (in their native language, where possible). They were all delighted with the gift, and promised to read the materials. Sharing the gospel with these enthusiastic, inquisitive young people was an uplifting, exhilarating experience for our family."

What is needed to be missionaries is testimony and commitment. President Benson encouraged this commitment, saying, "We must prove, every day of our lives, that we are willing to do the will of the Lord—to spread the restored gospel, to bear testimony to the world, to share the gospel with others." (CR, *Ensign*, November 1990, p. 5.)

Remember, we explained that principles and promises go together? Here is another one: "If it so be that you should labor all your days in crying repentance unto this people, and bring, save it be one soul unto me, how great shall be your joy with him in the kingdom of my Father!" (D&C 18:15.)

And here's a thought we heard once to go with it: If that person you bring unto Christ is your own self, how *great* shall be your joy!

Genealogy

Genealogy is a fascinating, rewarding work that will bind our families for eternity. Many times, however, we think Aunt Marge or Uncle Frank is taking care of the genealogical work for our family. Or, we may see the task as overwhelming, if no one in our family has done it before.

The Church has greatly simplified the work of researching our ancestors. Elder Richard G. Scott gave an excellent talk on this subject in the October 1990 conference. In conclusion he said,

But what about you? Have you prayed about your own ancestors' work? Set aside those things that don't really matter in your life. Decide to do something that will have eternal consequences. Perhaps you have been prompted to look for ancestors but feel that you are not a genealogist. Can you see that you don't have to be anymore? It all begins with love and a sincere desire to help those who can't help themselves. . . . Anywhere you are in the world, with prayer, faith, determination, diligence, and some sacrifice, you can make a powerful contribution. Begin now. I promise you that the Lord will help you find a way. And it will make you feel wonderful. (CR, *Ensign*, November 1990, p. 7.)

Our daughter tells this story about the help she received from the Lord in doing genealogical research:

> I was trying to find some information about several of our family lines. I ran into a problem and was unable to make two of the lines connect. I knew that these ancestors lived in South Carolina, and that they had donated the land for a church to be built. I learned about a centennial celebration for this church, and when I inquired, they sent me a publication about the celebration. It didn't help me in my research, but as I looked at it and pondered the problem, the words kept coming to me, "The answer is in this church."
>
> I decided to see if I could find information from anyone still living there. I called a man who lived in the area and asked if he knew of anyone with our family name who attended this church. To my surprise he said that *he* was a member of that church, and that he would ask around the next Sunday. When he called me back he said that he had found a man with one of our family names who had been doing research into his family lines. When I contacted the man he graciously agreed to share his work.
>
> This man's genealogical research added four additional generations on our family line, and he sent me precious photographs and other materials. We have since submitted these ancestors' names to the temple, and we had the privilege of doing their work ourselves. I feel that genealogical work involves us in a companionship with those on the other side, and I know that the Lord helps us as we seek to perform temple work for our kindred dead.

You can also begin work on your descendant's genealogy. How? By writing your life history and keeping a journal. This will be a treasured record to loved ones in future years.

Temple Attendance

Make yourself ready to go to the temple as soon as you possibly can, if you have not already done so. This will be the sweetest, most consistently strengthening activity you can engage in. Temple attendance should be a regular occurrence. We should go as often as we possibly can. When we go to the temple, we separate ourselves from worldly influences and attune ourselves to the voice of the Spirit. The more often we go, the more our minds are filled with righteous impressions and experiences.

President Gordon B. Hinckley outlined these blessings of temple attendance: "Temples are there to be used, and those who use them will reap a blessing of harmony in their lives. They will draw nearer unto the Lord, and He will draw nearer unto them." (CR, *Ensign*, November 1985, p. 60.)

President Ezra Taft Benson gave us this promise: "I promise you that, with increased attendance in the temples of our God, you shall receive increased personal revelation to bless your life as you bless those who have died." (CR, *Ensign*, May 1987, p. 85.)

Sometimes when I have a serious problem I go to the temple in an attitude of prayer. I have silent prayer in the temple. Before the time I have completed my work in the temple I have an answer to my problem. I personally recommend this method of solving problems to you.

Church Service

We should go the extra mile in all of our church service. If you don't hold a church calling, go in and discuss it with your bishop. Make yourself worthy to serve in the Church. Do your visiting teaching and home teaching with integrity and compassion. Fast monthly and contribute your fast offerings.

Use the Sabbath day as a holy day for scripture study, journal writing, family home evening, attending all your church meetings, visiting the sick or the lonely. Sanctify the day by listening only to sacred music. Magnify your calling in the Church. Ask yourself what activities you should engage in to cultivate the proper spirit for the Sabbath.

It Will Show in Your Face

Have you ever noticed that people who live a righteous life have a certain light in their eyes? Do you radiate that light? As you live the gospel and fill your life with good, you will find a zest for life and a joy that will transform even your countenance. It will show in your face.

President Spencer W. Kimball once told the following fable to illustrate how pure thoughts and righteous living affect a person:

Lord George had led an evil life. He had been dishonest. He had been a drunkard, a gambler and a cheat in business, and his face reflected the life he had led. It was a very evil face.

One day he fell in love with a simple country girl to whom he proposed marriage. Jenny Mere told him that she could never marry a man whose face was so repulsive and so evil-looking; . . . she wanted a man with a saint-like face which was the mirror of true love. . . .

Lord George went down to [a man who] made waxen masks for people . . . [This man] selected a mask, heated it over a lamp, [and] fixed it to Lord George's face; and when Lord George looked in the mirror, he found that he had the face of a saint who loved dearly. So altered was his appearance that Jenny Mere was soon . . . won.

He bought a little cottage in the country, almost hidden in an arbor of roses, with a tiny garden spot. From then on his entire life changed. He became interested in nature. . . . He was engrossed in kindliness and the world around him.

He was not content with starting life anew, but tried to make amends for the past. . . . He restored his ill-gotten gains to those whom he had cheated. Each day brought new refinements to his character, more beautiful thoughts to his soul.

By accident, his former companions discovered his identity. They visited him in his garden and urged him to return to his old evil life. When he refused, he was attacked and the mask torn from his face.

He hung his head. . . . [He thought:] Here was the end of his new-found life and his love. . . . As he stood with bowed head, with the mask at his feet on the grass, his wife ran across the garden and threw herself on her knees in front of him. When she looked up at him, what do you suppose she found? Lo! Line for line, feature for feature, his face was the same as that of the mask. Lines of beauty, [truly, the face of a saint].

President Kimball continued, "There is no doubt that the life one leads and the thoughts one thinks are registered plainly in his face." (CR, *Ensign*, May 1975, pp. 80-81, adapted.)

We have seen this very change occur in the lives of those who transform themselves with the help of the gospel. As their lives fill with good, their countenances fill with light. One day I saw a man whom I had not seen for years. His face had always looked worldly to me. When I met him this time I was surprised. His face was softened, his eyes kind. He told me that he was now working in the temple.

For some time we taught a dear brother and his wife the temple preparation lessons. This man was a heavy smoker and had never availed himself of the temple blessings. As we helped him to realize the love Heavenly Father has for him, and the eternal beauty of the gospel principles, he gained spiritual strength and was able to put aside some lifelong habits that had been holding him back. People who knew him began to comment on the gentleness his face was assuming. When we went to the temple with him, his countenance was as though it glowed. His happiness was so penetrating, it showed as light in his eyes and in his face. His wife was so happy, she wept tears of celestial joy.

As we continually engage ourselves in good causes, filling our minds and our lives with good, we will become more righteous. We will be able to be successful husbands and wives, parents, brothers and sisters, friends, and servants in the Church. All of these things come through lives dedicated wholeheartedly to the Lord, because through His strength we can succeed.

The five steps we have discussed in these chapters: pray for the Lord's help, accept responsibility for your thoughts, cut off the flow of trash, replace evil thoughts with something good, and be engaged in a good cause, are the foundation for understanding how to control our thoughts. They start us firmly on the way to purification of our hearts.

We will continue our upward quest by presenting other basic gospel principles, which, if taken to our hearts and made part of our lives, will enrich us, ennoble us, and enable us to become more Christlike—our objective and our goal. We testify to this truth, and encourage you to go on and firmly establish these principles as guides in your onward pursuit.

Section II

Understanding the Battle
Between Good and Evil

The Eternal Plan

Life's Purpose

We were each sent to the earth with a mission. Our children learn this in Primary as they sing the words to this sweet song:

My life is a gift; my life has a plan.
My life has a purpose; in heav'n it began.
My choice was to come to this lovely home on earth
And seek for God's light to direct me from birth.
I will follow God's plan for me,
Holding fast to his word and his love.
I will work, and I will pray;
I will always walk in his way.
Then I will be happy on earth
And in my home above.
(*Children's Songbook*, pp. 164-65.)

President George Q. Cannon spoke eloquently of the purpose of earth life, and the missions each of us accepted when we came here:

We are sent here as missionaries, so to speak. God has given to each of us a mission. He has sent us forth and has said unto us: "Go, now, and be faithful. I have blessed you with everything that is necessary to fill a good mission on the earth. You are going in to new scenes, and you will be exposed to temptations such as you have never known. You are going to take upon you a tabernacle of flesh, and Satan is going to be there with you. He has tempted you here; you have been exposed to his allurements and his sophisms, but you resisted his propositions, and you clung to me and to Jesus, my well-beloved Son.

"Now, go down on the earth and receive tabernacles of flesh and bones and be proved there and see whether you will be faithful there in the midst of the darkness that will prevail; for there will be a veil drawn between your present life and that life, and you will have to live by faith. If you will exercise faith in Me, I will always be with you; My spirit will be with you; and if you will keep My commandments, you will come back into My presence, and you will dwell with Me eternally, and you will enter upon a career of never ending glory. Now, go and be faithful."

I have just described to you in my crude way something of that which I know occurred when we came from the abode of our Father in Heaven. He wants us to be faithful. He does not want us to listen to Satan. (*Gospel Truth*, p. 12.)

Some people think the purpose of life is to be successful in a career, to make a lot of money, or to receive worldly fame. They give these projects their time and energy. They leave little opportunity or attention to the building up of their spiritual life. Their wealth controls them.

There are others who, although not burdened with riches nor obsessed with the desire for them, nevertheless miss the spirit of love and feel that life has somehow cheated them, that there should have been more than what they had. Still others feel that the world owes them a living. They have no sense of community with other human beings, no feeling of responsibility to them. These have failed to catch the insight that there is a more important dimension to life, one that applies to people, families, love, caring, and goodness. They have missed the spiritual awareness that properly befits children of an eternal Father, who has stated that His "work and [His] glory" is to "bring to pass the immortality and eternal life of man." (Moses 1:39.)

In actuality, each and all of us came here with a mission and a purpose. Nothing in this grand universe happened randomly or by chance. Our Father planned a grand design for His creation, with the focus on you and me and all of His children. Each of us has a role, an appointed mission to perform, in this great work of salvation. His plan will succeed. "The final outcome is certain," President Benson said. "The forces of righteousness will finally win. But what remains to be seen is *where* each of us personally, now and in the future, will stand in this battle—and how tall will we stand?" ("You Are a Marked Generation," *Ensign*, April 1987, p. 73.)

The principal purpose of life is the same for all of us: to receive our physical bodies and prove whether we will remain true to our Heavenly Father's eternal plan. Beyond that, we have personal, specific missions within that plan which are tailored to the talents, abilities, and interests we have, and the time and locality frames in which we live. Our Father has something exciting and challenging awaiting each of us as we ready ourselves to accept and perform it. These individual missions are revealed to us gradually, line upon line and precept upon precept, as we are faithful, and prepared to receive.

The control of our thoughts is a very basic and important part of individual success in our own lives and missions. As we gain in self-control, we gain in purity. As we increase in purity, we increase in personal strength and ability to perform, not only in society, but in the Lord's kingdom. We are able to draw in a greater way on the powers of priesthood and revelation, those heavenly enablers.

Nephi teaches us in beautiful language what we should do "after [we] have entered in by the way." (2 Nephi 32:1.) "Wherefore, I said unto you, feast upon the words of Christ; for behold, the words of Christ will tell you all things what ye should do" (v. 3.), and further, "again I say unto you that if ye will enter in by the way, and receive the Holy Ghost, it will show unto you all things what ye should do." (v. 5.)

With such plain and precious promises available to us, why do we hesitate and continue to struggle with our mortality? If you have received the laying on of hands, you are entitled to feel the Holy Spirit in your life daily if you are living by the light. Every day when you wake up, pray that the Spirit will be with you all day long, and then live in such a way as to invite the Spirit to be with you. With joy you can work out your salvation here upon the earth, and reach out to others to assist them in your own special way. You can return to your Father with gladness.

In the dispensation of the Fulness of Times, the Lord teaches us, "Seek not for riches but for wisdom, and behold, the mysteries of God shall be unfolded unto you, and then shall you be made rich. Behold, he that hath eternal life is rich." (D&C 6:7.)

Our Premortal Estate

We were in the premortal state for eons—thousands of earth-years—preparing to come here. Although our lives may seem long, in the eternal view it is a very short time.

Church members were faithful spirits in the pre-mortal existence: "We were true in keeping our first estate. The people that are here today stood loyally by God and by Jesus, and they did not flinch. If you had flinched then, you would not be here with the Priesthood upon you. The evidence that you were loyal, that you were true and that you did not waver is to be found in the fact that you have received the Gospel and the everlasting Priesthood." (*Gospel Truth*, p. 7.) We stood firm with our Father and our Savior.

President George Q. Cannon said that we rejoiced when we knew we would come down to earth and be allowed to work out our salvation: "Now, the Lord our God has given unto us this probation, which we call our second estate. . . . We consented to come here. For when the foundations of the earth were laid, the sons of God sang together, and rejoiced because an earth was prepared to which they could come and receive tabernacles and enjoy the blessings connected therewith. It was a step in our progress towards the glory that our Father has attained unto." (*Gospel Truth*, p. 17.)

Our Second Estate

We are here in what the Lord terms our "second estate," to receive our physical bodies, and to see if we will prove faithful (see Abraham 3:22-26). When we return, will we be able to report happily to our Father in Heaven after these few short years? Will we remain faithful until the end? For this purpose we came to earth.

Elder Bruce McConkie uses this interesting metaphor to emphasize the importance of this second estate:

"In the sense that mortality is the great probationary period of eternal existence, in the sense that 'this life is the time for men to prepare to meet God' (Alma 34:32), this life becomes the most important part of all eternity. In it we take the final examination for all the life we lived in pre-existence, and in it we take the entrance examination which will determine the kingdom of glory we shall inherit in the life hereafter." (*Mormon Doctrine*, p. 443.)

President Cannon urged us not to waste the advantage we forged through our faithfulness in the first estate: "Therefore, make good use of the time you have. Now is the time of your probation; now is the time of harvest; now is the summer of your days. Let it not be said, 'the harvest is past, the summer is ended, and my soul is not saved.' But let us bear in mind that now is the probation that God has given us. Let us make use of it by doing the works of righteousness, by keeping the commandments of God, by having our eye on the mark of our high calling in Christ Jesus." (*Gospel Truth*, p. 19.)

Can you imagine the torment of soul we would suffer if we failed this test? After this life when our memories are returned to us, we will know how valiant we were before we came here. If we have retrogressed, if we have become less than we were, oh, how unhappy we will be.

This life is a time to grow, to develop, and to advance. President Cannon said, "The life of a Latter-day Saint is a life of progress—a life of continued improvement. The Latter-day Saint who is living as he should do is better today than he was yesterday; he will be better tomorrow than he is today. If there be any imperfections in his life, he is eager to discover and correct them, that he may become more perfect and more like our Father." (*Gospel Truth*, p. 19.)

Seeking continual improvement gives a focus to our daily endeavors. It gives us challenge and stimulates imagination and creativity. Our kind and loving Heavenly Father blesses us with talents, abilities, aptitudes, insights, and intellect. There is no limit to the ideas, achievements, and attainment available to us, His children.

No earthly achievement should take precedence over one's own personal salvation. President Cannon writes, "There is nothing as important to me as an individual as my own salvation. This is the most important thing to me that can be—that I myself shall be saved, that I myself shall so live as to be counted worthy by the Almighty to receive an exaltation in His Kingdom." (*Gospel Truth*, p. 75.) By living in such a way that your soul is saved, you can best help your husband or wife, your children, and your friends and neighbors.

And we can do it! We have two wonderful gifts to help us be successful in this life. One of them is the Light of Christ, and we were born with this gift. If we live by it and cherish it, it will lead us to truth.

In addition, faithful members of the Church have the gift of the Holy Ghost, which has many offices to perform in helping us with our heavenly goal. President Kimball said, "The Holy Ghost is a revelator. He is a reminder and will bring to our remembrance the things which we have learned and which we need in the time thereof. He is an inspirer and will put words in our mouths, enlighten our understandings and direct our thoughts. He is a testifier . . . a teacher . . . a companion and will walk with us, inspiring us all along the way guiding our footsteps, impeaching our weaknesses, strengthening our resolves, and revealing to us righteous aims and purposes." (*Teachings of Spencer W. Kimball*, p. 23.)

President Cannon said, "God has reserved spirits for this dispensation who have the courage and determination to face the world and all the powers of the evil one, visible and invisible, to proclaim the Gospel and maintain the truth and establish and build up the Zion of our God fearless of all consequences. . . . There is a constant stream of emigration from the spirit world of noble spirits . . . anxious to emerge into this sphere of existence, pressing forward, a vast column of them, noble and holy beings, ready to take their part in the probation which God has assigned unto all his children." (*Gospel Truth*, p. 18.)

This is us, noble and holy beings, offspring of Deity. Our Father in Heaven spent thousands of years (earth time) preparing us for this majestic task. It is truly possible for us to improve our situations, to become better than we now are, to rise above our earthly tendencies and find happiness in His way of life. Let's be faithful; let's prayerfully work at building up the kingdom of God. In doing this noble work, we can save our own souls as well.

Our Physical Bodies

One of the most important reasons for coming to earth was to receive our physical bodies, which when united with our spirits, comprise our souls: "The spirit and the body are the soul of man." (D&C 88:15.)

We need to care for the bodies which house our eternal spirits, so we can accomplish all we are meant to in this life. Some tend to forget the sacred nature of our physical selves, and abuse their bodies in one way or another. The body being the tabernacle of the spirit should be always regarded with respect and honor. Elder Bruce R. McConkie writes, "To point up the sacred and holy nature of the human body, the Lord calls it a *temple*. 'Know ye not that ye are the temple of God, and that the Spirit of God dwelleth in you? If any man defile the temple of God, him shall God destroy; for the temple of God is holy, which temple ye are.' (1 Corinthians 3:16-17.)" (*Mormon Doctrine*, p. 781.)

All of us on this earth kept our first estate and merited coming here to receive our bodies. We should observe all the laws of good health, and respect our physical bodies as gifts from God. The Doctrine and Covenants has many precise physical instructions which point up this truth, and help us to treat our bodies in such a way that they may remain active and able to help us with the test of our second estates. (Specifically see D&C 29:30-35, Sec. 88, and Sec. 89. Also see 1 Corinthians 6:19-20.)

Our mortal existence has both temporal and spiritual aspects. Alma refers to this when he admonishes us to pray "for whatsoever things ye stand in need, both spiritual and temporal." (Alma 7:23.) We have heard it said that one of the major problems we have in reconciling our lives in the present framework is that we think we are mortal creatures looking for spiritual experiences. We should remember that we are spiritual beings having a mortal experience. This should give us a correct perspective. Remember also that there are good reasons for keeping the commandments, for they are the tools and rules to achieve happiness in this life and eternal life hereafter.

As part of the eternal plan, when we came here we partook of the fallen nature, brought about by the Fall of Adam. We are to struggle against this necessary human condition and overcome by obedience to divine law. President Cannon said that "the dross of our nature should be cleansed by obedience to the laws of God and that by obedience to His laws these tabernacles which we have received . . . may be redeemed and be fitted and prepared to dwell in a higher and purer abode." (*Gospel Truth*, p. 11.)

King Benjamin explained the dual nature of God's blessings: "And moreover, I would desire that ye should consider on the blessed and happy state of those that keep the commandments of God. For behold, they are blessed in all things, both temporal and spiritual; and if they hold out faithful to the end they are received into heaven, that thereby they may dwell with God in a state of never-ending happiness." (Mosiah 2:41.)

Jesus Christ, our Elder Brother, not only set the example and marked the way, He broke the bands of death and paid the price to redeem us from the Fall. He also paid the price for the sins we commit while in this estate. Our test is to follow Him, keep His commandments, and accept His sacrifice in our behalf. If we thus keep our second estate, we "shall have glory added upon [our] heads for ever and ever." (Abraham 3:26.)

It is our privilege and our mission to come here "foreordained to do good, to keep the commandments of God and to be saved; for God loves all His children and would save every human soul. He would not that any one should be lost; but He desires the salvation of all." (*Gospel Truth*, p. 113.)

With this confidence that our Heavenly Father desires us to succeed, to be at peace and happy on this earth and return to His presence when we have finished, don't you think we can do it? He has shown us the way.

The Savior said, "Come unto me, all ye that labour and are heavy laden, and I will give you rest.

"Take my yoke upon you, and learn of me; for I am meek and lowly in heart: and ye shall find rest unto your souls.

"For my yoke is easy, and my burden is light." (Matthew 11:28-30.)

We came here under covenant to perform our assigned missions. As members of this church we have pledged again with our Elder Brother Jesus Christ to obey Him. As we strive to keep His commandments we start to feel that rest to our souls that He promised. We come to know that the Lord's way is the happiest way. As we take up His work and faithfully serve, He makes our burdens light.

The Millennial Reign

The next phase of this mortal existence is an exciting time when the Savior, our Lord and King, returns to this earth to cleanse it and make it a fit abode for the just and honorable people who will live under His personal rule. We do not know when this will happen, but we should strive to be ready in case it should be in our lifetimes. This will be a marvellous time when Satan will be bound. Communication will be open for the righteous dead to assist the righteous on the earth with the portentous work of the millennium, that of preaching the gospel, perfecting the Saints, and redeeming the dead. The Savior will reign personally upon the earth—another era of great elation when heaven and earth will resound with shouts of joy.

Beyond the Veil

There is a veil drawn between the spirit world and earth life. We can't remember what happened in the spirit world. This was done so we can be fully tested in this life. After death, our lives continue on, and our memory of the previous life will be returned to us. In the film *Man's Search for Happiness* Richard L. Evans states that after death, "Your memory of this life will remain with you, and your knowledge of your life before birth will be restored." Think of knowing again the person we were before we came here, and of knowing our loved ones again as we did then. Our lives cover these three phases of existence as a continuance. Keeping faithful will result in "glory" being "added upon" our heads "forever and ever." (Abraham 3:26.)

President George Q. Cannon talks of the joy with which we shall greet our Heavenly Parents: "I believe that when we see our Father in heaven we shall know Him; and the recollection that we were once with Him and that He was our Father will come back to us, and we will fall upon His neck, and He will fall upon us, and we will kiss each other. We will know our Mother, also. We will know those who have begotten us in the spirit world just as much as we will know each other after we pass from this state of existence into another sphere." (*Gospel Truth*, p. 5.)

Alma 40:11-12 tells us:

Now, concerning the state of the soul between death and the resurrection—Behold, it has been made known unto me by an angel, that the spirits of all men, as soon as they are departed from this mortal body, yea, the spirits of all men, whether they be good or evil, are taken home to that God who gave them life.

And then shall it come to pass, that the spirits of those who are righteous are received into a state of happiness, which is called paradise, a state of rest, a state of peace, where they shall rest from all their troubles and from all care, and sorrow.

"Wickedness Never Was Happiness"

Alma 41:10 reminds us, "Wickedness never was happiness."

The wicked seek happiness in doing iniquity, but it never was part of the eternal plan. Happiness comes from righteousness and following our Savior, Jesus Christ. The wicked cut themselves off from His influence by their choice of unrighteous actions, and continually seek but never find happiness and the freedom they anticipate:

"All men that are in a state of nature, or I would say, in a carnal state, are in the gall of bitterness and in the bonds of iniquity; they are without God in the world, and they have gone contrary to the nature of God; therefore, they are in a state contrary to the nature of happiness." (Alma 41:11.)

Mormon gave us a vivid description of the condition of people who had entirely forgotten the things of God, and took pleasure in their wickedness until they were totally depraved:

"But . . . their sorrowing was not unto repentance, because of the goodness of God; but it was rather the sorrowing of the damned, because the Lord would not always suffer them to take happiness in sin.

"And they did not come unto Jesus with broken hearts and contrite spirits, but they did curse God, and wish to die. Nevertheless they would struggle with the sword for their lives." (Mormon 2:13-14.)

What we set our hearts on in this second estate will become the direction of our lives, and also what we receive for our eternal reward. Brother Bruce C. Hafen of Brigham Young University wrote, "Not only will the righteous desires of our hearts be granted, the unrighteous desires of our hearts will also be granted. Over the long run, our most deeply held desires will govern our choices, one by one and day by day, until our lives finally add up to what we have really wanted." (*The Believing Heart*, p. 23.)

One of Satan's favorite tools is to affirm to us that the gospel truths are real, but that there is no hurry—it doesn't matter if we wait a little longer before we put them into effect in our lives. Samuel the Lamanite spoke to those who believed these lies in his day. He first described to them the awful situation they would find themselves in if they procrastinated their repentance until they found themselves "surrounded by demons, yea . . . encircled about by the angels of him who hath sought to destroy [their] souls."

Then, speaking to them as though they were already in this state he said, "But behold, your days of probation are past; ye have procrastinated the day of your salvation until it is everlastingly too late, and your destruction is made sure; yea, for ye have sought all the days of your lives for that which ye could not obtain; and ye have sought for happiness in doing iniquity, which thing is contrary to the nature of that righteousness which is in our great and Eternal Head." (Helaman 13:37-38.)

Alma describes the state of the souls who have waited too long to repent and return to God, finding themselves in a state of torment between death and the resurrection:

> And then shall it come to pass, that the spirits of the wicked, yea, who are evil—for behold, they have no part nor portion of the Spirit of the Lord; for behold, they chose evil works rather than good;

therefore the spirit of the devil did enter into them, and take possession of their house—and these shall be cast out into outer darkness; there shall be weeping, and wailing, and gnashing of teeth, and this because of their own iniquity, being led captive by the will of the devil.

Now this is the state of the souls of the wicked, yea, in darkness, and a state of awful, fearful looking for the fiery indignation of the wrath of God upon them; thus they remain in this state, as well as the righteous in paradise, until the time of their resurrection. (Alma 40:13-14.)

The negative effect of losing our opportunity to prove ourselves faithful in this estate will go on throughout the eternities to come. This penalty would be almost more than one could bear. Elder Melvin J. Ballard said pointedly, "but if we miss [our hope of eternal life], if we lose it, we whose right it is to obtain it, I cannot tell you the sting of conscience and remorse, the hell of torment we shall endure endlessly, if we miss it, through our own ignorance and foolishness. May God save us from that affliction." (*The Three Degrees of Glory*, p. 37.)

Consider for a moment the plight of the wicked:

1. They miss the rest of soul that God gives the righteous.
2. They lack the peace and happiness the Comforter brings.
3. They have lost the Light of Christ; they walk in spiritual darkness.
4. They do not have the Holy Ghost to lead, guide, and direct them.
5. They have not the hope of eternal life hereafter.

Elder Theodore M. Burton said,

I have since wondered how anyone could knowingly prefer to live where it is dark and cold. How could anybody willingly prefer darkness and misery over light and warmth? Yet darkness, cold, and misery will be the lot of those who willingly and knowingly reject the Lord. John wrote, "God is light, and in him is no darkness at all." (1 John 1:5.)

I would like to speak about God's realm of light in contrast to the dark realm of Satan. Those who follow Satan will be cast into outer darkness, "where there is weeping, and wailing, and gnashing of teeth." (D&C 133:73.) How terrible to live in such a place of darkness and cold. It is entirely different from what we usually think of as "burning in hell." That burning is the lasting regret one feels who has chosen the darkness of Satan in preference to the light of Christ.

Through modern revelation we have been taught that "the glory of God is intelligence, or, in other words, light and truth." Such light and truth forsake the evil one. (See D&C 93:36-37.) (CR, *Ensign*, May 1981, pp. 28-29.)

Can you imagine the horror of living in such a place of darkness and cold? In a place with Satan and his evil spirits? Surely such a thought will give us the encouragement we need to help us walk in the light, keep the commandments and follow our Savior.

Let's not take a chance on losing this estate. Let's vigorously pursue a life of righteousness. Let's always be found building the kingdom, caring for God's children, repairing our weaknesses and losing ourselves in His service.

The Glories of Eternal Life

In his book *The Three Degrees of Glory*, Elder Melvin J. Ballard describes the rewards of those who inherit eternal life:

Reading . . . from the 53rd verse [of Doctrine and Covenants, Section 76]:

"And who overcome by faith, and are sealed by the Holy Spirit of promise, which the Father sheds forth upon all those who are just and true.

"They are they who are the church of the Firstborn.

"They are they into whose hands the Father has given all things—"

Is there anything that you have ever dreamed of that you wanted, that you longed for? Into the hands of those who attain [the celestial glory] shall all things be given.

What a world of meaning! You can ponder over that all the rest of your lives . . . every thought and aspiration of the human heart in righteousness . . . will be but a fraction of that which is comprehended in this statement, that "unto them shall be given all things".

Reading again:

"They are they who are priests and kings, who have received of his fulness, and of his glory;

"And are priests of the Most High, after the order of Melchizedek, which was after the order of Enoch, which was after the order of the Only Begotten Son.

"Wherefore, as it is written, they are gods, even the sons of God—"

We have frequently said that perhaps the grandest thought that has ever been brought forth to the children of men is the Mormon truism, namely: "As man is God once was, and as God is man may become." The foundation of that truism is in this revelation and these words we have just read. Let me read them again:

"Wherefore, as it is written, they are gods, even the sons of God—" (pp. 8-9.)

Think of it. The highest degree of the Celestial Kingdom will exceed every hope, every wish, every aspiration of righteousness that it is possible for us to envision. And we can receive it.

Paul stated it thus: "But as it is written, Eye hath not seen, nor ear heard, neither have entered into the heart of man, the things which God hath prepared for them that love him." (1 Corinthians 2:9.) All this is the result of loving God with all our heart, might, mind, and strength. It is a matter of choosing the right. Selfless, loving service, having one's eye single to His glory, seeking first the Kingdom and His righteousness bring this about.

There are those who have received an affirmation while still in this life that they are among the Lord's anointed, and will receive eternal life. This is not to be confused with the notion of receiving salvation in spite of anything we do on this earth, but rather a confirmation of comfort and assurance to those who have made the effort to put Jesus Christ and His service first in their lives, to the exclusion of self. It is possible while yet in this second estate.

Elder Melvin J. Ballard said,

Let us be earnest in this work. It will cast an influence over your whole families. It will strengthen your faith. It will add testimony to your faith. Surely there is peace and joy in it. May you find it, and may everyone under the sound of my voice this evening, go hence with a firm resolve, such as we have never had before, that we will make our calling and election sure, that at the last day our records may be clear, that there may be no clouds upon our titles, that we may receive our inheritance in the celestial glory of our God. If that shall be our reward, our joy will be full, beyond all my power to tell you. May the Lord help us to have a clear conscience and to do every day that which we ought to do. . . . If we succeed, oh, my brethren and sisters, if we win that prize we shall be compensated beyond all expectations. We shall receive more than we have ever dreamed of joy and happiness and eternal satisfaction. (*The Three Degrees of Glory*, pp. 36-37.)

The purpose of this eternal plan is our happiness. Our Father set it into operation to enable us to continue on and eventually receive eternal happiness. President Cannon assured us, "I think that God has created us to be happy, and my belief is that he placed happiness within the reach of all, and it is man's own fault if he is not happy and does not enjoy himself every day of his life. This is one of my reasons for liking my religion, . . . because it bestows full happiness and joy upon its believers." (*Gospel Truth*, p. 125.)

No matter where you are in your progression, don't give up. Don't lose hope. Continue to resist temptation. Never let Satan enlarge on his insidious, evil thoughts. Use the many ways you have learned to withstand his enticements.

The more we practice righteous principles as we learn them, the more we feel the comforting spirit of the Holy Ghost with us. Our minds become clear and focused, our opportunities multiply. In ways we cannot anticipate, our joy and happiness increase.

We testify to you that this is true, and add our prayer with yours that the Lord will bless you with strength to keep your second estate with peace in your heart, and with other advantages that come to the faithful, in the name of the Holy One of Israel.

10

Light Versus Darkness

An essential idea in learning to control our thoughts and purifying our hearts is understanding our nature as human beings, and understanding the conflict we are undergoing day by day. An integral component of our life experience is the basic conflict between light and darkness, or between good and evil. Careful reading of the scriptures reveals this confrontation to be fundamental to our mortal experience. Moroni exhorts us to seek to distinguish good from evil: "Wherefore, I beseech of you, brethren, that ye should search diligently in the light of Christ that ye may know good from evil; and if ye will lay hold upon every good thing, and condemn it not, ye certainly will be a child of Christ." (Moroni 7:19.)

Jesus Christ, our Savior and Redeemer, is the Light. John calls Him the "true Light which lighteth every man that cometh into the world." (John 1:9.) He explains further that this Light "shineth in darkness; and the darkness comprehended it not." (v. 5.)

The Doctrine and Covenants helps us understand, "The glory of God is intelligence, or, in other words, light and truth. Light and truth forsake that evil one." (D&C 93:36-37.)

Christ, the gospel, truth, intelligence, spirit, and life are some of the synonyms used in the scriptures for "light." Darkness is the opposite. It refers to sin, ignorance, and apostasy. (See *Mormon Doctrine*, pp. 179 and 444.)

Light and Truth

A deep study of the principles of Light and Truth could last a lifetime, so we are going to point out only some of the magnificent details of this exalted concept.

Let's start with the Doctrine and Covenants, regarding Jesus Christ, "the true Light," and the glory of His position in the universe.

> He that ascended up on high, as also he descended below all things, in that he comprehended all things, that he might be in all and through all things, the light of truth;
> Which truth shineth. This is the light of Christ. As also he is in the sun, and the light of the sun, and the power thereof by which it was made.
> As also he is in the moon, and is the light of the moon, and the power thereof by which it was made;
> As also the light of the stars, and the power thereof by which they were made;
> And the earth also, and the power thereof, even the earth upon which you stand.
> And the light which shineth, which giveth you light, is through him who enlighteneth your eyes, which is the same light that quickeneth your understandings;
> Which light proceedeth forth from the presence of God to fill the immensity of space—
> The light which is in all things, which giveth life to all things, which is the law by which all things are governed, even the power of God who sitteth upon his throne, who is in the bosom of eternity, who is in the midst of all things. (D&C 88:6-13.)

Light (or Intelligence, or Truth, all synonyms) is that which actually, both physically and spiritually, governs the universe and this earth on which we stand. It set in motion and regulates the order and function of the cosmos. It warms and lights this earth, giving and enhancing life, enabling plants and animals to take nourishment and grow.

Elder Bruce R. McConkie reaffirmed this, saying, "Christ is the *light of life*. Life exists in and through and because of the light of Christ. . . Without this light of life, the planets would not stay in their orbits, vegetation would not grow, men and animals would be devoid of "the breath of life" (Gen. 2:7), and life would cease to exist." (*Mormon Doctrine*, p. 447.)

The Light of Christ enlightens the minds and spirits of humanity, increasing our ability to think and do. This light is given to all people who come into the world. Indeed it is that from which our spiritual beings came forth.

"For the word of the Lord is truth, and whatsoever is truth is light, and whatsoever is light is Spirit, even the Spirit of Jesus Christ.

"And the Spirit giveth light to every man that cometh into the world; and the Spirit enlighteneth every man through the world, that hearkeneth to the voice of the Spirit." (D&C 84:45-46.)

We will include here some definitive statements from our church leaders to help us better understand what light is and what it does.

Elder Bruce R. McConkie:

1. Through the Light of Christ [the Lord] governs and controls the universe and gives life to all that therein is.
2. By this same immensity-filling light—and also to certain faithful ones, by the power of the Holy Ghost!—he enlightens the mind and quickens the understanding.
3. By his own upright, sinless, and perfect course, in preexistence, in mortality, and in resurrected glory, he sets a perfect example and is able to say to all men: "Follow thou me." (2 Nephi 31:10.) (*The Promised Messiah*, p. 208.)

Elder Theodore M. Burton:

God's light includes the physical light we see, which makes us feel so warm and comfortable. God's light is also the power to understand and comprehend all things. In other words, all kinds of light are related to intelligence and truth. (CR, *Ensign*, May 1981, p. 29.)

Elder Bruce R. McConkie:

Christ is the light; the gospel is the light; the plan of salvation is the light; "that which is of God is light; and he that receiveth light, and continueth in God, receiveth more light; and that light groweth brighter and brighter until the perfect day." As the light of the sun enters the body *through our natural eyes*, so the light of heaven—the light of the Spirit which illuminates our souls—enters through our spiritual eyes." [See D&C 50:24.] (*The Mortal Messiah*, 2:153, emphasis added.)

Elder Ted E. Brewerton:

The light of the gospel illuminates the path of life to eternity that otherwise would be dark and nondirecting.

We can be like a mirror and direct light even into dark places. We are not the sources of light; nevertheless, through us light can be reflected to others. (CR, *Ensign*, November 1991 p. 12.)

Elder Bruce R. McConkie:

Light comes from God (2 Ne. 31:3), and the cry of righteous men has always been, "O send out thy light and thy truth: let them lead me." (Ps. 43:3.) The Lord's word is a light to the path of the faithful (Ps. 119:105), and men are commanded to "walk in the light of the Lord." (Isa. 2:5; John 11:9-10; 12:35.) Parents are commanded to bring up their children "in light and truth." (D&C 93:40-42.) Light is a protection against evil of every sort, and the saints should "put on the armour of light." (Rom. 13:12.) (*Mormon Doctrine*, p. 445.)

What have we learned so far?
1.   Through light, Christ governs and controls the universe.
2.   God's light includes physical light. We see and feel its warmth.
3.   God's light is also the power to understand and comprehend all things.
4.   All kinds of light are related to intelligence and truth.
5.   Gospel light includes Christ, the gospel, the plan of salvation.
6.   The light of the gospel illuminates the path of life.
7.   Light is a protection against all kinds of evil.
8.   The Spirit of Christ, sometimes called our conscience, is given "to every man that cometh into the world."
9.   This Spirit of Christ helps us know right from wrong.

Darkness or Light

Darkness is the absence of light, either physical or spiritual. Darkness is a condition of rebellion and apostasy against the gospel, its light, and its Author. Darkness persuades us to sin; darkness is sin. Darkness is oppression, fear, confinement, despair; darkness is enmity; darkness is any malicious or unkind feeling. Dark thoughts are sinful thoughts.

Elder Bruce McConkie writes: "In the gospel sense, *darkness*—the opposite of light—reigns where there is ignorance, iniquity, and apostasy. Light is of God, darkness is of the devil; Christ is the true light, Lucifer the fountain of gross darkness and apostasy. 'I am the light which shineth in darkness, and the darkness comprehendeth it not,' our Lord said. (D. & C. 6:21; John 1:5.) 'God is light, and in him is no darkness at all.' (1 John 1:5.) Where the true gospel of Christ is, there is light; and where that gospel is not found, darkness reigns. 'The whole world lieth in sin, and groaneth under darkness and under the bondage of sin, . . . because they come not unto me,' The Lord said. (D. & C. 84:49-54.)" *Mormon Doctrine*, p. 179.)

Just as light is an essential, universal principle, so darkness is also necessary in the plan of progression. Opposition is a necessary principle, or we could not choose, thereby we could not advance, neither could we receive any judgment or reward.

Speaking of God's children, Moses says, "And they taste the bitter, that they may know to prize the good. And it is given unto them to know good from evil; wherefore they are agents unto themselves." (Moses 6:55-56. See also 2 Nephi 2:11-14.)

Nephi explains how the transgression of Adam in the Garden of Eden brought the conflict between light and darkness into this sphere of existence, so that mankind could experience this necessary opposition. Were it not for the opposition between good and evil, and the intercession of Jesus Christ, we could not know joy.

> But behold, all things have been done in the wisdom of him who knoweth all things.
>
> Adam fell that men might be; and men are, that they might have joy.
>
> And the Messiah cometh in the fulness of time, that he may redeem the children of men from the fall. And because that they are redeemed from the fall they have become free forever, knowing good from evil; to act for themselves and not to be acted upon, save it be by the punishment of the law at the great and last day, according to the commandments which God hath given. (2 Nephi 2:24-26.)

Light, truth, and good emanate from God and Christ. Evil is the province of the devil. In his vindictiveness, he is actually providing a necessary portion of the plan for our advancement. Part of passing our mortal probation is to meet the conflict between light and darkness or good and evil, thereby gaining experience, learning to recognize both, and choosing the light or the good.

After their expulsion from the Garden of Eden, Adam and Eve were taught the Law of Sacrifice, which includes the indispensable principle of repentance, and they understood that this was a type of the sacrifice of Jesus Christ who would come as a redeemer to pay the price of justice for their transgression. Understanding at last the full gospel plan, Adam prophesied these things for the benefit of us all:

> And in that day Adam blessed God and was filled, and began to prophesy concerning all the families of the earth, saying: Blessed be the name of God, for because of my transgression my eyes are opened, and in this life I shall have joy, and again in the flesh I shall see God.
>
> And Eve, his wife, heard all these things and was glad, saying: Were it not for our transgression we never should have had seed, and never should have known good and evil, and the joy of our redemption, and the eternal life which God giveth unto all the obedient.
>
> And Adam and Eve blessed the name of God, and they made all things known unto their sons and their daughters. (Moses 5:10-12.)

Immediately Satan began to tempt mankind (the children of Adam and Eve) to disregard these important principles. Some believed and followed him: ". . . and they loved Satan more than God. And men began from that time forth to be carnal, sensual, and devilish." (v. 13.)

President George Q. Cannon talked of the influence of unseen spirits around us:

> Those evil spirits, . . . invisible to our eyes, yet palpable to our senses, are constantly seeking to instill into our minds evil thoughts and wrong desires, to prompt us to commit sin and thereby grieve the Spirit of God and to lead us, as Cain was led to perpetrate crime which resulted in his becoming Perdition. But there are also angels around us. Though invisible to us they are continually inviting us and pleading with us to do that which is right. The Spirit of God, too, rests upon us, and it prompts us to keep the commandments of God. By means of these influences, therefore, we are receiving experience and we are growing in knowledge. (*Gospel Truth*, p. 66.)

Satan is angry, hateful, and vicious, but not all-powerful. President Cannon said,

> If he had power, he would sweep this entire people from the face of the earth. If he could, he would destroy us all. . . . It is because

he has not the power that he does not do it; it is because our Father and God checkmates him and restrains him and overrules his acts that he does not do this. The disposition is there; the willingness is there; the murderous spirit is there. . . . We know this. . . . We have this kind of a foe to contend against. (*Gospel Truth*, pp. 15-16.)

Our Father in Heaven restrains Satan. His evil influence is necessary in the gospel plan of progression, but he can only do what we allow him to do in our lives. He is not supreme.

President Cannon instructed us, "He who is imbued with the Spirit of God is sensibly aware when the evil power approaches, but he does not welcome it to his bosom; he resists it with all the might and strength God has given unto him; he obtains power over it, and it no more troubles him; if it does, its influence is more weakened than previously." (*Gospel Truth*, p. 65.)

Each time we resist the evil spirit, we become stronger and the influence of the evil spirit on us becomes weaker.

When our Father put us into this earthly situation, He did not leave us without help to accomplish our life's purposes. President Cannon told us that the commandments (laws) which God has given us provide ways and means to overcome the spirit of darkness:

My view of the Gospel is that when it is obeyed by mankind the power of the devil will cease. That is my view respecting a part of the power that will be brought to bear to bind Satan. Satan will be bound because he will not have power over the hearts of the children of men. Why? One reason will be because they will have obeyed the more perfect law which will have relieved them from his power. . .

In the Gospel of the Lord Jesus Christ as God has revealed it unto us *there are laws so perfect that when this people called Latter-day Saints shall obey them they will be so far lifted up above the power of Satan that he will have but little power to tempt them.* We never shall be emancipated from the power of Satan until we do obey these laws of God. An obedience thereto will bring emancipation to us and to every human being on the face of the earth, and it is upon no other principle that emancipation can be brought. (*Gospel Truth*, p. 69, emphasis added.)

The most basic of these laws is obedience. As we have noted, the Spirit of Christ is given to every person who is born on the earth. That light has many functions, one of which is to let us recognize darkness and avoid it. It is that inner guide that lets us feel comfortable with right choices and uneasy with poor ones. Obedience to its influence keeps us "on the beam." It leads us toward truth, the true Church, and the higher light, which is the Holy Ghost.

President Joseph F. Smith said that the Spirit of Christ "strives with . . . men, and will continue to strive with them, until it brings them to a knowledge of the truth and the possession of the greater light and testimony of the Holy Ghost." (*Gospel Doctrine*, pp. 67-68.)

We receive the Holy Ghost by obedience to the first principles of the gospel: first having faith in Jesus Christ, then repenting of all our sins, after which we are baptized and confirmed by one who has authority. We keep the Holy Ghost with us by continued obedience, by remaining worthy and faithful.

The Holy Ghost is the greater light. President N. Eldon Tanner spoke of it thus:

> We are encouraged to remain faithful through a promise of increased light and knowledge, for He said:
>
> "That which is of God is light; and he that receiveth light, and continueth in God, receiveth more light; and that light groweth brighter and brighter until the perfect day." (D&C 50:24.)
>
> "And if your eye be single to my glory, your whole bodies shall be filled with light, and there shall be no darkness in you; and that body which is filled with light comprehendeth all things." (D&C 88:67.)
>
> How glorious and how desirable! Who would not want to strive for such a blessing? (CR, *Ensign*, November 1977, p. 49.)

We Can Exchange Dark Thoughts for Light

Such a concept of enlightenment and glory kindles desire and hope in all of us who are struggling to control our minds and hearts. Elder Dallin H. Oaks taught us that this desire can enable us to exchange one thought for another thought. "Our Heavenly Father knows the desires of our hearts and will judge us accordingly. He will punish evil desires and reward righteous ones.

"We can suppress evil desires and substitute righteous ones. This involves education and practice." (*Pure in Heart*, p. 149.)

Elder Oaks said further, "Through our divinely granted willpower we have ultimate control over our desires. But the desires of our hearts are so deep-seated that it may take many years of practice for us to be sure that education and practice have perfected our desires to the point where all are entirely righteous." (*Pure in Heart*, p. 150.)

We have previously discussed ways to exchange a bad thought for a righteous thought. Here is another way, based on the glorious concept of light and truth. Contemplate the beautiful passages of scripture describing the effect of light in your life. Cultivate that desire, and make an agreement with yourself that next time Satan tries to put a bad thought into your mind you will instantly exchange it for light—you will think about light. Follow these steps; this can be done in the mind instantly.

1. Visualize yourself being filled with light.
2. Visualize that light increasing in you because of your faith.
3. Visualize this light within you growing "brighter and brighter until the perfect day."
4. Visualize your body without any darkness in it.
5. Visualize your eye being single to the Glory of God.
6. Visualize yourself in the straight and narrow path that leads to eternal life.
7. Visualize the Holy Ghost enlightening your mind and quickening your understanding.
8. Visualize Jesus Christ lifting you up and making you equal to your temptation.
9. Visualize a sweet stream of light coming into your soul as answer to your prayer.
10. Visualize yourself a fountain of light, overflowing with gratitude and thanking your Father for this help, when the strength comes.
11. Finally, visualize yourself not listening to Satan.

After this fullness of light, the effect of a thought about Satan, even of *not listening* to him, will be a shock. What a contrast!

Following this approach, every time Satan tries to put a bad thought into your mind you will automatically exchange that thought for a thought of light. Look into the light in the area you are in. Feel the warmth of the sun. Let the light fill your mind. If you practice this procedure you will find that without even trying when Satan attacks you will be ready. In an instant your mind will automatically change to thoughts of light.

You will find great joy in controlling your mind in this manner. You can then go on with light in your mind to whatever you want to think about. Don't let your mind go idle. Keep it busy thinking about constructive things. Always have projects you are working on, projects that challenge your mind. Keep busy. Pray for the blessings you need. Ponder the scriptures. Store up ideas for a talk or lesson you will give in the future.

Elder Boyd K. Packer recommends singing an inspirational hymn, then tells us why singing a hymn dislodges an evil thought: "As the music begins and as the words form in your mind, the unworthy thoughts will slip shamefully away. The hymn will change the whole mood on the stage of your mind. Because it is uplifting and clean, the baser thoughts will disappear, for while virtue, by choice, *will not* associate with filth, evil *cannot* tolerate the presence of light." (*Teach Ye Diligently*, p. 47.)

You might try singing this hymn about light when you are bothered with a bad thought.

> Teach me to walk in the light of his love;
> Teach me to pray to my Father above;
> Teach me to know of the things that are right;
> Teach me, teach me to walk in the light. (*Hymns*, #304.)

Other hymns that will help exchange a bad thought for good thoughts are, "I Am a Child of God," "Because I Have Been Given Much," "Lord, I Would Follow Thee," "How Gentle God's Commands," "I Need Thee Every Hour," "I'll Go Where You Want Me to Go," "Sweet Hour of Prayer," and "I Believe in Christ." Singing the hymns is a good way to keep the Spirit with you. Any of the hymns will have the same effect—memorize several of your favorite hymns, then when a bad thought comes, exchange it for your hymn.

Desire the Light

The light will come brighter and truer into our lives when we have a strong desire for it. If we heed the Light of Christ, our conscience, and continually do as it directs, the desire to do right will become stronger. Alma told us to let desire "work" in us and it would grow up into full fruited faith (see Alma 32). The desire to do right increases in the same way.

Elder Joseph B. Wirthlin spoke of this principle:

> The springs of human action are inherently in the feelings, not the intellect. . . .

Only in accepting our Savior and doing his will do we acquire the "feeling to do right." . . . Fundamental to most wrong-doing is a lack of desire [to do right]. . . . Individuals who do right and "hunger and thirst after righteousness" (Matthew 5:6) get and keep alive through their actions the feeling to do right. Inherent in the first principles of the gospel is the "desire principle"—the desire to love God and fellowmen "with all thy heart, and with all thy soul, and with all thy mind." (Matthew 22:37) (CR, *Ensign*, May 1976, p. 56.)

Elder Dallin Oaks explained how educating our feelings will cause us to desire higher and better principles:

We can begin the education of our desires by attempting to alter our feelings. The desires of our hearts are fundamental, but our feelings are closer to the surface and easier for us to identify and influence.

I have sometimes heard a person say: "I hate him. I can't help how I feel." I have also heard someone say: "I can't stand to have anyone tell me what I must do. I can't help it. That's just the way I am." These assertions are mistaken. Feelings *are* subject to change. Our feelings are subject to our will.

My widowed mother understood that principle. "Pray about your feelings," she used to say. She taught her three children to pray for the right kind of feelings about their experiences—positive or negative —and about the people they knew. If our feelings are good, we are more likely to have appropriate desires, to take right actions, and to act for the right reasons.

We can perfect our desires. God commands us to do so, and he will strengthen us in this effort if we will seek his help. (*Pure in Heart*, pp. 150-51.)

Pray for the Light

God has commanded us to pray for the blessings we desire. "Ask, and ye shall receive; knock, and it shall be opened unto you." (D&C 4:7.) Through humble fervent prayer we can learn to "hunger and thirst" after righteousness.

In the struggle between light and darkness, prayer is vital. "If ye would hearken unto the Spirit which teacheth a man to pray ye would know that ye must pray; for the evil spirit teacheth not a man to pray, but teacheth him that he must not pray." (2 Nephi 32:8.)

The powers of darkness are opposed to prayer. The evil spirit uses every trick he can think of to try to discourage us from praying. He knows that if we pray sincerely and humbly we will get answers to our prayers, strengthening us and making us more able to combat him. Each time our prayers are answered our faith becomes stronger. Through prayer we grow closer to our Father in Heaven, our desire to keep the commandments of the Lord expands, and our spirituality increases. We become more faithful to Him. Satan knows that if we sincerely offer humble prayers over a long enough period of time, we will win and he will lose the battle. We will have filled our souls with light, and put ourselves beyond his enticements.

President Cannon taught us we should pray in our hearts as well as aloud: "It is a good thing to know how to pray; and we are not heard for our much speaking in prayer. It seems to me we should be full of the spirit of prayer, and we should pray in our hearts as well as with our lips and on our knees and cultivate the habit of praying in our hearts. We cannot stop always to get down on our knees to ask for that which we need; but we can ask the Lord in our hearts, no matter what we are engaged in." (*Gospel Truth*, p. 414.)

Don's personal testimony: "I testify that this is true. I know that God will answer our prayers even as President Cannon has said. He has answered my prayers in this manner many times. My life has been enriched by this counsel. When I learned to let a silent prayer run through my mind at the very moment of need, I found I could work more closely with my Father in Heaven. I can ask Him for blessings as I drive my car, as I talk in difficult interviews with bankers or buyers, as I arise to speak before a congregation. It opens my heart to wisdom through the Holy Ghost, and softens my business dealings. I make fewer errors, and find life runs much more smoothly.

"I recently had such an experience in my business as a building contractor. We were having difficulty keeping to our time schedule in building homes. Some of the homes would sit for long periods with very little progress, so I prayed to my Father in Heaven that He would show me a faster way to get these homes built. It came into my mind that I should give time limits for each job to be done, then check the progress of every home every day with my foreman. I told the foreman to work closely with the subcontractors so they knew how long they would each have to do their work, then monitor their progress. I strove to follow the instructions from the Spirit, knowing that when I ask for specific help, I am under obligation to do as directed. All areas began to move faster. It was a forthright answer to my prayer."

We know that the Lord also wants to help you in all your righteous endeavors. Though you may be facing problems that are difficult to solve, never forget that your Father in Heaven knows the solution to all problems. To those who are faithful and pray to Him, He gives solutions.

Prayer is especially important in our homes. President Cannon taught us the disastrous effects of neglecting our family prayers: "No family that fails to attend to family prayers in the proper season can keep up with the progress of the Kingdom of God. Such families fall behind in everything. They become dark in their minds, dull in their spirits and lose what little faith they may possess. They are guilty of gross ingratitude, and this is a great sin. The Spirit of God is grieved and will withdraw itself from every person who does not appreciate the goodness of God to him and who fails to render Him that worship and thanksgiving which are due to Him as our Creator and Protector." (*Gospel Truth*, p. 411.)

President Cannon thought it would be better to go without breakfast than to go without our morning prayer! "We trust that every reader will make it a fixed rule to attend to secret and family prayers. Better go without a meal than to neglect this duty. If your stomach is empty, you will feel faint and be reminded that you must give it food. Remember that the spirit also needs food, and make it your business to attend to supplying it in the way that God has appointed. Then your spirit and your body will be developed alike, and strength will be maintained." (*Gospel Truth*, p. 412.)

We enjoy our family prayers as well as personal prayers. We feel it is important to begin the day with an invocation of His blessings on the various activities of the family members. We express gratitude for the opportunities of the day, and ask for His assistance in our projects. We ask for the gospel to enlighten our minds. Then as the day proceeds, we often pray silently, to ask for the blessings we need and to thank Him for the many blessings we receive as the hours go by.

Rules are Tools—Commandments Are Enablers

Our Father in Heaven will never ask us to do something we cannot do. He will make a way for us to fulfill His commandments. If we think of the laws and commandments as "enablers," means by which we can accomplish worthwhile goals, we will be encouraged in our efforts to keep them. Keeping His laws makes it possible for us to do something we could not otherwise do.

Every day heavier-than-air machines, designed and engineered to function under the known laws of aerodynamics, transport people and goods thousands of air-miles. Obeying the laws or rules makes this possible. We have come to depend on this method of transportation, observe the achievement daily and do not think it worth a remark. Only recently in terms of human history we have put laws of electronics to work, and daily watch pictures of events thousands of miles away, receive FAX messages, use computers, E-mail and the "Internet." These things are only available if all laws are obeyed. We become impatient if someone tells us a question cannot be handled because "the computer is down."

In like manner, but on a grander and more exalted scale, obedience to gospel laws and commandments enables us to reach personal spiritual planes we never thought possible. If we stubbornly refuse to believe that obedience to the laws of the gospel is important, we are the losers.

Spiritual laws empower, facilitate, and enable the accomplishment, not only of spiritual things, but of temporal activities as well, because our lives are an extension of a previous spiritual experience, and everything we are engaged in has spiritual consequences. Commandments are not restrictions, but implements. Rules are tools.

President Cannon assured us that God will empower us to do anything He commands. It requires our faith.

> [God] never gave a commandment unto the children of men without opening a way by which they could fulfill it; if they do not fulfill it, therefore, through lack of diligence or faith on their part, they must be the losers. He has done all that He can, consonant with justice, in revealing the law, with the rewards and penalties attached to obedience and disobedience, and in promising the necessary assistance to enable them to fulfill it if they will but seek for it. All who have ever sought for this assistance have obtained it and have proved for themselves that the Lord requires nothing of mankind but what, if they seek it, he gives them power to perform; and there are no circumstances—however seemingly difficult—which conspire to prevent them from obeying His commandments but what the Spirit of the Lord will enable them, in His own due time, to surmount and control. (*Gospel Truth*, p. 80.)

Likewise, with every test received, there is the ability to pass it appropriately. Heavenly Father will not allow you to be tempted above what you are able to stand. He will make a way for you to escape. Alma exhorted us to: "watch and pray continually , that ye may not be tempted above that which ye can bear, and thus be led by the Holy Spirit." (Alma 13:28.) The Lord also assures us: "I prepare a way for [your] deliverance in all things out of temptation." (D&C 95:1.) (See also 1 Corinthians 10:13.)

Obviously, that does not mean nobody fails—but they did not have to fail. If you heed the light, if you go to your Father in Heaven in all humility and ask Him to strengthen you, He will do so. Many times you will feel the strength coming into your soul while you are still praying or soon after. When the strength comes, offer thanks to Him who gave the gift.

Elder Delbert L. Stapley said that keeping our spiritual lights bright enables us to overcome temptation:

> The Lord has never promised that the overcoming of evil would be easy, but everyone can, if he wills, win the battle against the power of Satan.
>
> The gospel of Christ is a lamp in our hands to guide us in righteous paths. Light can always dissipate darkness, but darkness can never replace light. It is only when the light of the Spirit within us is dimmed or goes out that the darkness of temptation and sin enters in, and Satan takes over. (CR, *Improvement Era*, June 1968, p. 52.)

Prayer will strengthen us and fortify us against temptations. When you are tempted, pray until the temptation goes away. It will soon go away. Please take time now to commit yourself to this self-improvement program.

Now, having done so, don't you feel more confident you can win over your temptations?

Not only does our Father in Heaven enable us to keep his commandments, but the keeping the commandments enables us to accomplish all the worthwhile tasks of life. Most of our efforts in life center around our gainful employment, our family responsibilities, our learning, both in school and in other areas, our interpersonal relationships, and our recreational pursuits. Keeping the commandments enables us to do better in every one of these facets of life. When our minds are clear, we are able to focus our energies better. Seeking the Lord first empowers us with faith and optimism. Confidence beams in a radiant countenance. Avoiding covetousness enables us to concentrate on our own productivity. Honesty not only avoids trouble with others, it faces life and its problems squarely, and with good results. The strength we receive from keeping the Word of Wisdom is physical and spiritual. Being worthy of the Holy Spirit enables us to make correct decisions. Right choices avoid troublesome entanglements. Prayer strengthens and fortifies us. Wise use of time frees us for doing more of what we want and need to do. Love begets love. By learning and keeping God's commandments, our personal accomplishments increase, our personal relationships improve, our satisfactions multiply.

"Light Cleaveth unto Light"

The Spirit of Christ, light and truth, leads people to a repentant attitude and a godly sorrow for things they have done wrong. D&C 88:40 tells us that "light cleaveth unto light." He who responds to the light that he has received, gains more light. That light leads us in an upward movement away from darkness and sin, and toward happy, heartening, encouraging feelings which are the natural companions of light and truth.

Elder Orson Pratt explained how the Spirit, through the light within us, quickens our minds when we keep the commandments: "We need the influence of the Spirit of God to quicken the light that is within us, for light cleaves to light, and the Spirit of God is light, and it cleaves unto the light that enters into the composition of the spirit of man; and when we keep his commandments the Lord is ever ready and willing to quicken the judgment, inform the mind, and lead us along in our thinking and reflecting powers, that we may have power to understand a great many truths." (*Journal of Discourses*, 17:327.)

One of the phrases repeated often in the latter-day revelations is that "The light . . . shineth in darkness, and the darkness comprehendeth it not." (See D&C 6:21; 10:58; 11:11; 39:2; etc.) What a tragedy not to recognize the Light of the World. Those who choose darkness and ignore the pleadings of the Spirit of Christ lose the light they have previously received. This warning should encourage us to have a repentant spirit and seek for more light and truth, which will cleave unto that which we have already received.

The happy way to live is to repent immediately when we become aware that we have done something contrary to the will of God. He will forgive us and we will not have a build-up of unrepented sins. This will keep our slates clean. A repentant spirit is a protection against losing our light.

We gain more light by searching out the truth and living by it. We can also lose light in little, insidious ways, without even being aware of it, if we are not careful and watchful. A *Church News* editorial quoted Elder Neal A. Maxwell who said,

"In these darkest hours, we must keep our individual lights shining. The moment of greatest danger is when there is so little light that darkness seems normal. Church members can be models of morality, a glow of goodness like a perpetual midnight sun."

As he emphasized the need to keep our lights bright by our constant faithfulness to the Lord, he added:

"We must remember, however, that it is not necessary, either, that Satan extinguish our light, if he can simply keep it dim." . . .

When we stay away from our meetings we dim our light. When we withhold our tithes and offerings, we dim our light. When we break the Word of Wisdom, when we profane, when we are dishonest, we dim our light. And when we submit to immorality, we come near to extinguishing it.

The Light of Christ is given to us freely if we will accept it, but when we turn our backs upon it, we are left in darkness indeed! (*Church News*, August 23, 1975, p. 16.)

Is the small dishonest act of accepting too much change at the register worth the light we lose? Is the item we "must have" from the store on Sunday worth the light we lose? Is the small deception we put forth to avoid inconvenience worth the light we lose? Is the dirty joke or the R-rated movie worth the light we lose?

Elder Delbert L. Stapley adds, "'And that wicked one cometh and taketh away light and truth, through disobedience, from the children of men. . . .' (D&C 93:39.) It is through disobedience and man's failure to hearken unto the voice of the Spirit and the counsels of God that Satan is able to come and take away from man the light and truth of the gospel. When the light within us begins to dim, Satan moves in. When the light within us goes out, we are in his power and under his control." (CR, *Improvement Era*, June 1968, p. 52.)

We should do everything in our power to brighten our light. Don't forget simple everyday things like daily prayer and scripture study, sustaining the leaders of the Church, doing one hundred percent quality home teaching and visiting teaching, getting along with our neighbors and the people at the office, staying away from stores on Sunday, paying generous fast offering, being kind, charitable, and loving, in many ordinary ways being the light that is set upon the bushel so it can shine forth to the children of men (see Matthew 5:14,15), and building God's kingdom here on the earth.

Sister Ardeth Greene Kapp, former General President of the Young Women, wrote,

> Every time we do right, we increase the light. Going contrary to the light within affects our power of concentration, our ability to learn, our access to light, and our ultimate success intellectually and spiritually. Every right choice, every good thought, every act of kindness, every commitment to obedience, every earnest prayer, every sacrifice in defense of truth, every ounce of self-discipline in response to the whisperings of the Spirit, every extra effort in diligent study and preparation, every honest act—these all add to the light. And when even one light gets dim or goes out as a result of wrong choices, the world is a little darker. (*The Joy of the Journey*, p. 61.)

When our souls are filled with light, we search for more light, we love truth, and we seek for that which is good, true, beautiful, and praiseworthy. We shun darkness and evil, and gravitate toward the light of Truth. Joy, cheerfulness, and optimism radiate from our hearts.

We can tell when we are in the strait and narrow path because the Spirit of the Holy Ghost will be with us. This Spirit makes us happy and confident. We are peaceful, hopeful, and joyful.

President George Q. Cannon said, "Do not allow darkness and gloom to enter into your hearts. I want to give you a rule by which you may know that the spirit which you have is the right spirit. The Spirit of God produces cheerfulness, joy, light and good feelings. Whenever you feel gloomy and despondent and are downcast, unless it be for your sins, you may know it is not the Spirit of God which you have. Fight against it and drive it out of your heart. The Spirit of God is a spirit of hope; it is not a spirit of gloom." (*Gospel Truth*, pp. 144-45.)

As a note, if you *are* gloomy and despondent *because* of your sins, take positive steps to put repentance into your life immediately. Make arrangements immediately to see your bishop, if this is necessary. Make full confession and do whatever he tells you to do. Repent of the sins that are darkening your soul. Put your life in order. When you have a free conscience you can feel the light of the Holy Ghost in your life daily.

The Apostle John summarized the conflict between light and darkness:

"And this is the condemnation, that light is come into the world, and men loved darkness rather than light, because their deeds were evil.

"For every one that doeth evil hateth the light, neither cometh to the light, lest his deeds should be reproved.

"But he that doeth truth cometh to the light, that his deeds may be made manifest, that they are wrought in God." (John 3:19-21.)

There is so much darkness throughout the world. It is heartbreaking when we see that many follow Satan's thinking, and choose to commit evil deeds. We must not only lift ourselves out of his power, but also reach out to others around us who are in danger. We are committed to save ourselves, and to let our light shine before the world to the glory of our Father in Heaven. (See Matthew 5:16.)

Our Savior constantly admonishes us to let our light shine: "Hold up your light that it may shine unto the world." (3 Nephi 18:24.) "Verily I say unto you all: Arise and shine forth, that thy light may be a standard for the nations." (D&C 115:5.) "Ye are my disciples; and ye are a light unto this people." (3 Nephi 15:12.)

Truly light cleaveth unto light and seeketh her own. The spiral leads upward or downward according to our choices. If we let the light shine into our lives and prefer it, we move upward in the light. Its might, power, beauty, and intelligence illuminate our souls. Let us always reach toward the light, and cleave unto it. Let us actively seek the Spirit in our lives daily. Let us choose to radiate the Spirit of God.

President Joseph Fielding Smith described the beautiful reward of living our life according to the Light of Christ: "If we will just be true and faithful to every covenant, to every principle of truth that he has given us, then after the resurrection we would come back into his presence and we would be just like he is. We would have the same kind of bodies— bodies that would shine like the sun." (*Take Heed to Yourselves!*, p. 345.)

Isn't that worth working for? Wouldn't it be wonderful if on the day of judgment our beloved Savior, Himself the True Light, would say to us something like this, "Enter thou into thy glory, thou good and faithful servant"? This can be our happy lot if we are willing to keep our lights bright.

11

Understanding Satan,
The "Father of Lies"

And it must needs be that the devil should tempt the children of men, or they could not be agents unto themselves; for if they never should have bitter they could not know the sweet." (D&C 29:39. See also 2 Nephi 2:11-14.)

The need for opposition in all things is a significant concept in the gospel plan of progression and salvation. To develop our understanding of it we need to review the origin of that "father of lies" who is the perpetrator of the opposition and evil we confront daily.

Who Is Satan?

Elder ElRay L. Christiansen taught in conference that the origin of Satan goes back beyond our mortal experience. We quote his excellent description at length:

> The scriptures teach us that we lived in the spirit world before we were born into mortality. That is, we lived in the presence of God who is literally the Father of our spirits.
>
> When the great council was held in heaven, in which all of us were involved, the Father presented his plan for peopling the earth, and for the salvation of man. Lucifer wanted to amend the plan. He proposed to destroy the agency of man and to save all mankind, that not one soul would be lost. This he would accomplish through outright force and coercion, denying all persons the right of choice.
>
> Satan's proposal of compulsion was rejected by the Father, and Lucifer "was angry, and kept not his first estate; and, . . . many followed after him." (Abr. 3:28.)

We must have witnessed that tragic scene when Lucifer—brilliant, capable, yet lacking in intelligence to properly apply his knowledge (along with one-third of the hosts of heaven)—rose in hateful rebellion against God. And they were expelled from heaven, retaining the malignant powers to tempt and to persuade men to disobey God.

The Father's plan, accepted by Jehovah, provided man the right of choice, that through its exercise he might become strong and advance in learning, wisdom, and righteousness by conquering weaknesses and by resisting the temptations to do wrong. Then God said: "We will take of these materials, and we will make an earth whereon these may dwell:

"And we will prove them herewith, to see if they will do all things whatsoever the Lord their God shall command them." (Abr. 3:24-25.)

Now, God said also (and this is most important to you and to me): "Wherefore, because that Satan rebelled against me, and sought to destroy the agency of man, which I, the Lord God, had given him, and also, that I should give unto him mine own power; . . . I caused that he should be cast down;

"And he became Satan, yea, even the devil, the father of all lies, to deceive and to blind men, and to lead them captive at his will, even as many as would not hearken unto my voice." (Moses 4:3-4.)

How does Satan operate? What are his tactics? Using his superior knowledge, his unique powers of persuasion, half-truths, and complete lies, the evil one uses the spirit children who follow him (which were many), plus mortal beings who have yielded to his evil ways, to wage war against Jehovah and his followers; and they will, if they can, influence us to become critical and to rebel against God and his work. Thus he destroys the souls of men.

The scriptures tell us: "Satan stirreth them up, that he may lead their souls to destruction." (D&C 10:22.)

"Yea, he saith unto them: Deceive and lie in wait to catch, that ye may destroy; behold, this is no harm. . . .

"And thus he flattereth them, and leadeth them along until he draggeth their souls down to hell; and thus he causeth them to catch themselves in their own snare.

"And thus he goeth up and down, to and fro in the earth, seeking to destroy the souls of men." (D&C 10:25-27.) (CR, *Ensign*, November 1974, pp. 22-24.)

Satan is a real being. He does not have a body of flesh and bones, but he has a spirit body. President Marion G. Romney explained the necessity of understanding the reality of Satan: "We Latter-day Saints need not be, and we must not be, deceived by the sophistries of men concerning the reality of Satan. There is a personal devil, and we had better believe it. He and a countless host of followers, seen and unseen, are exercising a controlling influence upon men and their affairs in our world today. . . . This is no time for Latter-day Saints to equivocate." (CR, *Ensign*, June 1971, p. 36.)

Enoch knew of the reality of Satan. This great prophet, who was able to bring his people to such perfection that his entire city was taken up from the earth while still in mortality, had an experience during which he saw Satan and the power he exerts over the earth: ". . . and Enoch was high and lifted up, even in the bosom of the Father, and of the Son of Man; and behold, the power of Satan was upon all the face of the earth. . . .

"And he beheld Satan; and he had a great chain in his hand, and it veiled the whole face of the earth with darkness; and he looked up and laughed, and his angels rejoiced." (Moses 7:24, 26.)

Can you imagine that vile deceiver looking up at this heroic prophet and exploding into the challenge of his sinister laugh? The struggle for men's souls continues, and he and his evil assistants rejoice when any person succumbs to their treachery.

This helps us see why it is so important for us to understand the nature of Satan: so we can recognize his methods and properly resist them. Rather than being able to defeat the plan of the great Jehovah, he actually worked into God's program by becoming the vehicle through which opposition would be presented to God's children in mortality. His only success is in those individuals who fall to his will. He will not triumph over Jehovah's plan. Each of us, being subjected to this necessary condition of opposition and growth, needs to become aware of Satan's methods so we may choose the true good over Satan's entrapments.

The First Presidency felt it important enough to tell us in plain words how Satan operates: "He is working under such perfect disguise that many do not recognize either him or his methods. There is no crime he would not commit, no debauchery he would not set up, no plague he would not send, no heart he would not break, no life he would not take, no soul he would not destroy. He comes as a thief in the night; he is a wolf in sheep's clothing." (*Messages of the First Presidency*, 1965-75, Vol. 6, p. 179.)

When we speak of evil, we are speaking of Satan. He is the ultimate source of evil, and he is actively at work trying to bring to pass the spiritual destruction of man. Elder James E. Faust used Job's experience in the Old Testament to explain how Satan's influence is everywhere: "The prince of darkness can be found everywhere. He is often in very good company. Job said, 'Again there was a day when the sons of God came to present themselves before the Lord, and Satan came also among them to present himself before the Lord' (Job 2:1). His influence is everywhere: 'And the Lord said unto Satan, From whence comest thou? And Satan answered the Lord, and said, From going to and fro in the earth, and from walking up and down in it' (Job 2:2)." (CR, *Ensign*, November 1987, p. 34.)

Satan and Man's Agency

Satan's desire has been and will always be to rob us of our God-given agency. It was because of this desire that he was cast out of heaven. (See Moses 4:3-4.)

What have we learned thus far? We have learned that Satan is a real being. He is moving about actively on the earth seeking to lead us astray. He will use any means he can, any deception he can invent, to destroy our right to choose, and to lead us away from the Light.

Nevertheless, we *have* our agency. Our Eternal Father gave it to us before we came here, and He will never abridge it. We *can* choose the course our lives will take. The war in Heaven still rages on this earth— Lucifer battling to control men's souls; Lucifer, or Satan, trying to take from us that agency which the Lord gave us. But the only way Satan can take away our agency is for us to surrender it to him voluntarily by the choices we make to follow him. Therefore we can successfully resist him by learning to avoid the traps set by the evil one. We can and must learn to recognize and shun the deceptions rampant in the world.

One way Satan binds us gradually is through enticing us to commit sin. Sin robs us of our ability to make choices. President Spencer W. Kimball explained the enslaving effects of sin: "Sin is intensely habit-forming and sometimes moves men to the tragic point of no return. Without repentance there can be no forgiveness, and without forgiveness all the blessings of eternity hang in jeopardy. As the transgressor moves deeper and deeper in his sin, and the error is entrenched more deeply and the will to change is weakened, it becomes increasingly near-hope-less, and he skids down and down until either he does not want to climb back or he has lost the power to do so." (*The Miracle of Forgiveness*, p. 117.)

Perhaps some feel that since they have not committed heinous sins, Satan has no power over them. However, we must be aware of the adversary's *subtle* temptations and the way he leads us step-by-step. President Kimball warned of the sly craftiness of Satan: "The adversary is subtle; he is cunning, he knows that he cannot induce good men and women immediately to do major evils so he moves slyly, whispering half truths until he has his intended victims following him, and finally he clamps his chains upon them and fetters them tight, and then he laughs at . . . their misery." (CR, *Improvement Era*, December 1962, p. 928.)

Since man is a creature of habit, we have to watch ourselves every minute lest we enter into the little sins which have a way of growing into large sins. Then we must make sure we repent daily so Satan does not get a hold on us through sinful habits which are hard to break. When we sin to that point, it may seem impossible to return. Satan, seeing he has led us to this wretched situation, delights in our misery.

However, we always have our agency, and it is always possible to return. President George Q. Cannon tells us how: "We may depend upon it, therefore, that the proper way to take away the power from Satan is to teach mankind not to listen to him. They are free agents. They can reject him. He has no power to lead them astray if they will not listen to him. When they cease to listen to him, he will be bound." (*Gospel Truth*, p. 109.) Referring to the time when the Nephites lived in purity and Satan had no power over them, President Cannon said, "In this land he did not have power, and he was literally bound. I believe that this will be the case in the millennium." (*Gospel Truth*, p. 68.)

Occasionally, in the scriptures and in today's experience, demons take possession of human bodies, and sometimes even the bodies of beasts. Speaking of this, Elder Melvin J. Ballard said, "The power is given to every man and woman that lives to speak as Christ did: 'Get thee hence, Satan;' and he will leave you as quickly as he left the Master. He cannot *capture* a single soul unless we are willing to go. He is limited. He must win men and women." ("Struggle for the Soul," *New Era*, March 1984, p. 37.)

Elder Bruce McConkie assured us: "We do know that all things are governed by law, and that Satan is precluded from taking possession of the bodies of the prophets and other righteous people." (*The Mortal*

Messiah, Vol. 2, p. 282.) Our personal righteousness would seem to be the key to safety.

Satan's Tools

In order to win over Satan's efforts, we must recognize Satan's tools, the methods he uses to do his evil work here on the earth. President Marion G. Romney stressed the importance of being aware of the way Satan works: "I am persuaded that if we are to 'conquer Satan and . . . escape the hands of the servants of Satan who do uphold his work' (D&C 10:5), we must understand and recognize the situation as it is. This is no time for us to bury our heads in the sand, to equivocate or panic. The difficulties of our times have not caught us unawares. . . . We know that as the second coming of the Savior approaches, the tempo of Satan's campaign for the souls of men is being, and will continue to be, accelerated." (*Look to God and Live*, p. 145.)

The gospel light helps us "understand and recognize" Satan's traps and snares.

Deception

Deception is one of Satan's most powerful tools. Satan is the "father of all lies" and he has deceived man since the Garden of Eden. One of his deceptions is that we can get gain from sin. In the Book of Mormon great wickedness came from the secret combinations that flourished when men believed this lie. Ether explained how secret combinations destroy civilizations: "For it cometh to pass that whoso buildeth [secret combinations] up seeketh to overthrow the freedom of all lands, nations, and countries; and it bringeth to pass the destruction of all people, for it is built up by the devil, who is the father of all lies; even that same liar who beguiled our first parents, yea, even that same liar who hath caused man to commit murder from the beginning; who hath hardened the hearts of men that they have murdered the prophets, and stoned them, and cast them out from the beginning." (Ether 8:25.)

Anything which tries to take away the agency of persons, whether governments, ideologies, gangs, or individuals using coercion and force, is working under Satan's power and influence. There is much of this in evidence today.

There are many lies Satan will try to tell us. Elder James E. Faust reveals some of them, saying, "Some of Satan's most appealing lines are,

'Everyone does it'; 'If it doesn't hurt anybody else, it's all right'; 'If you feel all right about it, it's OK'; or 'It's the *in* thing to do.' These subtle entreaties make Satan the great imitator, the master deceiver, the arch counterfeiter, and the great forger." (CR, *Ensign*, November 1987, p. 34.)

The result of listening to Satan is sorrow and disappointment. Many of our young people listen to these lies, and then discover too late that they have been led into deep unhappiness. The story is told of an unwed mother who learned this lesson as she gave her baby boy up for adoption. She anguished, "'[My boyfriend] lied to me when he said nobody would get hurt, and that because we loved each other, anything we did was all right. . . . Oh, if only I had known five minutes before I was immoral how I would feel five minutes after I gave my baby away!'

"For this girl not to have thought ahead about the consequences of her actions and not to have realized that lust is the mere image of love is indeed heartbreaking." (Jaynann Morgan Payne, *Remarkable Stories from the Lives of Latter-day Saint Women*, vol. 2, p. 204.)

We can avoid being deceived by Satan if we follow the brethren, our living apostles and prophets. This is so important today when there are many loud voices calling us away from the path of obedience and happiness. Satan tries to deceive some into believing that they have received "special" revelation that calls them to act in ways contrary to the counsel of our living prophets. This problem is not new. In the Book of Mormon we read of Korihor, the Anti-Christ who came among the people of Nephi preaching against a belief in Christ and trying to persuade the people to disbelieve "the prophecies which had been spoken by the prophets, concerning the coming of Christ." (Alma 30:6.) When he asked Alma to show him a sign to prove to him that there is a God, he was struck dumb.

Only then did Korihor tell his tragic story: "The devil hath deceived me; for he appeared unto me in the form of an angel, and said unto me: Go and reclaim this people, for they have all gone astray after an unknown God . . . and he taught me that which I should say. And I have taught his words . . . even until I had much success, insomuch that I verily believed that they were true." If Korihor had been following the words of the scriptures and the leaders of the church at that time, including the prophet Alma, he would not have been deceived by Satan's counterfeit "revelation."

In so many ways Satan deceives us. We must heed the Spirit of Christ, the Holy Ghost, the established principles of the gospel, and our own common sense to avoid being led astray. Enlightenment will prevent deception.

Rationalization

Often, if Satan cannot deceive us by getting us to believe a big lie, he will use small lies, or rationalization. President Spencer W. Kimball once emphasized how Satan uses rationalization to slowly draw us into a life of sin: "He will use his logic to confuse and his rationalizations to destroy. He will shade meanings, open doors an inch at a time, and lead from purest white through all the shades of gray to the darkest black." (CR, *Ensign*, November 1980, p. 94.)

Satan tries to get us to overlook a little sin, soothing our consciences by rationalizing that it is not that important. We are then in a position to commit a larger sin. We believe his half-truths. We rationalize through logic based on these misconceptions until we find ourselves disbelieving the words of the prophets and substituting the learning of the world for the simple gospel truths. By this method Satan is able to ensnare those who would never begin by committing a so-called "big sin."

Some of the phrases that are heard include "I can handle it," "The leaders are out of touch with today's world," "They are getting into an area that is outside the proper range of religion," or "It's my body (or my life)." "What I do doesn't affect anyone else." "They don't care about me." There are many other such rationalizations that, if indulged in, will lead us away from truth.

It is well to remember in this area the Lord's declaration that we are to learn all things, but to learn them with the Holy Spirit to guide us. (D&C 88:118, 50:19.) All truth is part of the gospel compass, and when the veil is removed and we know all things, we will realize that there is no conflict between truth in any area, and the true understanding of the revealed truths of the gospel. (See also D&C 1:38-39.)

Elder Melvin J. Ballard reminded us, "The most favorite method the enemy of our souls has employed in ages past and that he will employ today is to capture souls by leading them gently, step by step. . . . Men and women do not go far wrong in an instant. It is by slow degrees, step by step." ("Struggle for the Soul," reprinted in *New Era*, March 1984, pp. 38-39.)

President Kimball reiterated, "Serious sin enters into our lives as we yield first to little temptations. Seldom does one enter into deeper transgression without first yielding to lesser ones, which open the door to the greater." (*The Miracle of Forgiveness*, p. 215.) In this manner Satan binds us.

Contention

Another of Satan's tools is contention. "For verily, verily I say unto you, he that hath the spirit of contention is not of me, but is of the devil, who is the father of contention, and he stirreth up the hearts of men to contend with anger, one with another.

"Behold, this is not my doctrine, to stir up the hearts of men with anger, one against another; but this is my doctrine, that such things should be done away." (3 Nephi 11:29-30.)

Anger, strife, contention. All these things are Satan's tools. The home is our greatest tool in combatting Satan. In Mosiah 4:14-15 we read, "And ye will not suffer your children that they go hungry, or naked; neither will ye suffer that they transgress the laws of God, and fight and quarrel one with another, and serve the devil, who is the master of sin, or who is the evil spirit which hath been spoken of by our fathers, he being an enemy to all righteousness.

"But ye will teach them to walk in the ways of truth and soberness; ye will teach them to love one another, and to serve one another."

If children transgress the laws of God when they fight and quarrel, don't we as adults also transgress the laws of God when we fight and quarrel one with another? When we fight and quarrel we serve the devil. We must teach our children in the family by our peaceful example, and in family home evening by the scriptures and words of the prophets, to live in peace with one another, love one another, and serve one another. We do this by helping them understand their own feelings, and negotiate peaceful settlements when conflicts inevitably arise.

Anger can lead to more serious actions. Failing to control our tempers can cause us to lose our sweet relationships with our families, can cause us to commit acts of violence, and can even lead to the loss of our eternal lives. President Kimball said, "Killing is an act of aggression. But *anger is a thought sin*. It may be the forerunner of murder. But if one's *thoughts* do not get vicious nor violent he is unlikely to take life." (*The Miracle of Forgiveness*, p. 112, emphasis added.)

President Kimball calls anger a "thought-sin." Anger, where we fight and quarrel, is a sin and must be repented of the same as any other sin.

Contention may also arise when we discuss points of the gospel. When contention arises, even in a gospel discussion, the Spirit departs. In D&C 10:63 we read why the Lord established His gospel: "And this I do that I may establish my gospel, that there may not be so much contention; yea, Satan doth stir up the hearts of the people to contention concerning the points of my doctrine; and in these things they do err, for they do wrest the scriptures and do not understand them."

As a rule of thumb, we may conclude that when a spirit of contention arises, we have crossed over the line to Satan's influence, and it is time to retrace our steps and regain a spirit of peace, *especially* in the settling of differences between family members.

Complacency

Complacency is a wedge Satan uses often with faithful members of the Church. When everything seems to be going just the way we like it, we sometimes let down our guard and can slide into sin, ignoring the warning signs. Satan tries to convince us that all is well, and that we need not struggle against sin. "And others will he pacify, and lull them away into carnal security, that they will say: All is well in Zion; yea, Zion prospereth, all is well--and thus the devil cheateth their souls, and leadeth them away carefully down to hell." (2 Nephi 28:21.)

This is often the case with Sabbath breaking. It also creeps into our choices of entertainment, how we use our leisure time, even how we treat our family members. Elder Neal A. Maxwell describes such situations: "A sister gives commendable, visible civic service. Yet even with her good image in the community, she remains a comparative stranger to Jesus' holy temples and His holy scriptures. . . . An honorable father, dutifully involved in the cares of his family, is less than kind and gentle with individual family members. . . . Consider the returned missionary, skills polished while serving an honorable mission, striving earnestly for success in his career. Busy, he ends up in a posture of some accommodation with the world." (CR *Ensign*, November 1995, p. 23.)

We fail to achieve our spiritual potential; we waste our precious gift of time; we are content with things as they are rather than striving for excellence.

Nephi continues by describing how Satan, once he has convinced a person to establish some apathetic habits, lulls the worldly sinner into complacent indifference, and induces him to continue in his ways: "And behold, others he flattereth away, and telleth them there is no hell; and he saith unto them: I am no devil, for there is none—and thus he whispereth in their ears, until he grasps them with his awful chains, from whence there is no deliverance." (v. 22.)

Discouragement

After a person has sinned, Satan puts to use another of his tools—discouragement. President James E. Faust explained how Satan uses discouragement to stop someone from repenting: "One of Satan's approaches is to persuade a person who has transgressed that there is no hope of forgiveness. But there is always hope. Most sins, no matter how grievous, may be repented of if the desire is sincere enough." (CR, *Ensign*, November 1987, p. 35.)

Akin to discouragement is weariness. We are admonished to "be not weary in well-doing" (D&C 64:33) because when the struggle seems long and we grow tired, Satan can use those weak moments to penetrate our spiritual armor. President Howard W. Hunter warned that "there are times in our struggle with the adversities of mortality when we become weary, weakened, and susceptible to the temptations that seem to be placed in our pathways. . . . Such a time is always the tempter's moment—when we are emotionally or physically spent, when we are weary, vulnerable, and least prepared to resist the insidious suggestions he makes." (CR, *Ensign*, November 1976, p. 17.)

President David O. McKay explained the importance of guarding against such moments, saying, "Your greatest weakness will be the point at which Satan will try to tempt you, will try to win you; and if you have made yourself weak, he will add to that weakness." ("The Temptations in Life," *Improvement Era*, July 1968, p. 3.)

Fear

An area sometimes overlooked as a tool of Satan is fear. Sometimes when a righteous person is accomplishing great good, or is about to do some important work, Satan will attempt to use fear to stop him. The Prophet Joseph Smith said, "The nearer a person approaches the Lord, a greater power will be manifested by the adversary to prevent the accomplishment of His purposes." (*Life of Heber C. Kimball*, p. 132, as quoted in CR, *Ensign*, November 1987, p. 35.)

The Prophet Joseph Smith knew this to be true from his own personal experience. When he first called upon God in the Sacred Grove, this incident occurred:

> After I had retired to the place where I had previously designed to go, having looked around me, and finding myself alone, I kneeled down and began to offer up the desires of my heart to God. I had scarcely done so, when immediately I was seized upon by some power which entirely overcame me, and had such an astonishing influence over me as to bind my tongue so that I could not speak. Thick darkness gathered around me, and it seemed to me for a time as if I were doomed to sudden destruction.
>
> But, exerting all my powers to call upon God to deliver me out of the power of this enemy which had seized upon me, and at the very moment when I was ready to sink into despair and abandon myself to destruction—not to an imaginary ruin, but to the power of some actual being from the unseen world, who had such marvelous power as I had never before felt in any being—just at this moment of great alarm, I saw a pillar of light exactly over my head, above the brightness of the sun, which descended gradually until it fell upon me. (Joseph Smith-History 1:15-16.)

Moses also had such an experience. After he had his great visitation from the Lord, he was alone again when

> Satan came tempting him, saying: Moses, son of man, worship me.
>
> And it came to pass that Moses looked upon Satan and said: Who art thou? For behold, I am a son of God, in the similitude of his Only Begotten; and where is thy glory, that I should worship thee? . . .
>
> I will not cease to call upon God, I have other things to inquire of him: for his glory has been upon me, wherefore I can judge between him and thee. Depart hence, Satan.
>
> And now, when Moses had said these words, Satan cried with a loud voice, and ranted upon the earth, and commanded, saying: I am the Only Begotten, worship me.
>
> And it came to pass that Moses began to fear exceedingly; and as he began to fear, he saw the bitterness of hell. Nevertheless, calling

upon God, he received strength, and he commanded, saying: Depart from me, Satan, for this one God only will I worship, which is the God of glory.

And now Satan began to tremble, and the earth shook; and Moses received strength, and called upon God, saying: *In the name of the Only Begotten, depart hence, Satan.*

And it came to pass that Satan cried with a loud voice, with weeping, and wailing, and gnashing of teeth; and he departed hence, even from the presence of Moses, that he beheld him not. (Moses 1:12, 13, 18-22, emphasis added.)

Notice that the fear in Moses' heart opened up to his mind the bitterness of hell. Fear is familiar to all of us.

Elder Orson Hyde related to President Heber C. Kimball this experience with evil as they labored to spread the gospel in England:

Every circumstance that occurred at that scene of devils is just as fresh in my recollection at this moment as it was at the moment of its occurrence, and will ever remain so. After you were overcome by them and had fallen, their awful rush upon me with knives, threats, imprecations and hellish grins, amply convinced me that they were no friends of mine. While you were apparently senseless and lifeless on the floor and upon the bed (after we had laid you there), I stood between you and the devils and fought them and contended with them face to face, until they began to diminish in number and to retreat from the room. The last imp that left turned round to me . . . and said, as if to apologize, and appease my determined opposition to them, "I never said anything against you!" I replied to him thus: "It matters not to me whether you have or have not; you are a liar from the beginning! *In the name of Jesus Christ, depart!*" He immediately left, and the room was clear. That closed the scene of devils for that time. (*Life of Heber C. Kimball*, p. 131, emphasis added.)

This type of experience is indeed frightening, but what we need to understand in order to overcome this fear is that we, as living beings, have power over those who have not a physical body. Joseph Smith emphasized, "All beings who have bodies have power over those who have not." (*Teachings of the Prophet Joseph Smith*, p. 181.)

There are some consistent patterns in these accounts. Note that Satan may appear in person when something important is occurring. He tries to thwart the grand designs of the great Jehovah. When fear of the evil darkness seems about to overcome the individual, he is able to call upon God, and *command Satan to depart.* Satan has no choice but to obey that command. We can expect the same in our own lives. When we are about to be conquered by our fear, we should call upon the power of Jesus Christ, and in His name cast out any evil influence that may be present. Satan and his angels have no power when commanded in the name of the Only Begotten. They have to leave.

Faith in the Lord Jesus Christ Will Give Us the Victory

Though faced with fear, each of these great people: Joseph Smith, Moses, and Orson Hyde, were able to overcome Satan, and so can we. Satan can go no further than we let him. We have our agency. He can't force us to do anything. We make our own choices.

President James E. Faust said, "[Satan] is really a coward, and if we stand firm, he will retreat. The Apostle James counseled: 'Submit yourselves therefore to God. Resist the devil, and he will flee from you' (James 4:7). He cannot know our thoughts unless we speak them. And Nephi states that 'he hath no power over the hearts' of people who are righteous (see 1 Nephi 22:26). . . . [Joseph Smith] also stated, 'Wicked spirits have their bounds, limits, and laws by which they are governed' (*History of the Church,* 4:576). So Satan and his angels are not all-powerful." (CR, *Ensign,* November 1987, p. 35.)

Sometimes people are caught up in the fascination of experiences with evil spirits. We are well advised to avoid discussing experiences concerning evil spirits, because doing so tends to make us vulnerable to their power. President Harold B. Lee related this experience:

> A few years ago while touring the missions of South America, I heard President William Grant Bangerter of the Brazilian Mission make some interesting comments. He reported that there had been a wave of incidents in which evil spirits were afflicting the missionaries and the Saints. At every conference the missionaries were relating experiences they were having with evil spirits. The intensity of their influence was frightening. The mission president admonished them to cease talking about the works of the devil in the future and instead teach with power the works of the Lord and bear testimony of his works among them. There was an almost immediate cessation of the power of the evil spirits. (CR, *Improvement Era,* June 1966, p. 522.)

These missionaries found that when they concentrated on the power of the Lord and on bearing testimony of Him, the influence of Satan diminished almost immediately. We should follow this pattern in our own lives, emphasizing faith and testimony instead of fear. We can bind Satan, or overcome his power in our individual lives by ceasing to listen to him and ceasing to think of him.

Not everyone is in the power of Satan. Elder Bruce McConkie wrote, "Little children are without sin because 'power is not given unto Satan to tempt little children, until they begin to become accountable before me.' (D&C 29:47.) The Three Nephites, having overcome and being 'sanctified in the flesh,' are beyond the power of Satan, and he cannot tempt them. (3 Ne. 28:39.) Similarly, when the righteous saints go to paradise, they will no longer be tempted, but the wicked in hell are subject to the control and torments of Lucifer (D&C 132:26)." (*Mormon Doctrine*, p. 782.)

President Kimball said, "Not even Lucifer, the star of the morning, the archenemy of mankind, can withstand the power of the priesthood of God." (*The Teachings of Spencer W. Kimball*, p. 499.)

Our object in life is to bind Satan by becoming righteous. President Kimball also said, "When Satan is bound in a single home—when Satan is bound in a single life—the Millennium has already begun in that home, in that life." (*The Teachings of Spencer W. Kimball*, p. 172.)

Be Alert to Temptation in Your Own Life

Many other conditions and habits become tools for Satan to use to destroy us. He is not exclusive: he will use any means that works! Consider these.

Idleness. When we are not occupied with something goal-oriented and productive, we find ourselves tempted to use that time to experiment with Satan's ideas, or simply to drift into questionable entertainment that is always readily available. Much better to direct our own activities and choose what occupies our time and our minds than to wander into useless or dangerous pursuits.

Criticism and judging. When we allow critical, intolerant attitudes into our daily choices of what we do and say, we tread on Satan's territory. This is the opposite of Jesus' injunctions to "Love one another" (John 15:17), even "Love your enemies, . . . and pray for those which despitefully use you and persecute you." (Matt. 5:44.) This is perhaps one of the most difficult areas of our lives to control, but right choices here will ward off much turmoil and sorrow. Many of the horrible situations in personal lives began with criticism and judging, then grew into uncontrolled anger and violence. Much better to change or avoid these attitudes when they first appear, rather than try to mend the problems they produce.

Coveting or comparing. Coveting, like anger, is a thought-sin. As one of the "Basic Ten" commandments, it will forestall much suffering if stopped while it is still in the mind. All the procedures studied for controlling thoughts apply exactly to controlling the problem of coveting. If we find ourselves in the situation of comparing what we have, what we are, or what we do with what other people have, are, or do, we are beginning a downward road that will lead to anguish of mind at best, and to breaking the commandments against stealing, lying, whoredoms, or murder at worst. Avoid the big problems by turning off the unwholesome desires when they first appear in the mind. Paul, the Apostle, gave this little gem: "Not that I speak in respect of want: for I have learned, in whatsoever state I am, therewith to be content." (Philippians 4:11.) If we concentrate on being grateful for whatever we have, we, too, can be content. It is a sweet condition.

We offer the challenge to you as the reader to list on paper the tools Satan is specifically using in your personal life. Ponder prayerfully these particular challenges, and act today to make changes to correct them.

We are in the mortal world, in the midst of our test and trial. The eternal struggle between light and darkness, between faith and fear, between right and wrong, between good and evil transpires around us every day. It is necessary that we understand it and its significance to our lives. Opposition is essential to our growth and progression, and our victory over evil is the essence of passing our probation. Hope is always available. We can overcome the world as Christ said when He promised us peace. (See John 16:33.) Faith in the Lord Jesus Christ is the key to our victory. The choice is ours.

Jesus said, "Behold, I am the law, and the light. Look unto me, and endure to the end, and ye shall live; for unto him that endureth to the end will I give eternal life." (3 Nephi 15:9.)

That we may apply this understanding to our daily choices with faith in the plan of our Eternal Father, and come off conqueror, is our prayer.

12

Resisting Temptation

We have learned that the temptations of Satan are necessary to the plan of salvation. (See D&C 29:39.) God allows us to be tempted so we can use our agency and learn to choose correctly. Even though temptation is necessary, we are not left alone to face it. We were endowed when we came into this life with the Light of Christ, so we are able to choose good over evil. By exercising right choices we not only gain experience but develop spiritual muscle and grow in strength. We are promised that God will help us to resist. 1 Corinthians 10:13 says, "There hath no temptation taken you but such as is common to man: but God is faithful, who will not suffer you to be tempted above that ye are able; but will with the temptation also make a way to escape, that ye may be able to bear it."

Obviously this does not mean that no one falls to temptation, but it means we may take the available escape route if we choose to do so. What are some ways that we can resist temptation?

Exercise Faith

Our Heavenly Father sent us here with intent that we are to succeed. He provided means for us, His children, that we would be able to succeed. Our Elder Brother, Jesus Christ, came here in love and power to make it possible. They both stand by ready to assist us according to our individual needs, and in our times of trial, simple or hard. Our charge is to exercise faith, which empowers us to do Their will, resist evil, be faithful to Their commandments, and return to Them. They will help us. The Apostle Paul declared, "I can do all things through Christ which strengtheneth me." (Philippians 4:13.)

Realize that You Have the Power to Choose

We have learned that God's children have the power to choose. You have your agency. You have many roles to fulfill in this life, such as mother/father/child, friend, employer/employee, citizen, neighbor, advisor, and so on. In all these roles, you make choices continually. Through your agency you have the power to choose—specifically, the power to choose good over bad. You can do it! Nephi told us that "Men are free according to the flesh; and all things are given them which are expedient unto man. And they are free to choose liberty and eternal life, through the great Mediator of all men, or to choose captivity and death, according to the captivity and power of the devil." (2 Nephi 2:27.)

God will not allow Satan to force us to do evil, and He will not force us to do good. We are completely free to choose for ourselves. However, once we have chosen, good or bad automatically follows. We cannot choose the consequences.

The Prophet Joseph Smith taught that "the devil has no power over us only as we permit him. The moment we revolt at anything which comes from God, the devil takes power." (*Teachings of the Prophet Joseph Smith*, p. 181.)

So, the consequence of revolting against that which comes from God is that we empower the devil. This is how we *permit* Satan to have power over us. We make that choice! We must realize that we have the power to choose. Furthermore, we *do* choose, sometimes unintentionally. Sometimes we choose evil simply by failing to choose the right. We must understand that all our choices affect our lives for good or evil. Alertness will save us from many problems.

President Spencer W. Kimball encouraged us to follow the Savior's example in fortifying ourselves against temptation:

> Keep the door closed to temptation. It is extremely difficult, if not impossible, for the devil to enter a door that is closed. He seems to have no keys for locked doors. But if a door is slightly ajar, he gets his toe in, and soon this is followed by his foot, then by his leg and his body and his head, and finally he is in all the way.
>
> The importance of not accommodating temptation in the least degree is underlined by the Savior's example. Did not he recognize the danger when he was on the mountain with his fallen brother, Lucifer, being sorely tempted by that master tempter? He could have

opened the door and flirted with danger by saying, "All right, Satan, I'll listen to your proposition. I need not succumb, I need not yield, I need not accept—but I'll listen."

Christ did not so rationalize. He positively and promptly closed the discussion, and commanded: "Get thee hence, Satan," meaning, likely, "Get out of my sight—get out of my presence—I will not listen —I will have nothing to do with you." Then, we read, "the devil leaveth him."

This is our proper pattern, if we would prevent sin rather than be faced with the much more difficult task of curing it. As I study the story of the Redeemer and his temptations, I am certain he spent his energies fortifying himself against temptation rather than battling with it to conquer it. (*The Teachings of Spencer W. Kimball*, p. 162-63.)

Avoid Areas of Personal Weakness

President Kimball further explains that to stay on the strait and narrow, we must prepare ourselves beforehand to reject evil whenever it appears, and stay out of situations in which we are vulnerable: "Generally the evil way is the easier, and since man is carnal that way will triumph unless there be a conscious and a consistently vigorous effort to reject the evil and follow the good. . . . It is important that all the sons and daughters of God upon this earth . . . determine to walk the uncrowded path which is *strait* and which is *narrow*. The time to quit evil ways is before they start. The secret of the good life is in protection and prevention. Those who yield to evil are usually those who have placed themselves in a vulnerable position." (*The Miracle of Forgiveness*, p. 15, emphasis included.)

A "vulnerable position" is any situation in which we have difficulty obeying the Lord's commandments. We must not choose to allow ourselves to get close to a tempting situation. If we do, sooner or later we will succumb. Paul admonished, "Abstain from all appearance of evil." (1 Thessalonians 5:22.)

President Joseph Fielding Smith explained how Satan takes advantage of our weaknesses: "We should be on guard always to resist Satan's advances. . . . He has power to place thoughts in our minds and to whisper to us in unspoken impressions to entice us to satisfy our appetites or desires and in various other ways he plays upon our weaknesses and desires." (*Answers to Gospel Questions*, vol. 3, p. 81.)

Thoughts can be placed in our minds by the evil one. What we do with those thoughts is our choice. However, remember these important words from Brother Don Norton, a professor at Brigham Young University: "Feeling the power of Satan does not make you evil. Basically, a temptation is a struggle against his influence—which is both real and powerful. But the fact that you're struggling does not mean that you are in his power or that the Spirit of God is not also striving with you. Evil consists, not of recognizing temptation, but of yielding to it." ("I Have a Question," *Ensign*, August 1978, p. 33.)

Satan works on our weakest points. If we were to study ourselves and find out what our weaknesses are, to know ourselves as well as he knows us, we would be better able to avoid our areas of personal weakness. Then we should also determine specific ways of strengthening ourselves so we will not succumb to Satan's temptation. There are many suggestions on how to fortify ourselves in this and other chapters in this book.

President George Albert Smith admonished us to stay on the Lord's side of the line separating good and evil: "If I determined to be on the safe side, the Lord's side, I would do the right thing every time. So when temptation comes, think prayerfully about your problem, and the influence of the Lord will enable you to decide wisely. There is safety for us only on the Lord's side of the line." (*Sharing the Gospel with Others*, p. 43.)

We cannot walk the line separating good and evil like a tightrope, and expect never to fall on the evil side. We must remain firmly, immovably on the Lord's side, far away from the line. Whenever we find ourselves in a situation in which we feel inclined to sin, or might be led to feel so, we should remove ourselves from the situation immediately. Only in this way will we be able to constantly resist the temptations inherent in that situation.

We should avoid any situation which compromises our ability to reason or destroys our agency. The Word of Wisdom warns us against using substances which are habit forming and addictive. Wisdom also tells us to avoid the overuse or abuse of any medicines or drugs. Many people have committed crimes or performed deeds against their conscience when under mind- or body-altering chemicals. Recreational use of chemicals and drugs should never be indulged in. Seemingly harmless tampering leads to addictions that are almost impossible to overcome. Satan delights in taking away the freedom and reasoning power of individuals in this manner. If you or someone you love is involved, seek competent help and priesthood blessings.

Let's make a commitment right now to always be on the safe side, the Lord's side of the line. Always pray for strength when tempted. Continue to pray until the temptation goes away. In this way there is safety from the snares of Satan.

Remember Who You Are

Keep your eye on the big picture. Remember you are a child of God. Remember where you came from, why you are here, and your potential to have eternal life. This will give you strength to not only control your thoughts and resist temptation, but to cultivate many good new thoughts.

Remember, we as Latter-day Saints were withheld to come forth in the latter days to prepare the world for the coming of the Lord. Have you ever wondered what you may have been doing for those thousands of years while you waited your turn? Most certainly you were preparing yourself for your mission, possibly strengthening and teaching others who were also waiting.

President Wilford Woodruff said, "The Lord has chosen a small number of choice spirits of sons and daughters out of all the creations of God, who are to inherit this earth; and this company of choice spirits have been kept in the spirit world for six thousand years to come forth in the last days to stand in the flesh in this last dispensation of the fulness of times, to organize the kingdom of God upon the earth, to build it up and to defend it and to receive the eternal and everlasting priesthood." (As quoted in *The Teachings of Ezra Taft Benson*, p. 555.)

We are the Lord's chosen people. We hold His Holy Priesthood. We made covenants in our pre-mortal life to come down here and become valiant members of the Church and build the kingdom of God. If we are faithful and valiant in our missions we will be some of the happiest children our Father in Heaven has, receiving joy from our faith while here, and looking forward with hope to our reward of eternal life.

Elder James E. Talmage related how receiving the Aaronic priesthood affected his young life: "The effect of my ordination (as a deacon) entered into all the affairs of my boyish life. . . . When at play on the school grounds, and perhaps tempted to take unfair advantage in the game, I would *remember 'I am a deacon*; and it is not right that a deacon should act this way.' On examination days, when it seemed easy for me to copy some other boy's work, . . . I would say in my mind 'It would be more wicked for me to do that than it is for them, because I am a deacon.'" (*Incidents from the Lives of Our Church Leaders* [Deacons instruction manual, 1914], pp. 135-36, as quoted in Deacons Course A Manual, 1983, p. 90.)

A recognition of who he was enabled the young James E. Talmage to resist the temptations he felt as a boy. These choices and others he made during his lifetime led him to become a very influential Apostle, whose writings are still accepted as definitive standards of our faith. All Latter-day Saints should feel the same way about doing wrong. As Saints we know who we are. We know we are children of celestial parents, and we have made eternal covenants. We have been given much, and we know that much is expected of us. We know that, because we have been so blessed, we are required to live a higher standard.

Latter-day Saints know that our allegiance is to the Lord. When we sin, we are choosing to serve the devil. President Kimball warned us that "sin . . . is service to Satan." (*The Miracle of Forgiveness*, p. 20.)

This idea is supported by the scriptures. "Know ye not, that to whom ye yield yourselves servants to obey, his servants ye are to whom ye obey; whether of sin unto death, or of obedience unto righteousness?" (Romans 6:16. See also Matthew 6:24.)

Let us remember that as children of a divine Father, Latter-day Saints, servants of only the Lord, we must never allow ourselves to serve the devil by choosing sin.

Alma spoke plainly:

> And now if ye are not the sheep of the good shepherd, of what fold are ye? Behold, I say unto you, that the devil is your shepherd, and ye are of his fold; . . .
>
> Therefore, if a man bringeth forth good works he hearkeneth unto the voice of the good shepherd, and he doth follow him; but whosoever bringeth forth evil works, the same becometh a child of the devil, for he hearkeneth unto his voice, and doth follow him.
>
> And whosoever doeth this must receive his wages of him; therefore, for his wages he receiveth death, as to things pertaining unto righteousness, being dead unto all good works. (Alma 5:39-42.)

As stated before, we are free to choose good or evil, but we are not free to choose the consequences. They follow automatically. If we choose the devil for our shepherd, we will be rewarded with death as to things of righteousness, but if we remember who we are and choose to love and follow Jesus Christ, we will be rewarded with eternal life.

Strengthen Yourself Spiritually

The Prophet Joseph Smith taught that we do not hold still in a spiritual sense: "If we are not drawing towards God . . . , we are going from Him and drawing towards the devil." (*Teachings of the Prophet Joseph Smith*, p. 216.) We cannot stand still. We either go forward or backward.

How can we ensure that we are continually drawing closer to God?

Prayer is our greatest source of strength. In 3 Nephi 18:18 we read, "Behold, verily, verily, I say unto you, ye must watch and pray always lest ye enter into temptation; for Satan desireth to have you, that he may sift you as wheat."

As we pray to overcome temptation, the Lord strengthens us so we can succeed: "Pray always . . . that you may conquer Satan, and that you may escape the hands of the servants of Satan that do uphold his work." (D&C 10:5.) As Amulek is enumerating the things we should pray about, he includes the admonition to "cry unto him against the devil, who is an enemy to all righteousness." (Alma 34:23.) Prayer confirms our convictions of right and wrong. Through prayer we receive strength.

Scripture study fills our minds with good, and helps us to gain spiritual nourishment and strength. Elder Marion G. Romney recommended daily reading of the Book of Mormon: "If we would avoid adopting the evils of the world, we must pursue a course which will daily feed our minds with and call them back to the things of the Spirit. I know of no better way to do this than by daily reading the Book of Mormon." (CR, *Ensign*, May 1980, p. 66.)

President Harold B. Lee often reminded us, "Wherefore, stand ye in holy places, and be not moved, until the day of the Lord come." (D&C 87:8.) The temple is a holy place. We should go there as often as we can. Our personal experience is that when we go to the temple we come away with power to help us live better lives. Sacrament meetings, conferences, and other worship services are also holy places where we can be regenerated and spiritually uplifted.

Look to other spiritually strong people for companionship and support. Having a network of friends, such as those within your ward or branch, to whom you can turn is helpful. And reaching out a strong hand of support to another who is faltering can be an important prop to your own wavering determination.

Success brings more success. When we have overcome a temptation or succeeded in avoiding a difficult situation, looking back on that previous success will give us confidence to successfully meet a new challenge.

Having the support of others who are spiritually strong is heartening. Prayer, scripture study, church attendance and temple attendance give spiritual reinforcement and enable us to recognize and resist evil.

Casting out evil spirits

In the New Testament we may read the account of certain experiences in which evil spirits had taken possession of the earthly bodies of individuals. Jesus cast out these devils by his word: "When the even was come, they brought unto him many that were possessed with devils: and he cast out the spirits with his word, and healed all that were sick." (Matthew 8:16.)

Again, "When Jesus saw that the people came running together, he rebuked the foul spirit, saying unto him, Thou dumb and deaf spirit, I charge thee, come out of him, and enter no more into him. And the spirit cried, and rent him sore, and came out of him: and he was as one dead; insomuch that many said, He is dead. But Jesus took him by the hand, and lifted him up; and he arose." (Mark 9:25-27.)

Note that Jesus commanded him to "enter no more into him."

Jesus gave this power also to His Apostles: "And when he had called unto him his twelve disciples, he gave them power against unclean spirits, to cast them out, and to heal all manner of sickness and all manner of disease." (Matthew 10:10.)

We may also profit by taking note of the time when the Apostles were unable to cast out a spirit, told in Matthew 17:14-21. When the father brought the afflicted boy to Jesus, "Jesus rebuked the devil; and he departed out of him: and the child was cured from that very hour." (v. 18.)

The disciples asked Jesus privately why they had been unable to cast out the spirit, and he explained to them that they needed to bolster their faith through fasting and prayer. (v. 21.)

Casting out of evil spirits is possible through the power of the priesthood. In certain instances, this may be necessary.

Consider this scenario. You are living a normal life, and for the most part, control your thoughts and keep the Lord's commandments. One day, you notice that strange evil thoughts are coming into your mind, thoughts that you have not had before. You soon find yourself bombarded with these evil thoughts.

Some of these thoughts may be negative thoughts about yourself, ugly thoughts that tear you down, dark thoughts that make you feel unclean, thoughts to which you are not accustomed. Ugly thoughts then branch out into other areas of your life, making you negative, insecure, doubtful. They seem to be whispered into your ears.

You protest: "These are not my thoughts. Where do they come from? Why are they coming?" You refuse them, but even as you try to keep them out they keep on coming. This may continue for days, weeks, even years. What can you do about these evil thoughts?

It is possible for such a condition to be the influence of Satan and his associates, in other words, evil spirits. They will put all manner of evil into our minds, such things as hate, immorality, lies, deceit, and destructive thoughts.

Nephi taught us how Satan does this: "He whispereth in their ears, until he grasps them with his awful chains, from whence there is no deliverance." (2 Nephi 28:22.) Verse 20 explains how he will "rage in the hearts of the children of men, and stir them up to anger against that which is good."

Elder Bruce R. McConkie said, "Acting in conformity with laws which exist, evil spirits have power to tempt men, to entice them to work wickedness . . . (D. & C. 76:17, 105-106.)" (Mormon Doctrine, p. 246.)

President Joseph Fielding Smith stated, "That Satan has great power to deceive is a demonstrated fact. . . . We should be on guard always to resist Satan's advances. . . . He has power to place thoughts in our minds and to whisper to us in unspoken impressions to entice us to satisfy our appetites or desires and in various other ways he plays upon our weaknesses and desires." (*Answers to Gospel Questions*, vol. 3, p. 81.)

It is not necessary for Satan himself to be present at every situation of temptation. Elder McConkie explained that when Satan, or Lucifer, was cast out of heaven, one-third of the hosts of heaven were cast out with him, and "stand at his side to do his bidding. Their mission is to make war with the saints and to destroy the souls of all men. (Revelation 12.) Obviously there are many *evil spirits* available to seduce and lead astray each person on earth." (Mormon Doctrine, p. 246.)

Not only do these evil spirits influence us, entice us, and put thoughts into our minds, it is possible for them to actually enter our bodies and control us, as in the scriptural accounts. The Prophet Joseph Smith taught, "The punishment of the devil was that he should not have a habitation like men. The devil's retaliation is, he comes into this world, binds up men's bodies, and occupies them himself." Then he added the remedy for this frightful situation through the authority of the priesthood, "When the authorities come along, they eject him from a stolen habitation." (*History of the Church*, vol. 5, p. 403.)

Satan and his evil spirits can not withstand the power of the priesthood. This knowledge was restored with the temple endowment, and the power was restored with the restoration of the priesthood. The same power is available to us as was used in the scriptural accounts.

When a person recognizes a situation such as is described in this section, that person may want to humbly seek the Lord through a priesthood blessing. He or she should tell the one who is to give the blessing that he is to cast out Satan and his associates or evil spirits, and command them not to come back. This may require fasting and prayer, or repeated blessings if the problem is deeply entrenched, but these spirits must obey the power of the priesthood when exercised with the principle of sufficient faith.

O, how precious is the joy that comes with the return to peace and rest.

Follow the Promptings of the Holy Ghost

President Marion G. Romney reminds us of the tools we have as members of the Church of Jesus Christ of Latter-day Saints to prevail over evil: "We know that to qualify to prevail against Satan and his wicked hosts, we have been given *the gospel of Jesus Christ*. We know that *the Spirit of Christ* and the power of His *priesthood* are ample shields to the power of Satan. We know that there is available to each of us *the gift of the Holy Ghost*—the power of *revelation* which embraces the gift of discernment by which we may unerringly detect the devil and the counterfeits he is so successfully foisting upon this gullible generation." (CR, *Ensign*, June 1971, pp. 36-37, emphasis added.)

President James E. Faust calls this our "inner braking system" which, he says, "will stop us before we follow Satan too far down the wrong road. It is the still, small voice which is within us." (CR, *Ensign*,

November 1987, p. 34.) This voice is quiet, and might require care to be heard and heeded. But it is the surest warning of temptation.

President Spencer W. Kimball explained how the gift of the Holy Ghost helps to defeat the tempter: "If heeded, [the Holy Ghost] will guide, inspire, and warn, and *will neutralize the promptings of the evil one.*" (*The Miracle of Forgiveness*, pp. 14-15, emphasis added.)

We can learn to recognize the promptings of the Holy Ghost, and by following them, claim the blessings promised by the prophet. President Kimball further explained how the Lord helps us through the Holy Ghost, saying, "He who has greater strength than Lucifer, he who is our fortress and our strength, can sustain us in times of great temptation. While the Lord will never forcibly take anyone out of sin or out of the arms of the tempters, he exerts his Spirit to induce the sinner to do it with divine assistance. And the man who yields to the sweet influence and pleadings of the Spirit and does all in his power to stay in a repentant attitude is guaranteed protection, power, freedom and joy." (*The Miracle of Forgiveness*, p. 176.)

What choice blessings the prophet promised! No matter what our present circumstances, these words must inspire us with hope and the exhilaration of anticipation: "guaranteed protection, power, freedom and joy." Surely any effort required to lift ourselves to that secure state would be worth the sacrifice! Why would we want to listen to the tempter, or to give way to our old desires when these affirmations are ringing in our ears.

President Wilford Woodruff said that we should labor to get the Spirit, because it will enable us to overcome the evil spirits that are around us: "Every man and woman in this Church should labor to get that Spirit. We are surrounded by these evil spirits that are at war against God and against everything looking to the building up of the kingdom of God; and we need this Holy Spirit to enable us to overcome these influences." (*Deseret Weekly*, 7 Nov. 1896, p. 643, as quoted in CR, *Ensign*, May 1979, p. 24.)

And further, Elder ElRay L. Christiansen says that as we gain the companionship of this Comforter, He will help us resist evil: "Members of the Church may have the blessing of the Holy Ghost, the prompter, as a companion as well. And when the Holy Ghost is really within us, Satan must remain without." (CR, *Ensign*, November 1974, p. 24.)

So, the gift of the Holy Ghost helps us to resist temptation by helping us discern good from evil, by warning us before we go too far down the wrong road, by guiding, inspiring, and protecting us, *by neutralizing the promptings of Satan*, by inducing us to remove ourselves from tempting situations, and by making Satan remain outside of us. The whole tenor of our lives will be uplifted if we remain worthy and if we listen to that sweet, still voice.

Sister Ardeth Greene Kapp shared a precious account: "I felt God's presence in a letter received not too long ago from a young man who is an inmate in the state prison. He wrote:

> I couldn't understand what interest God would have in someone like me, for I was a drug addict and convicted felon who hadn't prayed or gone to church in almost ten years. Still the feeling persisted, and even intensified, until one afternoon I finally was drawn to my knees in prayer in the privacy of my steel and concrete prison cell. For perhaps the first time ever I opened my heart to God. I said, "Heavenly Father, I know that you are there, but I don't know why. Why would you want to help someone such as me?" And the answer came softly, but so clearly and deeply felt that I've never been able to think about it without feeling it once again and having tears come to my eyes. "Mark, it is because I love you." How inexpressibly wonderful it felt to know that the God of the universe knew me and loved me. I stayed on my knees praying and crying for hours, and from that day on, I was truly a changed person. Not only was my heart changed, but my entire life was changed. With God's help, old habits can be overcome. (*The Joy of the Journey*, p. 171.)

Our Father is mindful of each and every one of His children. He knows us personally, and loves us all.

Gird Yourself with the Armor of Righteousness

God is on our side. He tells us what He will do in our behalf if we live righteously: "Keep all the commandments and covenants by which ye are bound; and I will cause the heavens to shake for your good, and Satan shall tremble." (D&C 35:24.)

Captain Moroni was a righteous man. Helaman tells us what would happen if we were all as righteous as Moroni: "If all men had been, and were, and ever would be, like unto Moroni, behold, the very powers of hell would have been shaken forever; yea, the devil would never have power over the hearts of the children of men." (Alma 48:17.)

The Prophet Joseph Smith said, "As well might the devil seek to dethrone Jehovah, as overthrow an innocent soul that resists everything which is evil." (*Teachings of the Prophet Joseph Smith*, p. 226.)

As we become more and more righteous, the devil loses power over us. Imagine rearing a family in which the devil had no power! This could happen if all family members live righteously.

This will be the condition on the earth during the thousand years of the Millennium. Nephi describes it this way: "And because of the righteousness of his people, Satan has no power; wherefore, he cannot be loosed for the space of many years; for he hath no power over the hearts of the people, for they dwell in righteousness, and the Holy One of Israel reigneth." (1 Nephi 22:26.) This will take place in the near future. We surely want to be on the Lord's side when this happens!

There was a time in the Book of Mormon when a whole civilization lived in righteousness and happiness. In 4 Nephi 1:15-16, we read, "And it came to pass that there was no contention in the land, because of the love of God which did dwell in the hearts of the people.

"And there were no envyings, nor strifes, nor tumults, nor whoredoms, nor lyings, nor murders, nor any manner of lasciviousness; and surely there could not be a happier people among all the people who had been created by the hand of God."

Surely it is this happiness that we seek as children of our Father in Heaven. We can overcome the power of Satan, and we can become holy. What we need to do is to begin. President David O. McKay tells us how: "Resist him, and you will gain in strength. If he tempts you in another way, resist him again, and he will become weaker. In turn, you become stronger, until you can say, no matter what your surroundings may be, '*Get thee behind me, Satan* . . .' (Luke 4:8.)" ("The Temptations in Life," *Improvement Era*, July 1968, p. 3, emphasis added.)

We have learned enough now to be prepared against Satan. We know what his tools are, and we know how to fortify ourselves against temptation. Let us now seek to claim the happiness our Father in Heaven has promised those who overcome Satan and the world.

God has promised that in the end each righteous person will be "raised to happiness according to his desires of happiness, or good according to his desires of good; and the other to evil according to his desires of evil; for as he has desired to do evil all the day long even so shall he have his reward of evil when the night cometh.

"And so it is on the other hand. If he hath repented of his sins, and desired righteousness until the end of his days, even so he shall be rewarded unto righteousness." (Alma 41:5-6.)

Summary: Ways to Protect Yourself Against Satan

In conclusion, let us restate the tools *we* have for combatting the power of Satan.

1. *Exercise faith in Heavenly Father and His Son Jesus Christ, and expect them to help you. Realize that you can't do it alone, you need their help.* "I can do all things through Christ which strengtheneth me." (Philippians 4:13.)

2. *Stay on the Lord's side of the line.* "If I determined to be on the safe side, the Lord's side, I would do the right thing every time. So when temptation comes, think prayerfully about your problem, and the influence of the Spirit of the Lord will enable you to decide wisely. There is safety for us only on the Lord's side of the line." (George Albert Smith, *Sharing the Gospel with Others*, p. 43.)

3. *Recognize that Satan is the father of lies.* "And he became Satan, yea, even the devil, the father of all lies, to deceive and to blind men, and to lead them captive at his will, even as many as would not hearken unto my voice." (Moses 4:4.)

4. *Do not be seduced by Satan's half-truths.* "The adversary is subtle; he is cunning, he knows that he cannot induce good men and women immediately to do major evils so he moves slyly, whispering half truths until he has his intended victims following him, and finally he clamps his chains upon them and fetters them tight, and then he laughs at . . . their misery." (Spencer W. Kimball, CR, *Improvement Era*, December 1962, p. 928.)

5. *Realize that the devil is the father of contention.* "For verily, verily I say unto you, he that hath the spirit of contention is not of me, but is of the devil, who is the father of contention, and he stirreth up the hearts of men to contend with anger, one with another." (3 Nephi 11:29.)

6. *Remember that God will not allow us to be tempted above our ability to resist.* "There hath no temptation taken you but such as is common to man: but God is faithful, who will not suffer you to be tempted above that ye are able; but will with the temptation also make a way to escape, that ye may be able to bear it." (1 Corinthians 10:13.)

7. *Resist Satan and you will gain in strength.* "Resist him, and you will gain in strength. If he tempts you in another way, resist him again,

and he will become weaker. In turn, you become stronger, until you can say, no matter what your surroundings may be, '*Get thee behind me, Satan.*' (Luke 4:8)." (David O. McKay, *Improvement Era*, July 1968, p. 3, emphasis added.)

8. *Make an agreement with yourself right now.* Say, "Every time I am tempted to sin, I will pray for strength and continue to pray until the temptation goes away."

9. *Pray that you may conquer Satan.* "Pray always . . . that you may conquer Satan, and that you may escape the hands of the servants of Satan that do uphold his work." (D&C 10:5.) As Amulek is enumerating all the things we should pray about, he includes the admonition to "cry unto him against the devil, who is an enemy to all righteousness." (Alma 34:23.)

10. *Remember that we are either moving closer to God or going toward the devil.* "If we are not drawing towards God . . . , we are going from Him and drawing towards the devil." (*Teachings of the Prophet Joseph Smith*, p. 216.)

11. *Pray that you will abhor sin.* In prayer Nephi pleaded, "O Lord, wilt thou redeem my soul? Wilt thou deliver me out of the hands of mine enemies? Wilt thou make me that I may shake at the appearance of sin?" (2 Nephi 4:31.) In Alma 13:12 we read, "Now they, after being sanctified by the Holy Ghost, having their garments made white, being pure and spotless before God, *could not look upon sin save it were with abhorrence*; and there were many, exceedingly great many, who were made pure and entered into the rest of the Lord their God." (Emphasis added.)

12. *Don't allow yourself to get into a situation in which there is temptation.* Temptation exists in any situation in which we have difficulty obeying the Lord's commandments. Do not allow yourself to get close to a tempting situation. The risk is too great. Avoid temptation. "Abstain from all appearance of evil." (1 Thessalonians 5:22.)

13. *Remember that you will be tempted in times of weakness, when you are emotionally and physically tired.* "There are times in our struggle with the adversities of mortality when we become weary, weakened, and susceptible to the temptations that seem to be placed in our pathways. . . . Such a time is always the tempter's moment—when we are emotionally or physically spent, when we are weary, vulnerable, and least prepared to resist the insidious suggestions he makes." (Howard W. Hunter, CR, *Ensign*, November 1976, p. 17.)

14. *Fortify your weakest points.* Satan works on our weakest points. Each one of us should study ourselves and find out what our weaknesses are. Then we should come up with several ways of fortifying ourselves so we will not succumb to Satan's temptation.

15. *Remember that Satan and his angels are not all-powerful.* "[Satan] is really a coward, and if we stand firm, he will retreat. The Apostle James counseled: 'Submit yourselves therefore to God. Resist the devil, and he will flee from you' (James 4:7). He cannot know our thoughts unless we speak them. And Nephi states that 'he hath no power over the hearts' of people who are righteous (see 1 Nephi 22:26). . . . [Joseph Smith] also stated, 'Wicked spirits have their bounds, limits, and laws by which they are governed' (*History of the Church*, 4:576). So Satan and his angels are not all-powerful." (James E. Faust, CR, *Ensign*, November 1987, p. 35.)

16. *Remember that Satan has to leave when we say aloud, "Depart from me, Satan."* President Kimball declared, "He has to leave when you say, 'Depart from me, Satan.' Every soul who has mortality is stronger than Satan, *if that soul is determined.*" (Spencer W. Kimball, *Ensign*, March 1976, p. 71, emphasis added.)

17. *Remember that Satan can have no power over us unless we allow it.* Joseph Smith taught that "the devil has no power over us only as we permit him. The moment we revolt at anything which comes from God, the devil takes power." (*Teachings of the Prophet Joseph Smith*, p. 181.)

18. *Determine to walk the strait and narrow path which leads to eternal life.* "Generally the evil way is the easier, and since man is carnal that way will triumph unless there be a conscious and a consistently vigorous effort to reject the evil and follow the good. . . . It is important that all the sons and daughters of God upon this earth . . . determine to walk the uncrowded path which is *strait* and which is *narrow.* The time to quit evil ways is before they start. The secret of the good life is in protection and prevention. Those who yield to evil are usually those who have placed themselves in a vulnerable position." (Spencer W. Kimball, *The Miracle of Forgiveness*, pp. 14-15.)

19. *Study the Book of Mormon every day.* "If we would avoid adopting the evils of the world, we must pursue a course which will daily feed our minds with and call them back to the things of the Spirit. I know of no better way to do this than by daily reading the Book of Mormon." (Marion G. Romney, CR, *Ensign*, May 1980, p. 66.)

20. *Attend Church, attend the temple, and keep your covenants.* "Wherefore, stand ye in holy places, and be not moved, until the day of the Lord come." (D&C 87:8.) The temple is a holy place.

21. *Seek to have the companionship of the Holy Ghost, who will sustain us in times of great temptation.* "He who has greater strength than Lucifer, he who is our fortress and our strength, can sustain us in times of great temptation. While the Lord will never forcibly take anyone out of sin or out of the arms of the tempters, he exerts his Spirit to induce the sinner to do it with divine assistance. And the man who yields to the sweet influence and pleadings of the Spirit and does all in his power to stay in a repentant attitude is guaranteed protection, power, freedom and joy." (Spencer W. Kimball, *The Miracle of Forgiveness*, p. 176.)

"Members of the Church may have the blessing of the Holy Ghost, the prompter, as a companion as well. And when the Holy Ghost is really within us, Satan must remain without." (ElRay L. Christiansen, CR, *Ensign*, November 1974, p. 24.)

22. *Remember that all good comes from God.* "For I say unto you that whatsoever is good cometh from God, and whatsoever is evil cometh from the devil." (Alma 5:40.)

23. *Don't lose hope.* Satan uses discouragement to stop someone from repenting: "One of Satan's approaches is to persuade a person who has transgressed that there is no hope of forgiveness. But there is always hope. Most sins, no matter how grievous, may be repented of if the desire is sincere enough." (James E. Faust, CR, *Ensign*, November 1987, p. 35.)

Understanding the Atonement

Christ in the Premortal Existence

In making changes in our lives, an understanding of the mission of our Savior and Redeemer will encourage and assist us. It is through faith in Him that we gain the desire, even the power to repent and become purified. His sacrifice is the center point not only of the great gospel plan, but of our individual lives as we strive to become as He is.

To understand the Atonement we must understand what happened in the pre-earth life—who our Savior was, who we were, and what the plan was whereby we came to earth.

Elder Bruce R. McConkie tells us what happened before the foundations of this earth, when our Father in Heaven held a great council, calling all His spirit children together:

> [At this great] solemn session . . . the Father made formal announcement of his plan of redemption and salvation. It was then explained that his spirit children would go down to earth, gain bodies of flesh and blood, be tried and tested in all things, and have opportunity by obedience to come back again to the Eternal Presence. It was then explained that one of the spirit children of the Father would be chosen to be the Redeemer and work out the infinite and eternal Atonement. And it was then that the Father sent forth the call which said in substance and effect: Whom shall I send to be my Son in mortality? Who will go down, be born with life in himself, and work out the great atoning sacrifice by which immortality will come to all men and eternal life be assured to the obedient?
>
> Two mighty spirits answered the call and volunteered their services. Christ said, in effect: Here am I, send me; I will be thy Son;

I will follow thy plan; and "thy will be done, and the glory be thine forever." But Lucifer sought to amend the plan of the Father and to change the proffered terms of salvation. "Behold, here am I, send me," he said, "I will be thy son, and I will redeem all mankind, that one soul shall not be lost, and surely I will do it; wherefore give me thine honor." (Moses 4:1-4.) When the Father said, "I will send the first," then Lucifer was angry, kept not his first estate, rebelled, and he and one-third of the hosts of heaven were cast out down to earth to become the devil and his angels. (Abra. 3:25-28; D&C 29:36-40.) (*Mormon Doctrine*, p. 164.)

And who was Jesus Christ at that time? President Ezra Taft Benson said that even at the time of the great council our Savior Jesus Christ was a God: "Jesus was a God in the premortal existence. Our Father in Heaven gave Him a name above all others—the Christ." (*The Teachings of Ezra Taft Benson*, p. 6.) President Benson further said, "Jesus Christ was and is the *Lord God Omnipotent* (see Book of Mormon, Mosiah 3:5). He was chosen before He was born. He was the all-powerful Creator of the heavens and the earth. He is the source of life and light to all things. His word is the law by which all things are governed in the universe. All things created and made by Him are subject to His infinite power." (*The Teachings of Ezra Taft Benson*, p. 6.)

The plan of salvation required each of us to come to earth and prove ourselves so we could return to our Father in Heaven. We knew no unclean thing could return to our Father's kingdom. We also knew that in the course of this life we would make mistakes. Still, all who come to the earth made the choice to do so in the premortal existence. We knew there would be an Atonement made for us to enable us to return to our Father in Heaven.

The Fall

When man was first placed on the earth, his condition was different from ours. Adam and Eve lived in the Garden of Eden, where these conditions existed:

1. They would have no children (see 2 Nephi 2:22-23, Moses 5:11).
2. They would not experience death (see 2 Nephi 2:22).
3. They would have no joy, for they knew no pain (see 2 Nephi 2:22-23).

4. They would do no good, for they knew no sin (see 2 Nephi 2:22-23).
5. They lived in the presence of God (see 2 Nephi 9:6).
6. They had freedom to choose for themselves (see 2 Nephi 2:15-19).

When Adam and Eve partook of the forbidden fruit, they were driven out of the Garden of Eden into the world in which we live today. The conditions in this world are:

1. We must labor for our own support (see 2 Nephi 2:19, Moses 4:29).
2. We can bear children (see Moses 4:22).
3. We are cut off from the presence of God (see Alma 42:7).
4. All of us must die (see Moses 4:25).
5. We are that we might have joy (see 2 Nephi 2:25, Moses 5:10-11).
6. There is a Messiah (see 2 Nephi 2:27, D&C 43:34).
7. We are free to choose between good and evil (see Moses 6:56).
8. Some choose to follow Satan and become carnal, sensual, and devilish (see Moses 5:13).
9. We are taught the possibility of repentance and redemption through Jesus Christ (see D&C 29:42-43).

In similitude of the great sacrifice Jesus Christ would make, animal blood sacrifice was practiced in the Old Testament days. After the Savior wrought out His Atonement in the garden and on the cross, blood sacrifice ceased. Elder Bruce R. McConkie said, "For four thousand long years, from Adam to that bleak day when our Lord was lifted up by sinful men, all of his righteous followers sought remission of their sins through sacrifice. . . . After the final great sacrifice on the cross, the use for the similitude that looked forward to our Lord's death ceased. Blood sacrifices became a thing of the past." (*The Promised Messiah*, pp. 379-80.)

We now partake of the sacrament in remembrance of Jesus Christ and His Atonement. In this way we renew our covenant we made at baptism to keep His commandments. This is our personal acceptance of His sacrifice.

Our Savior and His Infinite Atonement

Because of the fall of Adam, all mankind was born into the world we have described. It is a "probationary state, yea, [a] preparatory state" (Alma 42:13) in which we live, and our work in this life is to become worthy to return to our Father in Heaven.

When we sin, we become unfit to dwell with God. Since all have sinned, none are able to return to the presence of God. "And thus we see that all mankind were fallen, and they were in the grasp of justice; yea, the justice of God, which consigned them forever to be cut off from his presence." (Alma 42:14.)

God is just, and cannot "destroy the work of justice." (Alma 42:13.) What then can be done to make us clean again? Alma tells us, "The plan of mercy could not be brought about except an atonement should be made; therefore God himself atoneth for the sins of the world, to bring about the plan of mercy, to appease the demands of justice, that God might be a perfect, just God, and a merciful God also." (Alma 42:15.)

So, the Savior atoned for our sins so that we might be able to repent and be forgiven. His Atonement allows mercy to become active in our lives, and thus, because of our Savior, we can be pure enough to return to our Father in Heaven. Alma continues, "God ceaseth not to be God, and mercy claimeth the penitent, and mercy cometh because of the atonement; and the atonement bringeth to pass the resurrection of the dead; and the resurrection of the dead bringeth back men into the presence of God; and thus they are restored into his presence, to be judged according to their works, according to the law and justice." (Alma 42:23.)

We all have need of the Atonement, as was explained to us before we came to earth. President Joseph Fielding Smith illustrated the Atonement this way:

> *The effect of Adam's transgression was to place all of us in the pit with him. Then the Savior comes along, not subject to that pit, and lowers the ladder.* He comes down into the pit and makes it possible for us to use the ladder to escape. . . . The pit was banishment from the presence of the Lord and temporal death, the dissolution of the body. . . . Therefore, in his infinite mercy, the Father heard the cries of his children and sent his Only Begotten Son, who was not subject to death nor to sin, to provide the means of escape." (*Doctrines of Salvation*, 1:123, 127, emphasis included.)

Brother George W. Pace explains in beautiful language what the Atonement does for each of us as mortals:

> Because of the fall of Adam, the circumstances of earth are such that all of us commit sins after we become accountable at eight years of age. The sins we commit cause us to become unclean and consequently unfit to return to the presence of God. When we sin, we actually contaminate both our body and our spirit. . . .
>
> . . . The Savior's infinite atonement . . . meets the demands of justice in our behalf and, in the process, not only are we forgiven of our sins but we become like the Savior. This change occurs because in the process of repenting and then living the gospel, we avail ourselves of the Savior's power and his divine nature enables us to become like him. (*Our Search to Know the Lord*, pp. 78-79.)

In order to return to the presence of God, we must repent of our sins, and this repentance is only possible because of the sacrifice made for us by Jesus Christ, called the Atonement. In this way the eternal law of justice, which says that for every broken law there must be a penalty paid, is satisfied by our Savior Jesus Christ, who paid the greatest price ever paid, and ransomed us all with His blood. This was done through His grace and mercy. It was a free gift, but to receive the gift we are to repent and take upon us His holy name.

When we truly understand the price our Savior paid for our individual sins, we will show our gratitude to Him for His sacrifice by avoiding sin. Surely we are grateful for the price He paid! President Joseph Fielding Smith said,

> When we violate a commandment, no matter how small and insignificant we may think it to be, we show our ingratitude to our Redeemer. It is impossible for us to comprehend the extent of his suffering when he carried the burden of the sins of the whole world, a punishment so severe that we are informed that blood came from the pores of his body, and this was before he was taken to the cross. The punishment of physical pain coming from the nails driven in his hands and feet, was not the greatest of his suffering, excruciating as that surely was. The greater suffering was the spiritual and mental anguish coming from the load of our transgressions which he carried. If we understood the extent of that suffering and his suffering on the cross, surely none of us would wilfully be guilty of sin. We would

not give way to the temptations, the gratification of unholy appetites and desires and Satan could find no place in our hearts. (*The Restoration of All Things*, p. 199.)

"Even So in Christ Shall All Be Made Alive"

The other part of the Atonement is that, because of the death and resurrection of Jesus Christ, we will all break the bands of death and be resurrected. Without Christ's sacrifice, death would be eternal, and none of us could live again.

After the Savior's death and resurrection, many of the bodies of the saints which slept arose. They became resurrected beings. "And the graves were opened; and many bodies of the saints which slept arose, And came out of the graves after his resurrection, and went into the holy city, and appeared unto many." (Matthew 27:52-53.)

President Marion G. Romney explained the two parts of the Atonement when he said,

> Now, I believe with Enoch, "Because that Adam fell, we are; and by his fall came death" (Moses 6:48) that every man must die. I believe that to meet the demands of justice, it took the atonement of Jesus Christ to redeem men from that death, that they may be raised again and have their spirits and their bodies, which are separated through death, reunited. I believe that through the atonement of Jesus Christ whatever "transgression" Adam committed was paid for, and that as in Adam all die, even so in Christ shall all be made alive, every living creature (1 Corinthians 15:22; D&C 29:24, 77). I believe, too, that through the atonement of Jesus Christ my individual sins, your individual sins, and the individual sins of every human being that ever lived or ever will live upon the earth were atoned for, upon condition that we accept the gospel and live it to the end of our lives. (*Look to God and Live*, pp. 251-52.)

Elder Melvin J. Ballard explained that, because the Savior overcame death, we became His. "The price he paid was his life; in some way not yet perhaps fully comprehended and understood by us, he . . . satisfied the claims upon these earth bodies. He has purchased us; he has redeemed us; he has bought us; and we belong to him." (*Sermons and Missionary Services of Melvin J. Ballard*, pp. 169-70.) It is a great joy to belong to the Savior!

Jesus Christ is our personal Savior. He wrought the atonement in the Garden of Gethsemane and on the cross. He made it possible for us to have faith in Him, repent of our sins, be baptized by one having authority, and receive the gift of the Holy Ghost.

If we keep His commandments the Holy Ghost will be our constant companion throughout our life. After repenting of our sins and being baptized, we are in the strait and narrow path that leads to eternal life. If we stay in this path it will lead us to that goal. We will be resurrected into a celestial body and live with our Father in Heaven forever.

The Great Gift of Love

As we contemplate the enormous gift of the Atonement, we need to realize what great love our Father in Heaven and His Son Jesus Christ have for us. Elder Melvin J. Ballard helps us to understand what they endured as Christ wrought the Atonement for each of us:

> Our Father in Heaven went through [what Abraham experienced when asked to sacrifice Isaac] and more, for in his case the hand was not stayed. He loved his Son, Jesus Christ, better than Abraham ever loved Isaac, for our Father had with him his Son, our Redeemer, in the eternal worlds, faithful and true for ages, standing in a place of trust and honor, and the Father loved him dearly, and yet he allowed this well-beloved Son to descend from his place of glory and honor, where millions did him homage, down to the earth, a condescension that is not within the power of man to conceive. He came to receive the insult, the abuse, and the crown of thorns. God heard the cry of his Son in that moment of great grief and agony, in the garden when, it is said, the pores of his body opened and drops of blood stood upon him, and he cried out: "Father, if thou be willing, remove this cup from me."
>
> I ask you, what father and mother could stand by and listen to the cry of their children in distress, in this world, and not render aid and assistance? I have heard of mothers throwing themselves into raging streams when they could not swim a stroke to save their drowning children, rushing into burning buildings, to rescue those whom they loved.
>
> We cannot stand by and listen to those cries without its touching our hearts. The Lord has not given us the power to save our own. He has given us faith, and we submit to the inevitable, but he had the

power to save, and he loved his Son, and he could have saved him. He might have rescued him from the insult of the crowds. He might have rescued him when the crown of thorns was placed upon his head. He might have rescued him when the Son, hanging between the two thieves, was mocked with, "Save thyself, and come down from the cross. He saved others; himself he cannot save." He listened to all this. He saw that Son condemned; he saw him drag the cross through the streets of Jerusalem and faint under its load. He saw that Son finally upon Calvary; he saw his body stretched out upon the wooden cross; he saw the cruel nails driven through hands and feet, and the blows that broke the skin, tore the flesh, and let out the life's blood of his Son. He looked upon that.

In the case of our Father, the knife was not stayed, but it fell, and the life's blood of his Beloved Son went out. His Father looked on with great grief and agony over his Beloved Son, until there seems to have come a moment when even our Savior cried out in despair: "My God, my God, why hast thou forsaken me?"

In that hour I think I can see our dear Father behind the veil looking upon these dying struggles until even he could not endure it any longer; and, like the mother who bids farewell to her dying child, has to be taken out of the room, so as not to look upon the last struggles, so he bowed his head, and hid in some part of his universe, his great heart almost breaking for the love that he had for his Son. Oh, in that moment when he might have saved his Son, I thank him and praise him that he did not fail us, for he had not only the love of his Son in mind, but he also had love for us. I rejoice that he did not interfere, and that his love for us made it possible for him to endure to look upon the sufferings of his Son and give him finally to us, our Savior and our Redeemer. Without him, without his sacrifice, we would have remained, and we would never have come glorified into his presence. And so this is what it cost, in part, for our Father in Heaven to give the gift of his Son unto men. (*Sermons and Missionary Services of Melvin J. Ballard*, pp. 153-55.)

"For God so loved the world, that he gave his only begotten Son, that whosoever believeth in him should not perish, but have everlasting life." (John 3:16.)

I, too, will be forever thankful to my Father in Heaven for letting His son make that sacrifice for us. Without Jesus Christ's Atonement, we would have remained in our sins, and we could never have come glorified into His presence.

When I think of the horrible pain and misery the Savior suffered in Gethsemane and on the cross, I feel sorry that my personal sins added to His pain and suffering. I love Him and realize that I am totally dependent on Him for the air I breathe, the food I eat, and the world I live on, for His Atonement in my behalf, for His grace or enabling power that has changed my life for the better. I love Him with all my heart and plan to spend the rest of my life in His service.

"And this is the gospel, the glad tidings, which the voice out of the heavens bore record unto us—

"That he came into the world, even Jesus, to be crucified for the world, and to bear the sins of the world, and to sanctify the world, and to cleanse it from all unrighteousness;

"That through him all might be saved whom the Father had put into his power and made by him." (D&C 76:40-42.)

The Atonement of Jesus Christ is the glad tidings to men on the earth that, with the help of Christ, they *can* change their lives, overcome the chains of sin, be purified, and return to their heavenly home.

President J. Reuben Clark, Jr., said, "We must stand adamant for the doctrine of the atonement of Jesus the Christ, for the divinity of his conception, for his sinless life, and for, shall I say, the divinity of his death, his voluntary surrender of life. He was not killed; he gave up his life. . . . It is our mission, perhaps the most fundamental purpose of our work, to bear constant testimony of Jesus the Christ." (CR, *Improvement Era*, December 1955, p. 916.)

The Atonement Is Central to the Gospel

Actually, the Atonement is *the central doctrine of the Church*. It is the most important message we receive through the gospel. The Prophet Joseph Smith expressed this when he said, "The fundamental principles of our religion are the testimony of the Apostles and Prophets, concerning Jesus Christ, that He died, was buried, and rose again the third day, and ascended into heaven; and all other things which pertain to our religion are only appendages to it." (*Teachings of the Prophet Joseph Smith*, p. 121.)

Elder Bruce R. McConkie spoke further of the central importance of the Atonement when he said, "Nothing in the entire plan of salvation compares in any way in importance with that most transcendent of all events, the atoning sacrifice of our Lord. *It is the most important single thing that has ever occurred in the entire history of created things*; it is the rock foundation upon which the gospel and all other things rest. Indeed, all 'things which pertain to our religion are only appendages to it,' the Prophet said.

"The doctrine of the *atonement* embraces, sustains, supports, and gives life and force to all other gospel doctrines. It is the foundation upon which all truth rests, and all things grow out of it and come because of it. Indeed, *the atonement is the gospel.*" (*Mormon Doctrine,* p. 60, emphasis added.)

How important is it that we receive the gift of the Atonement and cleanse our lives through repentance? In the words of our Savior,

> Therefore I command you to repent—repent, lest I smite you by the rod of my mouth, and by my wrath, and by my anger, and your sufferings be sore—how sore you know not, how exquisite you know not, yea, how hard to bear you know not.
>
> For behold, I, God, have suffered these things for all, that they might not suffer if they would repent;
>
> But if they would not repent they must suffer even as I;
>
> Which suffering caused myself, even God, the greatest of all, to tremble because of pain, and to bleed at every pore, and to suffer both body and spirit—and would that I might not drink the bitter cup, and shrink—
>
> Nevertheless, glory be to the Father, and I partook and finished my preparations unto the children of men.
>
> Wherefore, I command you again to repent, lest I humble you with my almighty power; and that you confess your sins, lest you suffer these punishments of which I have spoken, of which in the smallest, yea, even in the least degree you have tasted at the time I withdrew my Spirit. (D&C 19:15-20.)

Christ warns us that if we will not repent of our sins and accept His sacrifice, we must suffer even as He did. We are to forsake the natural, carnal man, that is, to repent, and become purified through the Atonement. If we fail to do this, our sufferings are beyond our ability to comprehend.

One of our great blessings is that we are free to choose. In 2 Nephi 2:26-27 we are told how the Atonement makes us free to chart our course in this life and in the eternities.

And the Messiah cometh in the fulness of time, that he may redeem the children of men from the fall. And because that they are redeemed from the fall they have become free forever, knowing good from evil; to act for themselves and not to be acted upon, save it be by the punishment of the law at the great and last day, according to the commandments which God hath given.

Wherefore, men are free according to the flesh; and all things are given them which are expedient unto man. And they are free to choose liberty and eternal life, through the great Mediator of all men, or to choose captivity and death, according to the captivity and power of the devil.

Our Savior loved us enough to suffer these untold agonies for us and make it possible for us to repent of our sins, understand good and evil, and gain power thereby. We show our love and gratitude to the Savior by choosing to repent of our sins, keep His commandments, build His kingdom. President Joseph Fielding Smith said, "If we really understood and could feel even to a small degree, the love and gracious willingness on the part of Jesus Christ to suffer for our sins we would be willing to repent of all our transgressions and serve him." (*The Restoration of All Things*, p. 199.)

One of our beautiful sacrament hymns closes with these lines:

Oh, dearly, dearly has he loved!
And we must love him too,
And trust in his redeeming blood,
And try his works to do. (*Hymns*, #194.)

Our love for Him is equal to our understanding of what He did for us. When we feel His love for us, accept it, and trust Him, our love for Him grows accordingly. So also does our willingness to keep his statutes and assist in His saving work.

A Prophet's Testimony

President Howard W. Hunter gave this stirring affirmation of the mission of our Savior:

As an ordained Apostle and special witness of Christ, I give to you my solemn witness that Jesus Christ is in fact the Son of God.

He is the Messiah prophetically anticipated by Old Testament prophets. He is the Hope of Israel . . . the Beloved Son who submitted to the will of his Father . . . he suffered in the Garden of Gethsemane and died on the cross, giving his sinless life as a ransom for every soul who enters mortality. He did in very fact rise from the dead on the third day, becoming the firstfruits of the resurrection and overcoming death.

The resurrected Lord has continued his ministry of salvation by appearing, from time to time, to mortal men chosen by God to be his witnesses, and by revealing his will through the Holy Ghost.

It is by the power of the Holy Ghost that I bear my witness. I know of Christ's reality as if I had seen with my eyes and heard with my ears. I know also that the Holy Spirit will confirm the truthfulness of my witness in the hearts of all those who listen with an ear of faith. (*Ensign*, January 1984, p. 70.)

Ask Yourself, "What Would Christ Have Me Do?"

"That Which Ye Have Seen Me Do"

You have probably heard from your childhood that the best way to decide what is right to do is to ask yourself what Christ would do in the same situation. This may seem like childish advice, but it is, in truth, a deep spiritual principle.

As we make Christ the center of our lives, trying to do as He would do, we obey His commandments. "For the works which ye have seen me do that shall ye also do; for that which ye have seen me do even that shall ye do." (3 Nephi 27:21.)

We should emulate our Savior. He lived on earth and had interaction with many people. By reading His life history in the scriptures, we can come to understand His life, His gospel, His commandments. If we strive to live worthy of His guidance, we will find fewer problems and less stress in our lives. If we use His methods to solve our problems, our lives will be more successful and happier. If we humble ourselves to learn His will we will gain more understanding and more compassion. If we have the courage to do His will we will become more like Him. Our plan is to become as Christ is. He is our ideal.

Consider this account of a man who tried to put this principle to work in his life:

A secondary school principal, deeply perceptive to the needs of his fellow beings, was loved and respected by students, teachers, and patrons alike. His decisions were uncommonly wise, and his methods in handling young people seemed to defy analysis. Even in those cases where action had to be firm and uncompromising, the students felt that Mr. Edwards was fair and had a special regard for them. At the end of a particular school day filled with troubles, two of the teachers sat in his office and asked, "Mr. Edwards, just what is your secret in solving all your difficulties?" "I have no secret," he replied humbly. "Any success I might have goes back to the Savior. In each instance I try to think, 'What would Christ have me do?' I've always tried to live worthy to receive an answer. Through earnest study and prayer and fasting, I make a great effort to determine what he would have me do. Sometimes it takes courage to do what I know I have to do, but it brings blessings. (Relief Society manual, 1985, p. 5.)

What a marvelous way to solve problems. We should do likewise. When faced with questions, challenges, decisions in the course of our lives, we should seek to learn the will of our Savior, and then seek the courage to do what He would have us do.

The question, "What would Jesus have me do?" is perhaps a better question than, "What would Jesus do?" He was perfect, and could judge others perfectly. We are not, so with our imperfect eyes cannot always relate to others in the way He would. Furthermore, we might despair in being able to do "what He would do" if we cannot imagine Him ever getting into the situation we find our imperfect selves embroiled in. "What would He have me to do in this situation" finds us a way to search His teachings, His example, and the guidance of the Holy Spirit to find an answer.

Elder Mark E. Petersen admonished us to become more like Christ in our everyday lives:

> The meaning of complete salvation is that we become like the Savior in word and thought and deed. We can measure our progress toward salvation merely by determining how Christlike we are. If we are not becoming more like Him in our everyday living, we are not advancing toward salvation as we should.
>
> Becoming Christlike is a matter of daily spiritual growth. As a flower develops from a seed, as a mature adult develops from a tiny child, so we can grow spiritually day by day, eventually into Christ-like personalities. . . .
>
> Jesus the Savior is the supreme example of how we should build our souls.
>
> "What manner of men ought ye to be?" He asked, and then replied, "Even as I am." (3 Ne. 27:27.)

Becoming like Him is not something we can achieve overnight. It is a lifelong and an eternal process, nothing less. In every hour and every day we must strive to become like Him." (CR, *Ensign*, November 1982, p. 16.)

Remember Your Covenants

We are a covenant-making people. At baptism we made a sacred covenant to keep the Lord's commandments. We renew that covenant when we partake of the sacrament. We promise to remember Him. He promises His Spirit to be with us.

Let's keep in mind this sacred covenant all the hours and days of our lives. God has commanded us to be pure in heart. When we are tempted to listen to suggestive music, look at indecent videos, shows, and magazines, or indulge in evil thoughts, remembering our covenants will help us dismiss or cast out the evil thought. Let's keep our minds clean.

We can replace evil or idle thoughts with thoughts of Christ: His love, His example, His suffering on the cross for our sins, our gratitude for His mercy. We can worship Him in prayer. We can plead for strength to overcome. With His help we can control all of our thoughts.

We are striving to learn how to control our thoughts with the goal of becoming pure in heart. We know it is His will that we gain control of our minds and bridle our thoughts so they become a positive force for good rather than a weight which drags us down toward a baser life. As we strive to become pure, we should keep in mind this statement from President David O. McKay, quoted in President Kimball's *The Miracle of Forgiveness*: "The thought in your mind at this moment is contributing, however infinitesimally, almost imperceptibly to the shaping of your soul, even to the lineaments of your countenance . . . even passing and idle thoughts leave their impression." (p. 105.)

Think of that. Every moment counts. Every thought counts. All either build or tear down our character. What we think, what we carry in our minds, shapes us to what we are. Even idle thoughts may be very harmful in our process of becoming saints. We must choose carefully what we allow into our minds. The Lord said, "Look unto me in every thought." (D&C 6:36.)

By remembering the covenants we have made with God we can keep the Big Picture, Christ and His gospel, in mind. As we thus stand firm with integrity to the promises we have made with Him, His Spirit attends us, and our thoughts and actions become more noble and worthy.

Humble Yourself

Jesus Himself told us what He would have us do. "And behold, I have given you the law and the commandments of my Father, that ye shall believe in me, and that ye shall repent of your sins, and come unto me with a broken heart and a contrite spirit." (3 Nephi 12:19.) He asks us to come to Him with faith. The broken heart is humble, meek, teachable, willing to do the Father's will. The contrite spirit is sorrowful for having sinned, eager to make restitution for wrongs, eager to leave behind past mistakes and move forward into a newness of life. These things are basic, the first principles of the Gospel. This is the foundation for the good life we are seeking to attain.

When we embark on this endeavor, we are in the process of becoming Christlike. Alma describes the kind of saints we should be: "And now I would that ye should be humble, and be submissive and gentle; easy to be entreated; full of patience and long-suffering; being temperate in all things; being diligent in keeping the commandments of God at all times; asking for whatsoever things ye stand in need, both spiritual and temporal; always returning thanks unto God for whatsoever things ye do receive." (Alma 7:23.) These are beautiful choices of what to do with our thoughts and our actions.

The Prophet Joseph Smith gave us a touching example of a humble plea for forgiveness in these words, speaking to the Twelve: "I have sometimes spoken too harshly from the impulse of the moment, and inasmuch as I have wounded your feelings, brethren, I ask your forgiveness, for I love you and will hold you up with all my heart in all righteousness, before the Lord, and before all men." (*Teachings of the Prophet Joseph Smith*, p. 106.)

President Ezra Taft Benson pled with us to "cleanse the inner vessel" through humility and repentance: "My beloved brethren and sisters, as we cleanse the inner vessel, there will have to be changes made in our own personal lives, in our families, and in the Church. The proud do not change to improve, but defend their position by rationalizing. Repentance means change, and it takes a humble person to change. But we can do it." (CR, *Ensign*, May 1986, p. 7.)

The Lord entreats us to repent and come unto Him, including our thoughts. "Let the wicked forsake his way, and the unrighteous man his thoughts: and let him return unto the LORD, and he will have mercy upon him; and to our God, for he will abundantly pardon." (Isaiah 55:7.)

Seek The Spirit of Forgiveness

One of the most Christlike attributes is the attitude of forgiveness. It is also one of the most difficult. We find our pride stands in the way of allowing charity and kindness to speak to our hearts. Yet the Lord warned us that "with what judgment ye judge, ye shall be judged" (Matthew 7:2) and "if ye forgive not men their trespasses neither will your Father forgive your trespasses." (3 Nephi 13:15.) Christ pled with us to love each other, to be meek and lowly, and to follow Him. He exemplified more than any other person the divine attribute of forgiveness, by humbly asking His Father in Heaven to forgive those who were in the process of taking His life! (See Luke 23:34.)

The Prophet Joseph Smith exhorted us to this spirit of forgiveness in these words: "Ever keep in exercise the principle of mercy, and be ready to forgive our brother on the first intimations of repentance, and asking forgiveness; and should we even forgive our brother, or even our enemy, before he repent or ask forgiveness, our Heavenly Father would be equally as merciful unto us." (*Teachings of the Prophet Joseph Smith*, p. 155.)

If one is really struggling with evil thoughts, and having a hard time securing control over them, there is a good chance that person is harboring some unforgiving feelings against someone. This is one of the most difficult areas in which to effect a change of heart. Grudges and feelings of offense sometimes linger tenaciously even if we have made an attempt to change them. If this is the circumstance you are in, give the Lord your entire heart and plead, not just ask, that He make you whole. "Create in me a clean heart, O God; and renew a right spirit within me." (Psalms 51:10.) Fasting may be necessary. We may need to seek a priesthood blessing. But if we are willing to pay the price, we can have the reward. Many have succeeded.

Sometimes in the process of getting rid of grudges or hurt feelings, it helps to be able to confront the person involved, and with a prayer in your heart and the Holy Spirit as your guide, express to them your feelings and your desire to overcome them. This requires humility, but as you discuss the problems with the guidance of the Spirit, you both can feel much better. This gives a further safeguard against those same feelings and thoughts coming back into your mind again.

When we truly forgive, the spirit of enmity, the burden of resentment, the shackles of self-pity fall away from our encumbered hearts. We no

longer "droop in sin," and "give place for the enemy of [our souls]."
Nephi cried, "Awake, my soul," and "rejoice, O my heart," after the
burden of anger was removed from His spirit. (See 2 Nephi 4:26-30.) In
this forgiving attitude, we are ready to come unto Christ.

Look to the Lord in Every Thought

To fulfill our life's purpose the way the Lord wants us to we should
be training ourselves to look unto the Lord in every thought. As we
make changes that bring our life closer to Him, our thoughts precede our
actions. If we want to live like the Lord we must think Christlike
thoughts.

Do not suppose your thoughts are secret. You are becoming what you
think about.

James Allen wrote,

> A man does not come to the almshouse or the jail by the tyranny
> of fate or circumstance, but by the pathway of grovelling thoughts
> and base desires. Nor does a pure-minded man fall suddenly into
> crime by stress of any mere external force; the criminal thought had
> long been secretly fostered in the heart, and the hour of opportunity
> revealed its gathered power.
>
> Circumstance does not make the man; it reveals him to himself.
> No such conditions can exist as descending into vice and its attendant
> sufferings apart from vicious inclinations, or ascending into virtue
> and its pure happiness without the continued cultivation of virtuous
> aspirations. And man, therefore, as the lord and master of thought is
> the maker of himself, the shaper and author of environment. (*As a
> Man Thinketh*, p. 21.)

The concept may sound a little bit out of date. It is fashionable in this
day to think that man is shaped by forces outside his control—by his upbringing, by his opportunities, by his education, by society. The popular
idea is to take from people the responsibility for their own actions, leaving the blame on others for the evil they do. This notion negates individual agency and says that man, like the animals, must survive however
he can and go through life satisfying his appetites wherever he can,
because he cannot control them. This familiar argument is completely
opposite to the plan of our Heavenly Father. It is Satan's reasoning from
pre-earth life, dressed in today's language, and propagated through his
insinuations.

But through the gospel, we know that we have our agency as a gift from God. We are taught right and wrong, and we know we are responsible for our choices. We also know we have the power to overcome whatever negative elements may have influenced our lives. We may have had a traumatic upbringing. We may have been subjected to abuse or neglect. We may have had a negative model of home life. The Lord knows what your trials have been, and He wants you to look forward, not backward. He wants you to rise above your problems, whether they are of your own making or of any circumstance beyond your control. He stands ready to help you. He wants you, and all of us, to succeed. We have the Light of Christ to help conquer our surroundings and the Holy Ghost to burn the dross out of our imperfect, unfinished selves. It can be done.

President Kimball corroborates this: "There are those today who say that man is the result of his environment and cannot rise above it. Those who justify mediocrity, failure, and even weakness and criminality are certainly misguided. Surely the environmental conditions found in childhood and youth are an influence of power. But the fact remains that every normal soul has its free agency and the power to row against the current and to lift himself to new planes of activity and thought and development. Man can transform himself. Man must transform himself." (*The Teachings of Spencer W. Kimball*, p. 169.)

If you have taken the downward road and blamed it on circumstances beyond your control, decide now to follow Jesus Christ and change your life. Perhaps you started by looking at a magazine with pornography in it. One magazine leads to another. Or perhaps you began with R-rated movies. Evil videos may have been brought into your home, or you may have seen some of the many crude shows on TV. As people foolishly consume coarse, outrageous, and obscene entertainment, they think about, even fantasize the evil acts portrayed. After a while they accept as normal and begin to perform the evil acts they have learned. Before they are aware they have hit the bottom of the ladder and Satan has them bound into his way of life.

Think on this. If you never see the first evil show, there will never be a second one. By complete abstinence, we run no risk. But if a person has indulged in some of this type of activity, he or she should quit immediately, cut it out completely, secure help from Father in Heaven, and get back on the strait and narrow way. We become what we think about. Turn from the past and become what you hope to be.

President Ezra Taft Benson pled with us to keep the Lord in our minds: "To become as He is, we must have Him on our mind—constantly in our thoughts. Every time we partake of the sacrament, we commit to 'always remember him.' (Moro. 4:3, 5:2; D&C 20:77,79.)

"If thoughts make us what we are, and we are to be like Christ, then we must think Christlike thoughts. Let me repeat that: If thoughts make us what we are, and we are to be like Christ, we must think Christlike thoughts." ("Think on Christ," *Ensign*, April 1984, p. 11.)

President Howard W. Hunter affirmed:

> To each of us Jesus says, "If any man serve me, let him follow me" (John 12:26).
> The Lord's invitation to follow him is individual and personal, and it is compelling. We cannot stand forever between two opinions. Each of us must at some time face the crucial question: "Whom say ye that I am?" (Matthew 16:15.) Our personal salvation depends on our answer to that question and our commitment to that answer. . . . Since Jesus is indeed the Christ, what must we do?
> Christ's supreme sacrifice can find full fruition in our lives only as we accept the invitation to follow him. This call is not irrelevant, unrealistic, or impossible. To follow an individual means to watch him or listen to him closely; to accept his authority, to take him as a leader, and to obey him; to support and advocate his ideas; and to take him as a model. Each of us can accept this challenge. (*Ensign*, September 1994, p. 2.)

If you haven't fully committed yourself to the Lord, decide right now. At this moment, make a permanent, irreversible decision to control your thoughts. From this moment forward do everything in your power to control your thoughts. This is one of the most important decisions you will ever make.

Follow the example of self-control set by the Savior. The Savior said, "I am the way, the truth, and the life: no man cometh unto the Father, but by me." (John 14:6.) Jesus followed the Father in every way, explaining to His disciples that He had done only what He had seen His Father do (see John 5:19,20; John 14:7). He asks us to likewise follow Him, do as He did, and be like Him.

The Lord Will Not Abandon Us

President George Q. Cannon writes that our Father in Heaven knows everything about us: "He is the God whom we worship. When we call upon Him, though he may be remote from us, dwelling in His holy habitation in the midst of the eternities, the very thoughts of our hearts, the very conceptions of our minds, the feeble whisperings of our voices, they ascend to Him, are carried to Him; His ear comprehends them; . . . His all-piercing eye penetrates eternity, and the glance of His vision reaches us." (*Gospel Truth*, p. 101.)

This idea that the Lord knows all the thoughts of your heart may make you uncomfortable. Perhaps you feel that you have not followed the Lord in the past, that you have done things to offend Him, and because of this He has abandoned you. Elder Joseph B. Wirthlin said, "The Lord will never forsake or abandon anyone. You may abandon him, but he will not abandon you. You never need to feel that you are alone." (CR, *Ensign*, November 1989, p. 75.)

Our Father in Heaven and His Son Jesus Christ love us infinitely. How do we know how much the Savior loves us? Read President Benson's moving assertion, "It was in Gethsemane that Jesus took on Himself the sins of the world, in Gethsemane that His pain was equivalent to the cumulative burden of all men, in Gethsemane that He descended below all things so that all could repent and come to Him.

"The mortal mind fails to fathom, the tongue cannot express, the pen of man cannot describe the breadth, the depth, the height of the suffering of our Lord—nor His infinite love for us." (*The Teachings of Ezra Taft Benson*, p. 14.)

Jesus Christ learned, by suffering through mortality, "how to succor his people." He *knows* all about us and our joy and pain, and He loves us infinitely. President Howard W. Hunter said, "He suffered so much more than our sins. He whom Isaiah called the 'man of sorrows' (Isaiah 53:3; Mosiah 14:3) knows perfectly every problem through which we pass because he chose to bear the full weight of all our troubles and our pains. Why? 'that [he] may be filled with mercy, according to the flesh, that he may know according to the flesh how to succor his people according to their infirmities' (Alma 7:12)." ("Fear Not, Little Flock," *Devotional Speeches of the Year*, 1988-89, p. 115.)

He knows us so well. He died for all of us collectively, but He suffered for each of us individually. He knows the struggles we suffer, and He feels our pain. Our Savior loves us, personally and deeply. He continually invites us to come unto Him, that He may heal us. He wants to help us out of the pit of sorrows we are in. He calls us out of our self-inflicted darkness into His marvelous light. In 3 Nephi 9:14 we read,

"Yea, verily I say unto you, if ye will come unto me ye shall have eternal life. Behold, mine arm of mercy is extended towards you, and whosoever will come, him will I receive; and blessed are those who come unto me." All that is required to obtain the help of the Lord is that we sincerely "call upon his holy name." Helaman 3:27-28 tells us, "The Lord is merciful unto all who will, in the sincerity of their hearts, call upon his holy name. Yea, thus we see that the gate of heaven is open unto all, even to those who will believe on the name of Jesus Christ, who is the Son of God."

We will find the strength we need in Jesus Christ. He is a part of our lives. President Ezra Taft Benson said, "He does not say, 'I stand at the door and wait for you to knock.' He is calling, beckoning, asking that we simply open our hearts and let Him in." ("A Mighty Change of Heart," *Ensign*, October 1989, p. 4.)

When we invite the Lord into our lives, He can help us with our burdens. President Howard W. Hunter explained that the Savior can strengthen us to solve our problems: "Some of our concerns may come in the form of temptations. Others may be difficult decisions pertaining to education or career or money or marriage. Whatever your burden is, you will find the strength you need in Christ. Jesus Christ is Alpha and Omega, literally the beginning and the end. He is with us from start to finish, and as such is more than a spectator in our lives." (*Devotional Speeches of the Year*, 1988-89, p. 115.)

The Lord is merciful unto all who will in the sincerity of their heart call upon His holy name. He will answer your prayers. He will draw you close to Him if you will exercise faith in Him and strive to keep His commandments. President Benson said, "Only Jesus Christ is uniquely qualified to provide that hope, that confidence, and that strength to overcome the world and rise above our human failings." (CR, *Ensign*, November 1983, p. 6.)

Through the Lord Jesus Christ we can gain the strength we need to "rise above our failings." Some, however, continue to seek to change their lives through self-improvement programs and the use of will-power alone. These are not sufficient to change our nature. Only Jesus Christ has the power to redeem us from our fallen nature. Let us subjugate our willpower to "Thy will be done."

Brother George W. Pace of Brigham Young University wrote, "The Holy One of Israel [is] the source of power . . . everything else in the gospel (ordinances, principles, and programs) is a means to obtain that power. If we see the Savior as the source of redemptive power, I believe we will stress the necessity of knowing him ever so well and the importance of obtaining the companionship of the Holy Ghost to change our lives instead of vesting our time, energy, and money in intricate systems of behavioral change that have a measure of lifting power but are bereft of godly power to change human nature." (*Our Search To Know the Lord*, p. 74.)

We should always strive to keep the Lord's commandments, knowing that if we are faithful and diligent He will prepare a way for us to succeed. So, as we seek to change our lives, let us seek to know the will of our Savior. Let us seek to emulate Him. Let us gain power from the Savior to overcome our weaknesses. As we do so, our hearts will become purified and filled with a joy that is as deep as was our pain.

Remember, your Savior loves you, and wants to replace the pain in your heart with joy and peace. President Hunter sums it up beautifully:

> Peace can come to an individual only by an unconditional surrender—surrender to him who is the Prince of peace, who has the power to confer peace. . . . If we look to man and the ways of the world, we will find turmoil and confusion. If we will but turn to God, we will find peace for the restless soul. . . . This peace shelters us from the worldly turmoil. The knowledge that God lives, that we are his children, and that he loves us soothes the troubled heart. The answer to the quest lies in faith in God and in his Son, Jesus Christ. This will bring peace to us now and in the eternity to follow. (CR, *Improvement Era*, December 1966, p. 1105.)

You Can Succeed!

The Holy Ghost Can Strengthen Us
to Overcome Our Weaknesses

You can succeed! The Lord has commanded us to purify our thoughts, and we know that, as Nephi said, "The Lord giveth no commandments unto the children of men, save he shall prepare a way for them that they may accomplish the thing which he commandeth them." (1 Nephi 3:7.) What is the way the Lord has prepared to help us govern our thoughts?

President John Taylor answered the question this way: "What will enable you, brethren and sisters, to govern yourselves? The Spirit of God; and you cannot do it without the Spirit of the living God dwelling in you,—you must have the light of revelation, or else you cannot do it." (*Journal of Discourses*, 10:57.)

How does the Spirit of God help us to overcome our weaknesses? President George Q. Cannon explained that we must seek for the spiritual gift that will help us to overcome whatever weakness is plaguing us:

> If any of us are imperfect, it is our duty to pray for the gift that will make us perfect. Have I imperfections? I am full of them. What is my duty: To pray to God to give me the gifts that will correct these imperfections. If I am an angry man, it is my duty to pray for charity, which suffereth long and is kind. Am I an envious man? It is my duty to seek for charity, which envieth not. So with all the gifts of the Gospel. They are intended for this purpose. No man ought to say, "Oh, I cannot help this; it is my nature." He is not justified in it, for the reason that God has promised to give strength to correct these things, and to give gifts that will eradicate them." (*Millennial Star*, 16 Apr. 1894, p. 260, as quoted in Melchizedek Priesthood Study Guide, 1989, pp. 87-88.)

We *can* overcome any weakness with the help of the Spirit. The Spirit of the Lord can even change our hearts and turn us from people who have a disposition to do evil to people who desire to do good continually. This happened to King Benjamin's people when the Spirit touched them as he spoke. When he finished, he asked them if they believed what he had said. Their response was a forceful tribute to the power of the Spirit on the repentant heart: "And they all cried with one voice, saying: Yea, we believe all the words which thou hast spoken unto us; and also, we know of their surety and truth, because of the Spirit of the Lord Omnipotent, which has wrought a mighty change in us, or in our hearts, that we have no more disposition to do evil, but to do good continually." (Mosiah 5:2.)

The Spirit of the Lord caused a grand and marvelous change in their hearts. They changed to proponents of good. The Lord, through the Holy Spirit, can do the same for us. If we exercise our faith in Jesus Christ and plead for His help, He will send the Spirit to lift us up and take away our desire to do evil. Only with the help of the Spirit can we achieve this goal.

Paul recognized that it was not enough to try to live the law by himself. He wrote: "For I know that in me, that is, in my flesh, dwelleth no good thing; for to will is present with me, but to perform that which is good I find not, *only in Christ.*' (JST, Romans 7:19, emphasis added.) He also said that, to live eternally, it was necessary to control the desires of the body through the Spirit: "For if ye live after the flesh, ye shall die: but if ye through the Spirit do mortify the deeds of the body, ye shall live." (Romans 8:13.)

But will the Lord change our nature without any effort on our part? Of course not. We must depend on the Spirit, while at the same time putting forth all our effort.

President Howard W. Hunter advised, "The gospel of Jesus Christ is the divine plan for . . . spiritual growth eternally. It is more than a code of ethics. It is more than an ideal social order. It is more than positive thinking about self-improvement and determination. The gospel is the saving power of the Lord Jesus Christ with his priesthood and sustenance and with the Holy Spirit. With faith in the Lord Jesus Christ and obedience to his gospel, a step at a time improving as we go, pleading for strength, improving our attitudes and our ambitions, we will find ourselves successfully in the fold of the Good Shepherd. That will require discipline and training and exertion and strength. But as the Apostle Paul said, 'I can do all things through Christ which strengtheneth me.' (Philip. 4:13)." (CR, *Ensign*, May 1979, p. 26.)

What must we do to seek for and obtain the companionship of the Holy Spirit? Elder Hartman Rector Jr. said, "I guess that the Holy Ghost has the tenderest feelings of anyone with whom you will ever associate. If you just think the wrong thought, he is gone, and he does not come back until you clean it up. To court the Spirit, you must keep your thoughts clean." ("The Talent of Spirituality," *1979 Devotional Speeches of the Year*, p. 230.)

Another way we can maintain and increase our spirituality is to partake of the sacrament worthily every week. President Marion G. Romney explained the importance of the sacrament to our spirituality: "The purpose of the sacrament is to promote the maintenance of spirituality. Both the revealed prayers over the bread and over the water contain the phrase, 'that they [who partake] may . . . have his Spirit to be with them' (see D&C 20:77, 79)." (CR, *Ensign*, November 1979, p. 16.)

We have seen people who have struggled for years to overcome difficult problems alone. When they finally surrendered their lonely struggle and asked for the help of the Lord, they were able to overcome enslaving habits. One such man we knew had tried to quit smoking for many years. Finally, he went to his bishop and said, "Bishop, help me quit smoking. I can't do it by myself. The craving for a cigarette is too strong." The bishop arranged for the executive priesthood leaders to fast and pray with him. At the end of the fast they gave him a priesthood blessing. Through the Holy Spirit the bishop blessed him with strength, and told him his cravings for cigarettes would leave. He told us he never had a craving for a cigarette again. He soon accomplished his long-held desire to go to the temple. In about a year he became a temple worker. His life changed. Even his countenance changed. His face took on the peaceful look of a saint. The Lord lifted this man up and strengthened him so he could overcome his problems.

Similar blessings have come into our lives. The Lord will do the same for you. He will send the Holy Ghost to bring you power to overcome any problem you are working on. He will comfort you and bring you peace.

The solution to problems in any area of our lives is applying gospel principles. A marriage counselor wrote, "Our personal problems as well as our relationship problems are spiritual in nature and must be solved through spiritual means.

"It is not within our own power to heal ourselves. If it were, we wouldn't need the Atonement or the first principles and ordinances of the gospel. Our part is to be humble enough to allow the healing to take place through faith in the Lord, repentance, and actually receiving the cleansing power of the Holy Ghost." (C. Richard Chidester, "No Place for Pride," *Ensign*, March 1990, p. 19.)

The Holy Ghost can take evil from our hearts; what is required is for us to have the desire, do our part and allow the spiritual healing to take place. Elder James E. Talmage attests, "The special office of the Holy Ghost is to enlighten and ennoble the mind, to purify and sanctify the soul, to incite to good works, and to reveal the things of God." (*Articles of Faith*, p. 167.)

This seems to be a well-attested concept, in the scriptures as well as by our Latter-day prophets. The way to cleansing and purification is through the Spirit. Elder Bruce R. McConkie said, "We can be sanctified by the Spirit, have dross and evil burned out of us as though by fire, become clean and spotless, and be fit to dwell with gods and angels." (*Priesthood*, p. 31.)

This is a description of that which we are earnestly seeking. The effort we must put forth to achieve it is nowhere near the value of what we receive. Truly the ministration of the Holy Ghost is a pearl of great price. It is worth anything we feel we will have to "give up" in order to obtain the companionship of the Spirit. Christian author C. S. Lewis said pointedly, "I believe . . . that any man who reaches Heaven will find that what he abandoned (even in plucking out his right eye) was precisely nothing." (Preface to *The Great Divorce*, p. 6.) When we give up the things that are holding us back, we will discover that it was really no sacrifice at all, as the peace and the blessings of the Lord surround us and fill us with joy unmeasurable.

"For with God, Nothing Shall Be Impossible"

Our climb will become easier if we strive to always have a positive attitude about our ability to overcome evil thoughts. We have a lot to be positive about. We are children of God. As a prince can become a king, so a child of God can become like the Father. Our Father did not send us here to earth to fail. He sent us here to succeed. Remember, "For with God, nothing shall be impossible." (Luke 1:37.)

Elder Marvin J. Ashton admonished us never to think of ourselves as a "nobody":

I am certain our Heavenly Father is displeased when we refer to ourselves as "nobody." How fair are we when we classify ourselves a "nobody"? How fair are we to our families? How fair are we to our God?

We do ourselves a great injustice when we allow ourselves, through tragedy, misfortune, challenge, discouragement, or whatever the earthly situation, to so identify ourselves. No matter how or where we find ourselves, we cannot with any justification label ourselves "nobody."

As children of God we are somebody. He will build us, mold us, and magnify us if we will but hold our heads up, our arms out, and walk with him. What a great blessing to be created in his image and know of our true potential in and through him! What a great blessing to know that in his strength we can do all things! (CR, *Ensign*, July 1973, p. 24.)

Sometimes we get discouraged because we feel we cannot live up to what is expected of us in this life. We see the faraway goal of perfection, and the distance between here and there seems insurmountable. In our discouragement, we feel that perfection is impossible. However, the scriptures are full of assurances: "The Lord knoweth how to deliver the godly out of temptations." (2 Peter 2:9.) "Ask with a firmness unshaken, that ye will yield to no temptation, but that ye will serve the true and living God." (Mormon 9:28.)

While Christ was the only perfect person, Elder Mark E. Peterson explains that in many ways we *can* become perfect in this life.

I believe that in many ways, here and now in mortality, we can begin to perfect ourselves. A certain degree of perfection is attainable in this life. I believe that we can be one hundred percent perfect, for instance, in abstaining from the use of tea and coffee. We can be one hundred percent perfect in abstaining from liquor and tobacco. We can be one hundred percent perfect in paying a full and honest tithing. We can be one hundred percent perfect in abstaining from eating two meals on fast day and giving to the bishop as fast offering the value of those two meals from which we abstain.

We can be one hundred percent perfect in keeping that commandment which says that we shall not profane the name of God. We can be perfect in keeping the commandment which says, "Thou shalt not commit adultery." (Ex. 20:14.) We can be perfect in keeping the commandment which says, "Thou shalt not steal." We can become perfect in keeping various others of the commandments that the Lord has given us. (CR, *Improvement Era*, May 1950, p. 378.)

We receive help from both sides of the veil. Elder Jeffrey R. Holland said, "In the gospel of Jesus Christ you have help from both sides of the veil and you must never forget that. When disappointment and discouragement strike—and they will—you remember and never forget that if our eyes could be opened we would see horses and chariots of fire as far as the eye can see riding at reckless speed to come to our protection. They will always be there, these armies of heaven, in defense of Abraham's seed." ("For Times of Trouble," *New Era*, October 1980, p. 15.)

In the Old Testament we read of an experience in which the eyes of the Prophet Elisha's servant were opened, and he saw the heavenly help sent by the Lord.

> And when the servant of the man of God was risen early, and gone forth, behold, an host compassed the city both with horses and chariots. And his servant said unto him, Alas, my master! how shall we do?
>
> And he answered, Fear not: for they that be with us are more than they that be with them.
>
> And Elisha prayed, and said, LORD, I pray thee, open his eyes, that he may see. And the LORD opened the eyes of the young man; and he saw: and, behold, the mountain was full of horses and chariots of fire round about Elisha. (2 Kings 6:15-17.)

In the latter-days, the Lord affirms this truth: "For I will go before your face. I will be on your right hand and on your left, and my Spirit shall be in your hearts, and mine angels round about you, to bear you up." (D&C 84:88.)

You see, we can succeed! We *can* overcome negative, idle, evil, defeating thoughts. The Lord has shown us the way. We can become perfect one step at a time. Take that first step. Dedicate yourself to a cleaner, happier life. Find the strength in the Lord to overcome enslaving habits and to receive the joy that comes through living righteously.

"Is any thing too hard for the Lord?" (Genesis 18:14.) No! With God's help we can succeed in this life. As we succumb to the enticings of the Holy Spirit and submit our will to the will of God, we will be purified in our thoughts, our confidence will "wax strong," His strength will become ours. We can become so clean in our hearts that we will be able to stand before our Father and say confidently with the psalmist, "Search me, O God, and know my heart: try me, and know my thoughts." (Psalms 139:23.)

Elder Neal A. Maxwell asserted: "Another cosmic fact: only by aligning our wills with God's is full happiness to be found. Anything less results in a lesser portion (see Alma 12:10-11)." (CR *Ensign*, November 1995, p. 23.)

The Lord lets us know that He is at the helm and that we are in His watchful care. His purpose is to raise up a pure people, and the trials that we experience are toward that end. Our part is to move forward under all circumstances until we become purified:

> And now I give unto you a word concerning Zion. Zion shall be redeemed, although she is chastened for a little season. . . .
>
> Therefore, let your hearts be comforted; for all things shall work together for good to them that walk uprightly, and to the sanctification of the church.
>
> For I will raise up unto myself a pure people, that will serve me in righteousness;
>
> And all that call upon the name of the Lord, and keep his commandments, shall be saved. (D&C 100:13, 15-17.)

Upward to the Light

"The Light of Life"

We have presented a lot of material on how to control thoughts. This chapter is intended to help you put all this information together so you can organize your tools and proceed with your heavenly and eternal project of controlling your thoughts. Let's get in hand the weapons the Lord has given us for this battle.

As we review and come to understand the Lord's plan for our redemption and salvation, we will become as the people spoken of by Isaiah, "The people that walked in darkness have seen a great light." (Isaiah 9:2.) Let us take our journey upward to that light—indeed, that great Light which is Jesus Christ, our Redeemer and our Savior, and the Author of our salvation. He has proclaimed Himself: "I am the light of the world: he that followeth me shall not walk in darkness, but shall have the light of life." (John 8:12.)

How do we embark on that upward path to Christ, the Light of Life? President Brigham Young defined the struggle to purify the mind when he said, "The greatest mystery a man ever learned, is to know how to control the human mind, and bring every faculty and power of the same in subjection to Jesus Christ; this is the greatest mystery we have to learn while in these tabernacles of clay." (*Journal of Discourses*, 1:46-47.) This pinpoints our problem. If we can control our thoughts and bring every faculty of our minds into subjection to Jesus Christ, we will become like Him. Our lives will radiate the glorious light of His gospel.

"My Son, Give Me Thine Heart"

Once again we ask, "Why is it so important to control our thoughts?" Because we become what we think. President Spencer W. Kimball reminded us that we are the product of our thoughts: "How could a person possibly become what he is *not* thinking? Nor is any thought, when persistently entertained, too small to have its effect. The 'divinity that shapes our ends' is indeed in ourselves." (*The Miracle of Forgiveness,* pp. 104-05.)

President George Q. Cannon spoke of the danger of giving way to evil thoughts:

> Words and actions are but the external fruits of the inward thoughts of the soul; they must be conceived there before they find their birth from the lips or the hands of the corporeal frame. . . .
>
> If a man be pure in thought, he will be correspondingly pure in action; but if he allow his mind to roam in unrestricted freedom through the various avenues of evil or to dwell unchecked upon the contemplation of forbidden indulgences, it will not be long before his feet tread those paths and his hand plucks the tempting but deceitful fruit. . . .
>
> Our first and chief efforts, therefore, should be directed to having our hearts cleansed from all evil by the sanctifying and purifying influences of the Spirit of the Lord. . . . Hence, the Lord says, "My son, give me thine heart." (Proverbs 23:26.) Not thy lip service, thy money, or anything else that may be possessed as an inseparable adjunct of life, but thine heart, knowing, as He does, that where this is given all else will follow. (*Gospel Truth*, pp. 435-36.)

Agency and Responsibility

The Gospel plan assures us that we have our agency, the right to choose. "For the power is in them, wherein they are agents unto themselves. And inasmuch as men do good they shall in nowise lose their reward." (D&C 58:28.)

President Cannon said,

> All the sons and daughters of God are also free agents. Satan, therefore, tempts them. It is necessary they should be tempted. Without this the plan of salvation would not be perfect. On the one hand the Father entreats us to obey His laws, to keep His commandments and to cherish His Holy Spirit. On the other hand Satan tempts us to do wrong, to commit sin, to disobey God. . . . [However,] he cannot force us to do evil. If we do wrong, it is because we choose to do so, for we are free agents.

The Lord Himself will not compel us to serve and obey Him. It is pleasing to Him to have us do so. But, when we do so, it is because it is our choice and in the exercise of our agency. (*Gospel Truth*, pp. 108-09.)

We are agents unto ourselves. We make choices as to what we do and must take the consequences of our deeds, good or bad. We are responsible for all of our acts. God tells us that when we receive any blessing from Him it is by obedience to that law upon which it is predicated (D&C 130:20-21). Likewise, any evil we choose to indulge in leaves its mark upon us. It is our responsibility to make the right choices, and to repent when we may have chosen unwisely. Accepting our own responsibility is the first step in controlling our thoughts and our actions.

Bishop H. Burke Peterson gives an exercise which illustrates this upward path toward the light. What we choose to do moves us up or down:

Run through an exercise with me for just a moment. Picture yourself on whatever level of . . . the ladder of faith and testimony. Whether you are low or high . . . doesn't matter nearly as much as which way you are going. Now assume that tonight or this evening you watch a movie or show in which there are obvious sexual conversation and implications of breakdown in morals. If you watch that show, whatever level you are on, in my opinion, your spirit will step down just a bit after having had the experience—just a bit—not much, but a bit. Or assume that this afternoon you are involved in retelling an off-color story; your spirit will step down again. . . . Every time you put some of this material into your mind, your righteousness and your power to do good, to think clearly, and to make decisions that are proper will be diluted. ("Clean Thoughts, Pure Lives," *Ensign*, September 1984, pp. 72-73.)

We Are Responsible for Our Thoughts

Elder Dean L. Larsen spoke of our responsibility for cleansing our thoughts: "Even as with unwelcome visitors who may occasionally seek to gain entrance into our homes, *we have the power* to usher out, almost instantaneously, those negative impulses that come into the antechamber of our minds. We have a responsibility to do this. No one can do it for us." (*Free To Act*, p. 97, emphasis added.)

President Cannon promises us that each one of us has the power to resist evil: "God has given us power to resist these [evil] things, that our hearts may be kept free from them and also from doubt; and when Satan comes and assails us, it is our privilege to say, 'Get thee behind me, Satan, for I have no lot nor portion in you, and you have no part in me. I am in the service of God, and I am going to serve Him, and you can do what you please. . . . I will not listen to you; I will close my heart against you.'" (*Gospel Truth*, p. 17.)

Everyone has the power to resist evil and to close his or her heart against destructive forces such as anger, hatred, malice, and envy. We have the power to close our hearts against darkness. This power is God-given.

Self-talk can strengthen you. As you fight the battle, say to yourself something like this:

1. I am an agent unto myself.
2. God has given me the power to resist evil thoughts.
3. I will resist all evil thoughts.
4. I will not let them into my mind.
5. I will only think clean thoughts.
6. I close my heart against all evil thoughts, and against Satan and his associates.
7. I will not put up with Satan's lies any longer.

Next time Satan tries to put an evil thought into your mind, pray to your Father in Heaven. Ask for His blessing to help you keep the evil thought out of your mind. Say out loud, as President Cannon admonished, "Get thee behind me, Satan, for I have no lot nor portion in you, and you have no part in me. I am in the service of God, and I am going to serve Him, and you can do what you please."

President Spencer W. Kimball said, "Satan tells us that black is white. He lies to us; therefore, we must be prepared to make a bold stand before Satan. . . . We need the whole armor of God that we may withstand." ("The Blessings and Responsibilities of Womanhood," *Ensign*, March 1976, p. 71.)

As we take our bold stand against Satan, with determination, at all times and in all situations, we will prevail. The whole armor of God, which the prophet advocates, is described in Ephesians: we are girt about with truth, righteousness becomes our breastplate, our feet are shod with preparation, faith becomes our shield, salvation becomes our helmet, and we are armed with the word of God. (See Ephesians 6:11-17.)

We must take upon ourselves this protection that comes through the gospel of Jesus Christ so we will be safe. We can't afford to vacillate on these issues. Elder ElRay L. Christiansen warns us to avoid the "little sin":

> Now, the adversary knows that a little sin will not stay little, and he welcomes any and all into his kingdom by first trying to get us to lie a little, then helping us to try to justify ourselves in so doing or to cheat or to steal. Some folks are indeed induced to desecrate the Sabbath day until it becomes habitual with them. Some people begin with the use of liquor just to "relax a bit." Also, drug abuse, evil speaking, disobedience to parents, or deceiving one's own companions—these are means he has of getting us to digress from the proper course. He knows full well that, if continued, such diversions soon result in regrets, sorrows, and losses, because they lead us into greater sinfulness. (CR, *Ensign*, November 1974, p. 24.)

Don't allow the adversary to penetrate your armor. Watch every thought. When an evil thought arrives immediately cast it out. Discard it! Resist future evil thoughts. Remember that you are the master of your mind. You are the agent of your actions. You are determined to only think good thoughts and do good deeds. Keep an "eye single to the glory of God" (D&C 4:5) and continue in your upward climb.

If we will dwell in righteousness, Satan will have no power over us. President Cannon said, "My view of the Gospel is that when it is obeyed by mankind the power of the devil will cease. That is my view respecting a part of the power that will be brought to bear to bind Satan. Satan will be bound because he will not have power over the hearts of the children of men. Why? One reason will be because they will have obeyed the more perfect law which will have relieved them from his power." (*Gospel Truth*, p. 69.) "The time is coming when for one thousand years Satan will be bound." (p. 109)

We must close our hearts against Satan. We must stop listening to him. We must obey the gospel. In this way we bind the devil in our own lives. President Cannon said further, "By the Saints refusing to be led by the influences of Satan and not yielding to his seductive temptations, he is virtually bound so far as they are concerned; and, when the head of the family can attain unto this power and persuade his wife and family to do likewise, the power of Satan will be bound in that habitation." (*Gospel Truth*, pp. 69-70.)

"Pray That You May Come off Conqueror"

President Ezra Taft Benson said, "We should not invite the devil to give us a stage presentation. Usually with our hardly realizing it, he slips into our thoughts. Our accountability begins with how we handle the evil thought immediately after it is presented. Like Jesus, we should positively and promptly terminate the temptation. We should not allow the devil to elaborate with all his insidious reasoning." ("Think on Christ," *Ensign*, April 1984, p. 11.)

Prayer is an effective way to terminate Satan's temptation. The scriptures teach: "Pray always, that you may come off conqueror; yea, that you may conquer Satan, and that you may escape the hands of the servants of Satan that do uphold his work." (D&C 10:5.) "Cry unto him against the power of your enemies. Yea, cry unto him against the devil, who is an enemy to all righteousness." (Alma 34:22-23.) When the evil one starts to put an idea into your mind, you can pray to your Father in Heaven to help you. Focus your mind on what you are doing, and what you want the Lord to help you solve. Prayer will help you conquer Satan.

When you are earnestly striving to think only good thoughts, put your name in the temple. This is a demonstration of faith in prayer that you can participate in, and will be a source of strength to you. Continue your own prayer in your own behalf.

Alma tells us to take our problems to Heavenly Father in prayer and let Him help us solve them: "Cry unto God for all thy support; yea, let all thy doings be unto the Lord, and whithersoever thou goest let it be in the Lord; yea, let all thy thoughts be directed unto the Lord; yea, let the affections of thy heart be placed upon the Lord forever." (Alma 37:36.)

Choose the Lord's Side of the Line

President George Albert Smith said,

There are two influences in the world. The one is the influence of our Heavenly Father and the other is the influence of Satan. We can take our choice which territory we want to live in, that of our Heavenly Father or that of Satan.

I have many times repeated what my grandfather said. He, too, talked from this stand, and it was he who gave me his name. In advising his family he said, "There is a line of demarcation, well defined. On one side of the line is the Lord's territory. On the other side of the line is the devil's territory." And he said, "If you will stay on the Lord's side of the line, you are perfectly safe, because the adversary of all righteousness can not cross that line."

What does that mean? It means to me that those who are living righteous lives, keeping all of the commandments of our Heavenly Father are perfectly safe, but not those who trifle with his advice and counsel." (CR, *Improvement Era*, November 1949, pp. 699, 789.)

When we choose to be on the Lord's side of the line, we will remove all the evil and negative influences from our environment and cut off the flow of trash. This means to stop feeding our minds with *any* unworthy material. This includes *all* sources—movies, television, videos, music, books, magazines, etc. Sometimes we think, "It won't hurt to go to an R-rated movie once in awhile." But it *will* hurt. "A man is literally what he thinks, his character being the complete sum of all his thoughts," says President Kimball. (*The Miracle of Forgiveness*, p. 103.) One can't go to an R-rated show and not think about it. Partaking of any unworthy material moves us to the devil's side of the line. President George Albert Smith also said, "If you cross to the devil's side of the line one inch, you are in the tempter's power, and if he is successful, you will not be able to think or even reason properly, because you will have lost the Spirit of the Lord. . . . If I determined to be on the safe side, the Lord's side, I would do the right thing every time." (*Sharing the Gospel with Others*, p. 43.)

Determination to do the right thing every time will keep us on the Lord's side. Absolute honesty, with others as well as with ourselves, insures that we can make right choices.

"Cast Away Your Idle Thoughts"

After we have cleaned up the material flowing into our minds, we need to make sure our brain is not allowed to be idle. In D&C 88:69 we are instructed, "cast away your idle thoughts." Don's father, Joseph M. Christensen, would say to him, "Son, the idle brain is the devil's workshop." This is certainly true. The devil may put unclean thoughts into a vacant mind. We may prevent this by making sure our minds are busy at all times thinking good thoughts, making plans, learning productive skills and truths.

President David O. McKay said, "It is said by one man: 'I will know what you are if you will tell me what you think about when you don't have to think.' What do you think about when no other men are guiding your thoughts and you yourself control them?" (*True to the Faith*, p. 270.)

Elder Dean L. Larsen admonished us to keep our minds busy with good things:

> One cannot always be on the defensive against bad thoughts. It is essential to develop a capacity for sustained positive thinking. Keeping one's mind actively involved with constructive, useful things is the best protection. An idle mind becomes a ready repository for thoughts that have a negative influence on our feelings and behavior. There is so much of good literature, music, and art, and so many constructive challenges to work through to conclusions in our minds. We can focus our minds upon only one thought channel at one time. When good actors are performing on the stage of our mind, it is difficult for the bad actors to intrude. (*Free to Act*, p. 99.)

Preventing the negative and evil thought from lodging in our minds could include quickly concentrating on the things we are doing at the time. We can force our minds to think about only the good things we are seeing, hearing, and doing.

One plan works like a wheel going around—something out, something else in. We program the mind to start the wheel turning automatically when a bad thought tries to enter the mind. This ushers out the intrusive thought and brings a good thought in its place. You can program the mind to jump back to reality, allowing you to enforce concentration on what you are doing. Then you can consciously choose a constructive thought, such as trying to solve a problem you have been working on. When the bad thought tries to come in, you start the wheel going around, thus throwing out the bad thought; then concentrate on solving your problem. You may want to say or think, "Roll it," thus starting the wheel to go around. After you have followed this program for a while, the wheel will automatically start up when a bad thought tries to enter your mind. Out with the bad, in with something constructive and good. Get rid of unwanted recurring thoughts by flooding your mind with productive ideas.

Elder Richard G. Scott, speaking in the priesthood session of general conference, gave this advice:

Some bad thoughts come by themselves. Others come because we invite them by what we look at and listen to. Talking about or looking at immodest pictures of a woman's body can stimulate powerful emotions. It will tempt you to watch improper videocassettes or movies. These things surround you, but you must not participate in them. Work at keeping your thoughts clean by thinking of something good. The mind can think of only one thing at a time. Use that fact to crowd out ugly thoughts. Above all, don't feed thoughts by reading or watching things that are wrong. If you don't control your thoughts, Satan will keep tempting you until you eventually act them out. (CR, *Ensign*, November 1994, p. 37.)

Prayer also helps us to cast away idle thoughts. It refocuses our minds on constructive things. Because God knows all our thoughts, all we need to do is let the prayer go through our mind. He will send us strength to overcome if we will ask sincerely. If we plead with our Father in Heaven to send His Spirit to be with us, after a short while we will notice that our thoughts have changed for the better, and we are now enjoying the Spirit, thinking positively, and succeeding at what we are working on.

We should prepare ahead with good materials for idle times. For example, when driving from work, listen to the Book of Mormon on tape. Carry a scripture card to memorize. Read the scriptures and other good books every day during free time. Meditate and pray when faced with idle moments. Commuting time riding the bus could be used to prepare a talk for future use.

Another way to change our thoughts is set forth by Brad Wilcox, a teacher on the Elementary Education faculty at BYU:

Do something active. We are all well aware of the connection between our brains and our bodies. . . . However, we do not use this interconnection to our advantage as often as we should. Just as the mind can affect body movement, body movement can affect the mind. . . . When your mind goes blank, . . . chances are you have moved your body. That simple movement totally erased a thought. So when we *want* our minds to go blank, let's move.

"Oh, sure," some might be thinking, "jumping jacks in the middle of biology class." Not necessarily. Just try crossing arms, legs, ankles, fingers, and then uncross them and do it again. Move your hands. Wiggle your toes. It sounds strange, but when someone asks you what on earth you're doing you might not remember, and that's the whole idea. (*Feeling Great, Doing Right, Hanging Tough*, p. 73.)

All of these methods are helpful as we seek to discipline our minds. If we truly desire it, our minds will be filled with righteousness, to the exclusion of evil. Persistance will win; the Lord will grant us our righteous desires. Eventually our "whole bodies shall be filled with light, and there shall be no darkness" in us. (D&C 88:67.)

Elder Orson Hyde called the mind "the agent of the Almighty": "It [the mind] is the agent of the Almighty clothed with mortal tabernacles, and we must learn to discipline it, and bring it to bear on one point, and not allow the Devil to interfere and confuse it, nor divert it from the great object we have in view." (*Journal of Discourses*, 7:153.)

Jesus Himself taught us plainly about the importance of choosing light over darkness: "This is the condemnation, that light is come into the world, and men loved darkness rather than light, because their deeds were evil.

"For every one that doeth evil hateth the light, neither cometh to the light, lest his deeds should be reproved.

"But he that doeth truth cometh to the light, that his deeds may be made manifest, that they are wrought in God. (John 3:19-21.)

How do we show we love the light? We spend our days doing good, magnifying our callings in the Church, attending our worship services, holding family prayer and family home evening, rearing our children in righteousness, doing our home teaching or visiting teaching, helping our neighbors, visiting the sick, serving in the temple on a regular basis, living as Zion people.

You Are Stronger Than Satan

President Spencer W. Kimball has written, "Temptations come to all people. The difference between the reprobate and the worthy person is generally that one yielded and the other resisted." (*The Miracle of Forgiveness*, p. 86.)

We need not fear Satan or his temptations. We know that learning to resist evil is part of our probation, and our Father has adequately fortified us to enable us to succeed.

Satan is a liar, even the father of lies. The evil thoughts he puts into our minds are lies. In Alma 5:40 we read, "Whatsoever is good cometh from God, and whatsoever is evil cometh from the devil." We come from God and we are good—actually His sons and daughters. We kept our first estate and came here to mortality with bodies and with our Father's confidence and blessing. Our goal is to go to heaven. Satan has no body. He has no hope of eternal life. His goal is to get us to go to hell by sinning, so we can be miserable like himself. He tries to tell us that we can live in sin and still go to heaven. This is one of Satan's big lies.

Remember that *you are stronger than Satan.* The Prophet Joseph Smith taught: "All beings who have bodies have power over those who have not. The devil has no power over us only as we permit him." *(Teachings of the Prophet Joseph Smith,* p. 181.) You have a body, and you have the spirit of Christ. You are headed upward to the light. Satan and his spirits do not have this advantage. Do not permit him to influence you.

His biggest tool against you is fear. If you detect an evil power manifested against you, use your faith, and do not fear. If you stand firm he will retreat. By understanding how to handle his wiles and even his presence, you can stand forth in righteous triumph as a child of your Heavenly Father.

President Kimball told us that to successfully resist Satan's presence or influence, we are to say: "Depart from me, Satan." He reminds us that "every soul who has mortality is stronger than Satan, if that soul is determined." *(Ensign,* March 1976, p. 71.) Next time Satan tries to put an evil thought into your mind, say aloud, "Depart from me, Satan." He has to leave if you command him to. If you resist the devil, he will flee from you. If you are determined and keep your face toward the light, Satan will have no power over you.

President Ezra Taft Benson said of those chosen to come to earth in the latter days: "God has saved for the final inning some of His stronger and most valiant children, who will help bear off the Kingdom triumphantly. . . . You are the generation that must be prepared to meet your God." *(Ensign,* April 1987, p. 73.)

As members of the Church we were reserved to come down to earth in these latter days to help prepare the earth for the Second Coming of the Lord. We were prepared for this assignment in the spirit world. We are strong spirits, and we can be valiant and loyal to Him in all areas of our life and under all circumstances.

The Light of Christ

Every person born into this life carries in his heart the Light of Christ. We receive its influence daily and hourly. This is God's gift to all to help us resist evil and guide us home to Him. It is often referred to as our conscience, the still small voice. Elder Bruce R. McConkie says of the conscience, "By virtue of [the Light of Christ] all men automatically and intuitively know right from wrong and are encouraged and enticed to do what is right. (Moro. 7:16.) The recognizable operation of this Spirit in enlightening the mind and striving to lead men to do right is called *conscience.*" (*Mormon Doctrine*, p. 156.)

The Spirit of Christ enlighteneth every person who cometh into the world (see John 1:4-9.) It is a comfort, an uplift, a guide toward light and truth. Scriptural passages refer to the Spirit of Christ, our conscience which is given to every person, and also to the Holy Ghost, the additional guide and Comforter given through the priesthood to worthy persons who have committed their lives to Christ through repentance and baptism. Members of the true Church have received the right to both of these gifts from God.

Elder Rulon G. Craven writes, "What a marvelous blessing can be yours if you will learn to control and consistently discipline your mind in obedience to God's commandments! You can learn to discipline your mind if you will study the gospel, keep God's commandments, follow the prophets, and act according to the feelings of your conscience. You will then experience the power of the Spirit influencing your mind to righteous thoughts, acts, and behavior. You will become a person of confidence, power, and righteous self-direction." (*The Pursuit of Perfection*, p. 43.)

You can change your thoughts. You have this power. You can decide what thoughts you will keep in your mind and what thoughts you will cast out.

The Holy Ghost Will Help Us Succeed

The second guide and light which is given to members of the Church to help them in their upward reach is the gift of the Holy Ghost. We receive this precious gift at baptismal confirmation, and it remains with us as long as we remain faithful. This marvelous gift is too often taken for granted by Church members, and even may frequently be ignored. But if we fail to heed it, it may be withdrawn from us. An understanding of this blessing in our lives will help us in choosing good over evil, and in overcoming the trials that we encounter along the way through our mortal probation.

The Holy Ghost is a member of the Godhead, and His mission is to transmit the will of God to us to help us in our own search for exaltation, and in our service to our fellowmen in helping to bring to pass their immortality and eternal life (see Moses 1:39).

When you wake up each morning, make sure the Holy Ghost is with you. If he isn't, pray to your Father in Heaven to send the Holy Ghost to you. Plead for the Spirit. Beg for the Spirit. Pray until the Holy Ghost comes. Do not leave the room without the companionship of the Holy Ghost.

How can we tell when we have the Holy Ghost with us? President George Q. Cannon said, "When a man or woman, or a boy or girl receives the Holy Ghost, it brings peace, joy, love and happiness; and the person who is in possession of this Spirit has a feeling of kindness and charity towards all mankind. His mind is enlightened and the things of God are made plain unto him. Society is benefited and the world is purified by its bestowal." (*Gospel Truth*, p. 502.)

When we feel the Holy Ghost with us we should strive to keep all the commandments of God so the Holy Ghost can stay with us throughout the day and the night.

Elder James E. Faust explained how the Spirit can help shield us against evil and temptation:

> Satan has had great success with this gullible generation. As a consequence, literally hosts of people have been victimized by him and his angels. There is, however, an ample shield against the power of Lucifer and his hosts. This protection lies in the spirit of discernment though the gift of the Holy Ghost. This gift comes undeviatingly by personal revelation to those who strive to obey the commandments of the Lord and to follow the counsel of the living prophets.
>
> This personal revelation will surely come to all whose eyes are single to the glory of God, for it is promised that their bodies will be "filled with light, and there shall be no darkness" in them (D&C 88:67). (CR, *Ensign*, November 1987, pp. 35-36.)

The Spirit of the Lord can be discerned from any spirit of evil. President Brigham Young received a visit from the Prophet Joseph Smith after Joseph Smith's death. In this vision Joseph told him that it is vitally important that the people get the Spirit of the Lord and follow it. Joseph told President Young that the people "can tell the Spirit of the Lord from all other spirits; it will whisper peace and joy to their souls; it will take malice, hatred, strife and all evil from their hearts; and their whole desire will be to do good, bring forth righteousness and build up the kingdom of God." (*Manuscript History of Brigham Young 1846-1847*, pp. 529-30, as quoted by Loren C. Dunn, CR, *Ensign*, May 1979, pp. 71-72.)

Elder ElRay L. Christiansen said that as we gain the companionship of this Comforter, He will help us resist evil: "In all his evil doings, the adversary can go no further than the transgressor permits him to go, and we can gain complete power to resist the evils caused by Satan through adherence to the principles of the gospel of Jesus Christ. Members of the Church may have the blessing of the Holy Ghost, the prompter, as a companion as well. *And when the Holy Ghost is really within us, Satan must remain without.*" (CR, *Ensign*, November 1974, p. 24, emphasis added.)

The Holy Ghost gives us an enlightened sense of good and evil, making us more able to discern and resist Satan's advances. If we resist him with all the might, mind, and strength that God has given us each time he approaches, we will win out in the end. We need to live near to God every day so we can keep the Holy Spirit with us.

President George Q. Cannon said, "He who is imbued with the Spirit of God is sensibly aware when the evil power approaches, but he does not welcome it to his bosom; he resists it with all the might and strength God has given unto him; he obtains power over it, and it no more troubles him; if it does, its influence is more weakened than previously." (*Gospel Truth*, p. 65.)

President Cannon encouraged us to live in the light of the Spirit and overcome the adversary:

> We see the power of Satan, the knowledge of Satan and his cunning. He understands the avenues through which he can approach us best; he knows the weaknesses of our character, and we do not know the moment we may be seduced by him and be overcome and fall victims to him. Our only preservation is in living near to God, day by day, and serving him in faithfulness and having the light of revelation and truth in our hearts continually so that when Satan approaches we will see him and understand the snare that he has laid for us, and we will have the power to say, "Oh no, God being my helper, I will not yield to it; I will not do that which is wrong; I will not grieve the Spirit of God; I will not deviate from the path that my Father has marked out for me; but I will walk in it." (*Gospel Truth*, p. 144.)

As we walk by the Spirit, our minds will be enlightened, and our souls will be filled with joy. We will be able to successfully resist evil thoughts and receive revelation concerning things of righteousness. Imagine the joy of that glorious light filling our minds, to the exclusion of any darkness!

Light Will Prevail over Darkness

Nephi speaks plainly of the fate of those who choose darkness over light: "For because they yield unto the devil and choose works of darkness rather than light, therefore they must go down to hell. For the Spirit of the Lord will not always strive with man. And when the Spirit ceaseth to strive with man then cometh speedy destruction, and this grieveth my soul." (2 Nephi 26:10-11.)

But this is not the fate of those who keep their eye single to the glory of God. Light will prevail over darkness. If we are worthy, the Holy Spirit brings light into our lives, and leads us on our upward path, drawing ever closer to Jesus Christ, who is the Light of the world.

> And now, verily, verily, I say unto thee, put your trust in that Spirit which leadeth to do good—yea, to do justly, to walk humbly, to judge righteously; and this is my Spirit.
>
> Verily, verily, I say unto you, I will impart unto you of my Spirit, which shall enlighten your mind, which shall fill your soul with joy;
>
> And then shall ye know, or by this shall you know, all things whatsoever you desire of me, which are pertaining unto things of righteousness, in faith believing in me that you shall receive. (D&C 11:12-14.)

When we have the Spirit of God with us we are happy. Darkness, gloom, and depression indicate we are stepping over the Lord's line. In your reach toward the light, do not linger in gloom. When you are upset, disturbed, and full of doubt, pray. President George Q. Cannon taught us this method for restoring the spirit of light in our hearts:

> The Spirit of God is a spirit of hope; it is not a spirit of gloom.
> . . . When you are disturbed in your feelings and assailed with doubt and do not feel happy, withdraw yourselves from the world, leave the cares that press you, lay them aside, withdraw to your secret chamber, and bow yourselves down before your God and entreat him, in

the name of Jesus, to give you his Spirit, and do not leave your chamber until you are, as it were, baptized in the Spirit of God and full of peace and joy, all your cares and troubles dissipated and dismissed. This is the course we should take as Latter-day Saints. (*Gospel Truth*, p. 145.)

Doing this really works. When we humble ourselves before God and ask for His Spirit to be with us, He listens. As we plead with Him for His Spirit we feel its sweet influence coming upon us. The disturbed and doubtful feeling will leave. We will find peace, joy, and happiness. We must not give up, but continue to pray until this happens.

Scripture study is another way of bringing light to our hearts and minds, and keeping the Holy Spirit active in our lives. Consider the effect in the daily lives of the people Elder Rulon G. Craven referred to in this occurrence:

A group of Latter-day Saints, after taking a twelve-week adult education class on scripture study, were asked if studying the scriptures had any effect on their lives. Some of their comments follow:

"I have been more thoughtful and considerate of others."

"I am more patient."

"I recognize the Spirit better."

"For the first time in my life I have wanted to get close to the Lord."

"I am more aware of my children's needs."

"I have a better feeling towards my companion." (*The Pursuit of Perfection*, p. 44.)

These people stated the benefits they realized from studying the scriptures. They followed the light, then received more light. Let the scriptures enrich every day of your life. Jesus said, "They are they which testify of me" (John 5:39) and "Ye shall know the truth, and the truth shall make you free." (John 8:32.) In 2 Nephi 32:3-4 we read, "Wherefore, I said unto you, feast upon the words of Christ; for behold, the words of Christ will tell you all things what ye should do. Wherefore, now after I have spoken these words, if ye cannot understand them it will be because ye ask not, neither do ye knock; wherefore, ye are not brought into the light, but must perish in the dark." The light and truth we receive from our scripture study casts out the darkness with which Satan seeks to enslave our minds.

Jesus promised that light will prevail: "That which is of God is light; and he that receiveth light, and continueth in God, receiveth more light; and that light groweth brighter and brighter until the perfect day." (D&C 50:24.)

Look unto the Lord, Who Is the Light of the World

President Ezra Taft Benson admonished us to look to the Lord in every thought:

> The Lord said, "Look unto me in every thought." (D&C 6:36.) Looking unto the Lord in every thought is the only possible way we can be the kind of men and women we ought to be.
>
> The Lord asked the question of His disciples, "What manner of men ought ye to be?" He then answered His own question by saying, "Even as I am." (3 Ne. 27:27.) To become as He is, we must have Him on our minds—constantly in our thoughts. Every time we partake of the sacrament, we commit to "always remember him." (Moro. 4:3; 5:2; D&C 20:77,79.)
>
> If our thoughts make us what we are, and we are to be like Christ, then we must think Christlike thoughts.
>
> Paul, en route to Damascus to persecute the Saints, saw a light from heaven and heard the voice of the Lord. Then Paul asked a simple question—and the persistent asking of the same question changed his life. "Lord, what wilt thou have me to do?" (Acts 9:6.) The persistent asking of that same question can also change your life. There is no greater question that you can ask in this world. "Lord, what wilt thou have me to do?" I challenge you to make that the uppermost question of your life.
>
> We are accountable for our thoughts and what we think about. Our thoughts should be on the Lord. We should think on Christ. ("Think on Christ," *Ensign*, March 1989, p. 4.)

Truly this is a powerful question, for when we ask the Lord what He would have us do and then do as He asks us to do, our lives will take the upward path. As we pray about the activities we are involved in, we should pray that the Lord make known to us what He would have us do. We will receive answers that will keep us on the strait and narrow path that leads to eternal life. Our Father in Heaven wants to answer our humble prayers and bless our lives. He will direct us in the way of truth and righteousness. We may even make a complete turn around, as Paul did when he asked the Lord this question.

If we are to come unto the Lord and partake of His marvelous light, we must be spiritually prepared. We must learn to be humble. We must be as the Savior when He said "I am meek and lowly in heart." (Matthew 11:29.)

The broken heart and contrite spirit is the sacrifice [see D&C 59:8] which we are to lay upon the altar, and when we do we can have confidence that God will hear and answer our prayers. A broken heart is a humble heart. A contrite spirit is a repentant spirit.

When we approach the Lord with a repentant attitude and a humble and sincere heart, we are becoming like Him. We are choosing light over darkness.

Faith, Prayer, and Following the Savior

Elder Bruce R. McConkie said, "*Faith is a gift of God bestowed as a reward for personal righteousness.* It is always given when righteousness is present, and the greater the measure of obedience to God's laws the greater will be the endowment of faith." (*Mormon Doctrine*, p. 264.)

As we increase our obedience to God's laws our faith increases. We demonstrate our faith by listening to His servants teach us the gospel, prayerfully reading and pondering the scriptures, magnifying our callings in the Church, fasting and praying, sustaining the leaders of the Church, partaking of the sacrament, keeping the Sabbath day holy, and keeping our covenants. We increase our faith in the same ways. It is an upward spiral. We desire to believe, we learn His will, we exercise our faith, we do His will, He increases our faith, we seek to be like Him, He rewards our faith.

Alma urges us "Counsel with the Lord in all thy doings, and he will direct thee for good; yea, when thou liest down at night lie down unto the Lord, that he may watch over you in your sleep; and when thou risest in the morning let thy heart be full of thanks unto God; and if ye do these things, ye shall be lifted up at the last day." (Alma 37:37.)

When we ask for blessings, we should be striving to do His will. In return, God will give us according to our faith: "Even as you desire of me so it shall be done unto you." (D&C 11:8.) We need to seek the Lord's will in all portions of our lives—our home lives, our vocations, our relationships with others, our personal needs, through private prayer and prayer in our families, morning and night, and a running prayer in our minds and hearts all day long thanking Him for our blessings as they occur and asking for the blessings we need.

"And again, I command thee that thou shalt pray vocally as well as in thy heart; yea, before the world as well as in secret, in public as well as in private." (D&C 19:28.)

God will help us attain our righteous desires. Wanting to think no evil thoughts is a righteous desire. "I know that [the Lord] granteth unto men according to their desire, whether it be unto death or unto life; yea, I know that he allotteth unto men, yea, decreeth unto them decrees which are unalterable, according to their wills, whether they be unto salvation or unto destruction." (Alma 29:4.)

The gift of charity, the pure love of Christ, will help us purify our lives. Among its other virtues, numerated in Moroni 7:45, charity "thinketh no evil" and "rejoiceth not in iniquity."

Speaking to the prophet Moroni, the Lord explained that "Faith, hope and charity bringeth unto me—the fountain of all righteousness." (Ether 12:28.) The enlightenment of this great vision enabled Moroni to attest (v. 33-34) that this charity or pure love is why Jesus Christ was willing to lay down His life for us, and affirm: "Except men shall have charity they cannot inherit that place which thou hast prepared in the mansions of thy Father."

Our Savior was the epitome of charity. He had pure love and trust in His Heavenly Father, and again, He had this same pure love for us, His brothers and sisters. He laid down His life for us (John 15:13) in obedience to the will of His Father, and out of love for us. He, in turn, exemplified the pure love of our Father in Heaven, who loved us so much He sent His beloved Son to redeem us (John 3:16) and enable us to return to His presence and become like He is. As we seek to purify our minds, we should seek to follow our Savior, and let our hearts and lives be filled with charity, or love.

Since we must obtain this gift of charity in order to truly become like Christ, and to be fully accepted with Him, we ought to pray daily for this gift. With this love in our hearts and His light in our lives, we can accept our total dependence upon Him as our Savior, be faithful to Him, and allow His grace or enabling power to change our nature so that we have no more desire to sin. He can purify our hearts. He can lift us up and help us to be more like Him. His is the true light to which we aspire.

If we fill our souls with His light and His love, and endure to the end, we will come to a time of peace and rest hereafter. After we leave this life, Satan will have no further power over the righteous. President Cannon stated a promise and a warning:

> Satan has no power over the faithful dead. Satan is bound as soon as the faithful spirit leaves this tabernacle of clay and goes to the other side of the veil. That spirit is emancipated from the power and thraldom [slavery] and attacks of Satan. Satan can only afflict such in this life. He can only afflict those in that life which is to come who have listened to his persuasions, who have listed to obey him. These are the only ones over whom he has power after this life.
>
> The Latter-day Saints who have been faithful, the men and the women who have kept the commandments of God, those who have lived according to the light that they have had, whether it be much or little, when they leave this state of existence, they are placed in such a position that Satan . . . can do nothing to interfere with their happiness; but the wicked, those who list to obey him, those who give heed to his spirit, will only be still more completely in his power in the life that is to come. . . .
>
> Already we have a foretaste of it. You watch the men who yield to the temptations and allurements of Satan; you watch the men and women who give heed to his spirit, and you will find written legibly upon their faces that misery that awaits them in the world to come. (*Gospel Truth*, p. 61.)

The Light and the Life of the World

The personal testimony of President Howard W. Hunter is a beautiful summary of all that is required of us, as we reach up in our mortal challenge and probation, onward and upward toward that eternal Light:

> Only Christ can be our ideal, our "bright and morning star" (Rev. 22:16). . . . The great standard! The only sure way! The light and the life of the world! How grateful we should be that God sent his Only Begotten Son to earth to do at least two things that no other person could have done. The first task Christ did as a perfect, sinless Son was to redeem all mankind from the fall, providing an atonement for Adam's sin and for our own sins if we will accept and follow him. The second great thing he did was to set a perfect example of right

living, of kindness and mercy and compassion, in order that all of the rest of mankind might know how to live, know how to improve, and know how to become more godlike.

Let us follow the Son of God in all ways and in all walks of life. Let us make him our exemplar and our guide. . . .

His beloved disciple John often said of Christ, "We beheld his glory" (John 1:14). They observed the Savior's perfect life as he worked and taught and prayed. So, too, ought we to "behold his glory" in every way we can.

We must know Christ better than we know him; we must remember him more often than we remember him; we must serve him more valiantly than we serve him. Then we will drink water springing up unto eternal life and will eat the bread of life.

What manner of men and women ought we to be? Even as he is. (CR, *Ensign*, May 1994, p. 64.)

When we have put all enemies behind us, when we have been moved to sing the song of redeeming love, when we have our eye single to the glory of God, we can then be filled with His light and with His love. We can know personally and eternally the glorious revelation embodied in our Savior's resounding declarations:

Behold, I am Jesus Christ, whom the prophets testified shall come into the world. And behold, I am the light and the life of the world. (3 Nephi 11:10-11.)

Hearken and listen to the voice of him who is from all eternity to all eternity, the Great I AM, even Jesus Christ—

The light and the life of the world; a light which shineth in darkness and the darkness comprehendeth it not. (D&C 39:1-2.)

Behold, I am Jesus Christ, the Son of the living God, who created the heavens and the earth, a light which cannot be hid in darkness. (D&C 14:9.)

And if your eye be single to my glory, your whole bodies shall be filled with light, and there shall be no darkness in you; and that body which is filled with light comprehendeth all things.

Therefore, sanctify yourselves that your minds become single to God, and the days will come that you shall see him; for he will unveil his face unto you. (D&C 88:67-68.)

We testify that the things we have discussed in this book are true. During the years it has taken to research and write this book, we have felt the sweet influence of the Spirit guiding us. We have felt the witness of the Spirit that these things, supported by the words of the living prophets, are true.

We testify that you are a worthwhile and remarkable individual. You have a unique mission in this life that you will fulfill as you overcome the temptations that beset you. The Lord has saved you to come forth now in this exciting and difficult time. Having problems does not make you a bad person. All of us have weaknesses, and all of us can overcome our weaknesses and be stronger for doing it. Overcoming problems is part of the training and development for which we came to this earth.

We testify that the principles we have outlined will work. We have tested them in our own lives, and we have observed them at work in the lives of others. We know that they can help you to control your thoughts and fill your mind and your life with good. As you do so, you will be filled with the happiness and joy that are your promised reward in this life. May the Lord bless you in this worthy goal.

The companion volume *You Can Become Pure in Heart* takes us further down the road of fulfilling our life's purpose. Did you know that it is possible to become pure in heart in this life? Elder Bruce R. McConkie wrote, "Many of the present day saints and many in former days . . . attained the status of the pure in heart." (*Mormon Doctrine*, p. 612.) It is true. If we love God with all our hearts lose ourselves in His service, we can become pure in heart while in this life. Many will attain it.

Purity of heart is our destiny, our goal, and our challenge. This is the test for which we came here to prove ourselves. It is not only possible, but is a divine commission from our Heavenly Father who sent us here. It is our purpose and mission in mortality.

You Can Become Pure in Heart will explore these lofty precepts one by one in simple language, so that we may all come to an understanding of them and know how they can be accomplished by us—ordinary members of the Church.

Works Cited

Allen, James. *As A Man Thinketh*. Fort Worth, Texas: Brownlow Publishing Co., Inc., 1985.

Ballard, Melvin J. *Sermons and Missionary Services of Melvin J. Ballard*. Compiled by Bryant S. Hinckley. Salt Lake City: Deseret Book Co., 1949.

———. *The Three Degrees of Glory*. A discourse delivered in the Ogden Tabernacle September 22, 1922. Salt Lake City: Magazine Printing & Publishing, 1975.

Benson, Ezra Taft. *Come Unto Christ*. Salt Lake City: Deseret Book Co., 1983.

———. "In His Steps." *1979 Devotional Speeches of the Year*. Provo: Brigham Young University Press, 1980.

———. *The Teachings of Ezra Taft Benson*. Salt Lake City: Bookcraft, Inc., 1988.

Brown, Hugh B. *You and Your Marriage*. Salt Lake City: Bookcraft, Inc., 1977.

Cannon, George Q. *Gospel Truth*. Edited by Jerreld L. Newquist, 1957. Reprint, Salt Lake City: Classics in Mormon Literature Series, Deseret Book Co., 1987.

Children's Songbook of the Church of Jesus Christ of Latter-day Saints. Salt Lake City: Church of Jesus Christ of Latter-day Saints, 1989.

Clark, James R., comp. *Messages of the First Presidency*. 6 vols. Salt Lake City: Bookcraft, Inc., 1975.

Craven, Rulon G. *The Pursuit of Perfection*. Salt Lake City: Bookcraft, Inc., 1988.

Featherstone, Vaughn J. "No Other Talent Exceeds Spirituality." *1976 Devotional Speeches of the Year*. Provo: Brigham Young University.

Grant, Heber J. *Gospel Standards*. Compiled by G. Homer Durham. Salt Lake City: An *Improvement Era Publication*, 1943.

Groberg, John H. "There Is Always Hope." *Brigham Young University 1983-84 Fireside and Devotional Speeches*. Provo: Brigham Young University.

Hafen, Bruce C. *The Believing Heart*. Salt Lake City: Deseret Book Co., 1986.

History of the Church of Jesus Christ of Latter-day Saints. 7 vols. 2nd ed. revised. Salt Lake City: Deseret Book Co., 1980.

Hunter, Howard W. "Fear Not, Little Flock." *Brigham Young University 1988-89 Devotional and Fireside Speeches*. Provo: Brigham Young University Press, 1989.

Hymns of the Church of Jesus Christ of Latter-day Saints. Salt Lake City: The Church of Jesus Christ of Latter-day Saints, 1985.

Journal of Discourses. 26 vols. Liverpool and London, 1867. Reprint, Salt Lake City: n.p., 1966.

Kapp, Ardeth Greene. *The Joy of the Journey*. Salt Lake City: Deseret Book Co., 1992.

Kimball, Spencer W. *Faith Precedes the Miracle*. Salt Lake City: Deseret Book Co., 1972.

———. *The Miracle of Forgiveness*. Salt Lake City: Bookcraft, Inc., 1969.

———. *The Teachings of Spencer W. Kimball*. Edited by Edward L. Kimball. Salt Lake City: Bookcraft, Inc., 1982.

Larsen, Dean L. *Free to Act*. Salt Lake City: Bookcraft, Inc., 1989.

Lewis, C.S. *The Great Divorce*. New York: MacMillan Publishing Co., Inc., 1946.

Maxwell, Neal A. *Of One Heart*. Salt Lake City: Deseret Book Co., 1975.

McConkie, Bruce R. *Mormon Doctrine*. Salt Lake City: Bookcraft, Inc., 1966.

———. *The Mortal Messiah*. 4 vols. Salt Lake City: Deseret Book Co., 1980-81.

———. *The Promised Messiah*. Salt Lake City: Deseret Book Co., 1978.

McKay, David O. *Pathways to Happiness*. Compiled by Llewelyn R. McKay. Salt Lake City: Bookcraft, Inc., 1957.

———. *Stepping Stones to an Abundant Life*. Compiled by Llewelyn R. McKay. Salt Lake City: Deseret Book Co., 1971.

———. *True to the Faith*. Compiled by Llewelyn R. McKay. Salt Lake City: Bookcraft, Inc., 1967.

Nicholson, William. *Shadowlands*. Garden City, New York: The Fireside Theater, 1989.

Oaks, Dallin H. *Pure in Heart*. Salt Lake City: Bookcraft, Inc., 1991.

Pace, George W. *Our Search to Know the Lord*. Salt Lake City: Deseret Book Co., 1988.

Packer, Boyd K. *Teach Ye Diligently*. Salt Lake City: Deseret Book Co., 1975.

————. *That All May Be Edified*. Salt Lake City: Bookcraft, Inc., 1982.

————. "To the One." *1978 Devotional Speeches of the Year*. Provo: Brigham Young University Press.

Payne, Jaynann Morgan. "If Only I Had Known Five Minutes Before." *Remarkable Stories from the Lives of Latter-day Saint Women, Vol 2.* Compiled by Leon R. Hartshorn. Salt Lake City: Deseret Book Co., 1975.

Porter, Blaine R., compiler. *Priesthood*. Salt Lake City: Deseret Book Co., 1982.

Rector, Hartman Jr. "The Talent of Spirituality." *1979 Devotional Speeches of the Year*. Provo: Brigham Young University Press, 1980.

Romney, Marion G. *Look to God and Live*. Compiled by George J. Romney. Salt Lake City: Deseret Book Co., 1973.

Sill, Sterling W. *The Best of Sterling W. Sill*. Salt Lake City: Bookcraft, Inc., 1983.

Smith, George Albert. *Sharing the Gospel With Others*. Compiled by Preston Nibley. Salt Lake City: Deseret News Press, 1950.

Smith, Joseph. *Teachings of the Prophet Joseph Smith*. Selected by Joseph Fielding Smith. Salt Lake City: Deseret Book Co., 1938.

Smith, Joseph F. *Gospel Doctrine: Selections from the Sermons and Writings of Joseph F. Smith*. 3rd ed. Salt Lake City: Deseret Book Co., 1977.

Smith, Joseph Fielding. *Answers to Gospel Questions*. 5 vols. Compiled by Joseph Fielding Smith, Jr. Salt Lake City: Deseret Book Co., 1957.

————. *Doctrines of Salvation*. 3 vols. Compiled by Bruce R. McConkie. Salt Lake City: Bookcraft, Inc., 1954.

————. *The Restoration of All Things*. Salt Lake City: Deseret Book Co., 1964.

————. *Take Heed To Yourselves!* Salt Lake City: Deseret Book Co., 1966.

Snow, Lorenzo. *The Teachings of Lorenzo Snow*. Compiled by Clyde J. Williams. Salt Lake City: Bookcraft, Inc., 1984.

Talmage, James E. *The Vitality of Mormonism*. Salt Lake City: Deseret Book Co., 1948.

Tate, Lucile C. *LeGrande Richards: Beloved Apostle*. Salt Lake City: Bookcraft, Inc., 1982.

Whitney, Orson F. *Life of Heber C. Kimball*. Salt Lake City: Bookcraft, Inc., 1979.

Wilcox, Brad. "Controlling Unworthy Thoughts." *Feeling Great, Doing Right, Hanging Tough*. Favorite Talks from Especially for Youth. Salt Lake City: Bookcraft, Inc., 1992.

Young, Brigham. *Discourses of Brigham Young*. Compiled by John A Widtsoe. Salt Lake City: Deseret Book Co., 1978.

Other Sources Cited:

Conference Reports. Salt Lake City: The Church of Jesus Christ of Latter-day Saints. Speakers, month and year cited in text.

Deacons Course A Manual. Salt Lake City: The Church of Jesus Christ of Latter-day Saints, 1983.

Ensign. Salt Lake City: The Church of Jesus Christ of Latter-day Saints. Month and year cited in text. Conference Reports designated CR.

LDS Church News, News of the Church of Jesus Christ of Latter-day Saints. Salt Lake City: Deseret News. Articles cited in text.

The Improvement Era. Salt Lake City: The Church of Jesus Christ of Latter-day Saints. Month and year cited in text.

The New Era. Salt Lake City: The Church of Jesus Christ of Latter-day Saints. Month and year cited in text.

Relief Society Courses of Study. Salt Lake City: The Church of Jesus Christ of Latter-day Saints, 1985.

"Seek to Obtain My Word." Melchizedek Priesthood Study Guide. Salt Lake City: The Church of Jesus Christ of Latter-day Saints, 1989.

Index